Praise for *Joe Burk:*

"In choosing Joe Burk as his subject, Ed Woodhouse documents the rarity of a powerful will channeled by an equally stout moral center. He seems to have interviewed every possible witness and scoured every extant document to create a multi-dimensional portrait of the complicated, remarkable man. Woodhouse has done rowing history, and American history, a great service with this biography of Burk, whose character should be studied by experts and known by citizens everywhere."
—Peter Raymond, 1968 and 1972 Olympian (Silver in 8s),
Coach Harvard Lightweights, Radcliffe Crew,
1980 U.S. Olympic Quad.

"I knew Joe Burk by reputation and through my equally enigmatic mentor, Harry Parker. Ed's work brings this extraordinary man back to life and fills in a void in US Rowing and Olympic history."
—Gregg Stone, US sculler and coach.

"Lest we forget one of America's greatest scullers and coaches, Ed Woodhouse has captured Joe Burk—his perseverance, his modesty, and his trust in science—in a definitive biography told in part by the many champions he mentored.
—Dotty Brown, author of *Boathouse Row,*
Waves of Change in the Birthplace of American Rowing

"I had the honor of being coached by, visiting and exchanging correspondence with Joe Burk for over 40 years. Joe was an anomaly. The strongest, bravest, most competitive, most creative of men, and the sweetest of souls."
—Ken Dreyfuss, Penn Captain '69, National Team 1974,
1975, Coach of Coach of Navy Plebe Heavyweights,
Stanford Men's Varsity, Potomac Boat Club Elite Scullers, U.S.
National Lightweight Teams

How did Joe Burk prepare for his triumph in the Diamond Sculls at Henley in 1938 and 1939 and set a course record that endured for decades? By himself, with nothing but an old stopwatch, determination, perseverance, and will power. He coached and trained himself.

Who was Joe Burk: this unusual champion, decorated war hero, widely respected coach, and self-reliant gentleman? Ed Woodhouse, who learned about Joe Burk while rowing against Penn for the arch rival Harvard Crew, has researched and meticulously pieced together the life and letters of Joe Burk, to reveal in this carefully prepared work the fascinating life of this extraordinarily unique man.

—Dr. Reed Kinderman, Penn Crew '67

There was no hot water in the Penn Boathouse. So I asked Joe: 'What should we do."

Joe's reply: "Take a cold shower."

I quickly realized that asking a man who had earned the Navy Cross, Silver and Bronze Stars, sunk more tonnage than any other PT Boat Captain, won Henley and the Sullivan Award about hot water was worse than idiotic and that it was time for me to "man up."

—Howard Greenberg, Penn Crew '67

"Joe was a remarkable man, a compassionate and loving husband and father, a war hero, an absolute phenomenal athlete and always understated."

—Steve Gladstone, Championship Coach Navy, Yale, Cal, Brown, Harvard

Joe Burk

An American Ideal

E. J. Woodhouse

Joe
Burk

An American Ideal

Lynnhaven Press, 7150 Island View Way Dublin, Virginia, 24084

ISBNs: 979-8-218-74885-2 (paperback); 979-8-218-74886-9 (eBook)

Front cover art/photo courtesy of "Wide World Photos Inc."
    and From the Collection of Thomas Weil, Esq.
Cover and book design by Mayfly book design

Library of Congress Catalog Number: 2025915987
First Printing: 2025

Dedication

This book is dedicated to all rowers coached or influenced by Joe Burk, who keep his memory alive. May this book aid in that effort, and allow young rowers, particularly female rowers, the opportunity to absorb and appreciate Burk's coaching methods in the light of the changing face of rowing.

Contents

Foreword

"The great ones do not set up offices, charge fees, give lectures, or write books. Wisdom is silent, and the most effective propaganda for truth is the force of personal example.

The great ones are indifferent, in the profoundest sense. They don't ask you to believe: they electrify you by their behavior. They are the awakeners."

—Henry Miller

I t is past time that a book about Joe Burk, champion oarsman, naval war hero, and beloved college rowing coach, be published. He is one of the "great ones" that Henry Miller describes above, and the truth he taught was by personal example, in sport, in war, and in coaching. This book seeks to illuminate Burk's life for those in danger of never learning of his great example.

Joe Burk was one of the Greatest Generation, born in 1914. His life falls into three stages. He was first an athlete, winning letters at Penn in rowing and football in the mid 1930s, followed by multiple rowing championships in America, Canada, and Great Britain, culminating in the James Sullivan Award in 1940 as America's greatest amateur athlete. Had the 1940 Olympic Games been held, in all likelihood, he would have won the Olympic gold medal in the single sculls.

The second stage of his life was as a warrior fighting in the Pacific Theatre as a PT boat commander, and later as a combat operations expert, where he always chose to lead the most dangerous assign-ments of multi-boat actions he had planned. He was awarded the nation's highest honor for valor save for the Congressional Medal of Honor.

In the years after the war, the third part of his life was spent as a coach, first as freshman coach at Yale, then as Head Coach at the Uni-versity of Pennsylvania from 1950 until his retirement after the 1969 season. The Penn boathouse is now named the Burk Bergman Boat-house, and the single which he rowed in the 1930s has been restored and hangs in the main room of the Boathouse.

Few modern rowers in America know of Joe Burk, and that is to their detriment, as his example is as instructive as the most influential figures in the sport. This book seeks to advance Burk as a model of the best in rowing, and allow modern rowers the chance to draw inspira-tion from his example.

America's past rowing history has been largely preserved by an oral tradition. The best coaches have for decades encouraged their charges with tales of past greats that rowed to glory by methods worth emulating. This book is a continuation of that tradition, but I seek to make a permanent record of Burk's time and place in the history of American rowing, relying upon the stories of those still alive who learned from him.

I am aided in this task by many of Burk's oarsmen, still living, whose devotion to their coach is unsurpassed. The story you will read here is what they told to me. They were uniform in their devotion to him, whether they had rowed in his fast crews or ones that were less successful. They all spoke in the same way about the lessons he imparted, the patience he showed in teaching, and in his quiet, stoic manner. As those he coached grew older, the importance of his ex-ample heightened. Burk represented for those men a standard to be sought—an American ideal.

American rowing, when I joined it fifty-five years ago, was a small world. Most of those deeply involved knew everybody else but did not necessarily like them. Tribal allegiance left little room for genuine friendship. Joe Burk was one of the few who seemed to maintain the ungrudging respect of all.

The American rowing world now is larger—and now delightfully full of female rowers, who were an oppressed minority when I started. I have also found that the tribalism I knew in the '60s and '70s has not disappeared, but has in large measure simply been spread over a larger population.

Burk's example of sportsmanship abiding alongside an earnest quest for victory is needed now as much as ever.

D. Baily,   Tamaqua, Pa.

CHAPTER ONE

The Burk Family

Joseph William Burk was born on January 19, 1914, in Philadelphia, the second son of Paul Burk and his wife, the former Marguerite Reber Templin, who both came from prosperous families in Reading, Pennsylvania. Paul's family were Episcopalian, and Marguerite's were Lutheran.

Paul Heber Burk graduated from Franklin & Marshall College in 1908, which had originally been founded by Lutherans. Paul had been given his middle name "Heber" because his great grandfather, William Black Burk, had been an Episcopal minister who greatly admired Reginald Heber (1783–1826), an Anglican clergyman and the second Bishop of Calcutta. The Reverend Burk had himself done missionary work, establishing new churches in both Pennsylvania and Indiana.

Marguerite's grandfather served as trustee of Franklin & Marshall. The two grandfathers lived in Reading at the same time, and doubtless knew each other.

Paul Burk and Marguerite Templin were married in 1911. They had three sons: Paul Heber Burk Jr. in November of 1912, Joseph William Burk in 1914, and James Reber Burk in 1916. The couple decided a farm was the ideal place to raise their three boys. Early in their marriage, Paul and Marguerite bought a farm along the banks of Rancocas Creek in Burlington County, New Jersey, where the Burks focused on the cultivation of apple and peach orchards. This farm was to become the couple's own quiet path to financial security apart from any inheritance and would provide a bucolic and active childhood for their three boys. Eventually, the income from the farm would far exceed Paul Sr.'s salary in non-farm jobs.

The farmland of southern New Jersey—the Garden State—has supported rich agricultural production since the early days of Revolutionary America. Raising fruit for human consumption near major urban areas such as Philadelphia, Trenton, and Wilmington, Delaware, proved a reliable path to prosperity. Nearby fruit storage facilities in Moorestown and extensive road and rail access out of the area made the operation profitable at scale.

Modern readers might mistakenly call up visions of migrant farm laborers. In the era in which the Burk family farmed, margins were such that the Burk family with their three boys plus a few occasionally hired hands could generate significant profits.

From this family experience in farming, Joe Burk and his brothers gleaned many habits valuable to them in later life. Perhaps most prominent among these habits was the proclivity to take apart, understand, and fix anything that needed fixing. Anyone with experience in farming knows that a successful farmer must be a determined—and often an inventive—tinkerer. Farms are always remote, and all farm equipment needs constant maintenance and repair—and almost never at a convenient time. Joe Burk would creatively "tinker" all his life—most famously with his repair, maintenance, design, and innovative modifications of rowing equipment, and, during wartime conditions, with the powerful patrol torpedo boats he would command as a naval officer. In his years as a coach, he would help develop machinery to measure his oarsmen's efforts with a precision never before attained—and go on to pioneer equipment that would later set the standard in rowing training. And in his retirement, Burk would build by hand his own cabin and outbuildings in Montana, merely for the pleasure of doing it.

But perhaps most obviously, Joe Burk grew up in an almost idyllic physical training ground for the development of a multisport athlete

Burk Family Photo

who would need strength and endurance in equal measure. Joe Burk had hugely muscled forearms and biceps because he spent his youth hefting baskets of apples and peaches from the treetops to the ground.

But beyond the monetary and physical benefits of the life Joe Burk and his brothers led as children, they had the gift of a close nuclear family. The Burk family cohesion can be glimpsed today from a photograph taken on the occasion of Joe Burk's travelling with his parents to England in 1938, where he would win the Diamond Sculls trophy at Henley Royal Regatta. In the picture, the Burk parents, their three boys, and Paul Jr.'s wife are shown in a triumphant and characteristically twentieth-century American photograph. Dressed formally for transatlantic steamship travel, Marguerite and Paul Burk stand proudly in the back, symbolic of their role as supportive parents.

Their son Joe, in a dark suit, whose athletic accomplishments in sculling gave rise to this important occasion, kneels at the front so as to give a more complete view of his family. Behind Joe stand his two brothers—the one to the left, with hands on hips, is the youngest brother, Jim, who at the time of the picture was rowing on the University of Pennsylvania heavyweight crew.

The oldest brother, Paul Jr., tall and slender, is dressed in a light-colored suit, and on the steps of the Burk farmhouse, seems a silent presence above the others. He appears quiet and studious—he would not finish college because of dyslexia but would persevere to become a skilled draftsman and invent and develop machines that are still used today in the harvesting of cranberries, a major crop in rural New Jersey.

Directly in front of Paul is his new bride Marion, the daughter of William and Edith Pennington, who owned the farm adjacent. Marion, like her husband, is dressed as if for church and wears a sweet expression—the epitome of the "girl next door." The health and vigor of the family and their natural pride in the athlete son approaching his first international athletic competition is obvious—and deeply appealing.

An American ideal.

CHAPTER TWO

The Burk Boys' Education

"As a Friends school, we take the mission of Quaker education seriously. We have built our curriculum in a manner that allows students to experience academics through the lens of the Quaker values of deep listening, waiting on the Spirit, a belief in continuing revelation and growth, and the testimonies of Simplicity, Peace, Integrity, Community, Equality, and Stewardship."

—Westfield Friends School website

Modern readers imagining the world of Burlington County in the 1920s and the options available to Paul and Marguerite Burk for the education of their three boys must first recognize that, in the past one hundred years, that county has experienced a dichotomy of change and continuity. Change has come primarily from increased population, which has exploded sevenfold. Change has also come from dramatic improvements in transportation between the area and the City of Philadelphia just across the Delaware River.

1919 Top row: Steve Gausler, Jack Frishmuth, William Parry, Henry Parrish, Ralston Fitler, Lea Warner, Willis DelaCour, William Edwards, Prof. Trillon, Miss Judd, Mrs. Borden, Miss Broadhurst, Miss James, Miss Bausman, Nancy Biddle, Elaine Groves, Ruth Caldwell, Katherine Graff, Carola Collings, Larene Rolfe, Alice Lippincott
Middle row: Lynn Hendrickson, Frances Allen, Charlotte Partridge, Eloise Boyer, Ruth Rolfe, Franklin D'Olier, Edith Lippincott, Robert Caldwell, Charlotte Parry, Walter Lippincott, Alice Parrish, Philip Somervell, Charlotte Dorrance, Sue Lippincott, Charles Biddle 3rd, Mary Tyler, Nelson Harris, Marion Biddle, Phyllis Boyer, Elizabeth Jessup
Bottom row: Helen D'Olier, Cornelia Murray, Paul Burke, Sharpless Richie, Richard Graff, Ruth McVaugh, Robert Biddle, Amy Bilyeu, Richard Biddle, Lucy Dickson, Ellen Richie, Barbara Lewis, Eleanor Lewis, Dora Parry, Joseph Burke, Faith Fitler [25]

Paul Burk is the first boy in the first row on the left. Joe Burk is the first boy in the front row on the right. Courtesy of Westfield Friends School.

Burlington County now boasts a number of beautiful commuter-based neighborhoods with large and comparatively new homes.

By contrast, one constant in the county has been the primary school that educated the three Burk brothers, which was established by some of the state's earliest settlers from the Old World—the Quakers. One of the best of the Quaker primary schools in the area played a central role in the education of the three Burk brothers. The Westfield Friends School, established by the Quakers of Moorestown in 1788, is the oldest Friends School in America under the care of a Meeting—the term used for an active Quaker congregation. It served in Joe Burk's day, and still serves students from preschool through the 8th grade. In 1918, Paul and Marguerite Burk enrolled both Paul Jr. and Joe in the same grade at Westfield Friends, located then as now on Riverston Road in Cinnaminson, New Jersey. The parents felt confident that Joe, only fourteen months younger than Paul, could keep up both academically and physically. Photo 3 shows a picture of Joe and Paul with their first grade class. Joe is in the first row on the far right, and Paul on the far left.

The Burks determined that Westfield was the best option available for the education of their boys. In 1919, Westfield's mission was much the same as that of today and would have resonated with the Burk and Reber families religious sensibilities.

The cultural influence of the Quakers in America, while still touched upon today in high school history classes, is rarely appreciated by modern Americans who possess little knowledge of or exposure to the religion or its core beliefs. Joe Burk was raised in a county in New Jersey that was founded when Quaker influence was at its height.

Moorestown, New Jersey is one such place. In the center of the town's grid of colonial streets sits the Quaker Meeting House, a handsome brick building immaculately kept, with large multipaned windows allowing in both the light and the curious eyes of non-Quakers. While it has a modern website (*moorestownfriendsmeeting.org*), its description of its mission adheres to the ancient tenets of the faith: "Together we gather in worshipful and expectant stillness, keeping an open heart to the Divine, to each other, and to the Light within us." The associated cemetery with its low gravestones is symbolic of no soul being greater than another—especially in death—and is striking to the eye.

Moorestown was heavily influenced by the establishment of Quakerism in the United States, for this part of New Jersey, bordering as it does Philadelphia, is naturally part of the Quaker diaspora which led directly to the establishment of the Commonwealth of Pennsylvania, paradoxically established by William Penn, an English member of the Anglican Church who in midlife became a Quaker convert.

William Penn was born in 1644, the son of an influential admiral in the British Navy. One historian described him as "of the elite," having attended Oxford and thereafter devoting himself to the management of the lucrative Penn family estates in Ireland. It was in Ireland that he first encountered Quakers, who called themselves "Friends." By 1667, Penn had joined them.[1]

Among the assets William Penn had inherited was a debt owed to his father by King Charles II. Within ten years after having joined the Quakers, Penn petitioned for a grant of land from the King as payment for the debt owed. The King, after due consideration, granted rights to land in the New World to the west of New Jersey, north of Maryland, and south of New York—what is today Pennsylvania.

The Commonwealth of Pennsylvania's own history described the Charter as "nebulous and contradictory," but Penn's rights as to key items were clear: "control of the land and waterways; use of the wildlife and natural resources; as well as possession of gold, silver and 'precious stones.'"

In return, Penn was required to "to deliver annually to the King one-fifth of all gold and silver and two beaver skins."[2] Penn could run the nascent state in any way he wished—subject only to the requirement that any laws Penn made had to be consistent with then current English law. Beyond that, there were no restrictions. Modern readers have heard the phrase "It's good to be King." Penn's experience suggests it is good to be a creditor of the King. Historian Thomas Hamm wrote:

> As sole proprietor, Penn had absolute power over the colony and the form of its government the settlement took. Not surprisingly, he framed it according to Quaker principles, making it the first society in the world to be so established. Penn was confident that if properly constituted, Pennsylvania and its capital, Philadelphia (Greek for "City of Brotherly Love") would be a model for the rest of the world.[3]

By the end of the American Revolution, the political power of the Quakers in both Pennsylvania and New Jersey had declined, and today the Friends conduct their work in outreach to the larger secular community, such as the running of schools like Westfield. The experience of being taught at Westfield inculcated in each of the Burk boys the fundamental beliefs of Quakerism. We will see those qualities of modesty and a quiet purposefulness in each of the Burk boys—Paul, Joe, and Jim. And just as Aristotle asserted: "Give me a child until he is seven, and I will show you the man."

Joe Burk would not, as an adult, routinely attend Quakers meetings, but he would live his whole life as if he had. The Quaker values Joe Burk absorbed during his formative years, while not necessarily expressing themselves in a change of denomination, would be reflected in Burk's character into adulthood. Joe Burk the coach would in turn inspire a legion of oarsmen who would learn to row under Burk's quiet guidance. Many would come to call him a second father.

When Paul and Joe Burk graduated the eighth grade at Westfield Friends in 1926, they joined the Class of 1930 at the Moorestown High School, walking almost a mile from the family farm to catch public transportation across Rancocas Creek and down Route 130 to the point at which Bridgeboro Road diverges from present Route 130. The boys would then have another long trek south toward the old Mooretown High School, then adjacent to today's city hall. One way, the trip was six miles.

In his later years, Joe Burk recalled a time when the bridge crossing the Rancocas Creek was being replaced. Burk told Reed Kindermann (Penn '69) that he and his brother Paul would row a boat south across the Rancocas to meet the bus on the south side. They would secure the boat on the shore and continue the trip to school. In the evening, they would reverse the process, rowing the boat north across the Rancocas, securing the boat, and walking home to the Burk farmhouse.

Kindermann remembers that when he visited Joe Burk in his retirement in Montana, and Joe would often ask him about the fate of certain houses located along Burk's old commuting route. Even in his retirement in the wide expanses of Montana, Burk was still recalling the tree-lined roads of Burlington County.

By the time Paul and Joe Burk reached high school, Paul was struggling with certain aspects of schoolwork. While he was never formally diagnosed in his lifetime, his family, and especially his son John, who himself would be diagnosed as dyslexic, grew to recognize that Paul's powerful intellect was not fully appreciated during his academic training. While both Paul and Joe were admitted to the University of Pennsylvania following high school, and both boys would find great success within their chosen fields, only Joe would graduate.

Joe Burk played on the high school football, basketball, and baseballs teams. The old gym where he trained, and the fields where he played, can still be viewed in Moorestown today, across the street from the town hall.

CHAPTER THREE

The Poughkeepsie Regatta

I n the nineteenth century, most North American rowing races were held mainly between professional oarsmen who themselves made a tough living plying the waterfronts of America or Canada. Races on the Hudson at Newburgh were frequent, as were races on lakes in upstate New York, New England, and Ontario.

The exploits of those professionals were frequently the subject of weeks-long pre-race publicity and lively betting, and their races were viewed by enthusiastic supporters, many of whom would follow the races on specially arranged railroad cars running along the tracks flanking the Hudson. These men laid the groundwork for what would become competitive intercollegiate rowing.

In the early 1890s, the crews of three eastern rowing schools, Cornell, Columbia, and the University of Pennsylvania, formed the Intercollegiate Rowing Association and held their first championship in Poughkeepsie in 1895. The Poughkeepsie Regatta, which came to include freshmen, junior varsity, and varsity races at respectively two, three, and four miles, would be held with an increasing number of participants through 1948. The annual IRA championship continues to this day at other venues.

At the end of Joe Burk's junior year at Moorestown High School, Burk's attention was drawn to the upcoming 1929 IRA race at Poughkeepsie. Most newspapers had widely previewed the event all spring. A week before the June race, *The New York Times* published an article saying the crews were already at Poughkeepsie and were tapering their practice schedules to rest before the big event:

CREWS ON HUDSON EASE UP IN WORK
Put in Dull Day, but Face Stern Tasks This Week for Race Preparation
CORNEL HAS LATE DRILL
California, Columbia, Penn, Navy and Syracuse Fail
to Extend Themselves

In the New York newspapers, much was made of Columbia University's co-favorite status with California, who, in the day when all travel had to be made by rail, had crossed the country to row at Poughkeepsie. Ky Ebright, who had coxed at the University of Washington and thus was among the brotherhood of those who trained under the watchful eye of George Pocock, was the coach of the heavily favored California team.

On June 24, 1929, the morning of the race itself, *The New York Times* published a story with a dateline of the previous day, and with the heading "No Coaches to Predict Results," and the sub-heading "All Say That Their Crews Are Ready for the Regatta—Ebright a Bit Gloomy."

A side headline announced that then New York Governor Franklin Roosevelt, Mrs. Roosevelt, their three sons, with Secretary of State Edward and Mrs. Flynn, would all be the guests on the yacht of the wealthy industrialist William Shaw of New York City for the finals.[4]

Joe Burk, then a rising high school senior and three-sport athlete, read these articles and absorbed some of the breathless excitement. Burk had never rowed, other than his rowboat commutes across Rancocas Creek. Nonetheless, he was sufficiently intrigued to make the trek by train to Poughkeepsie alone. And it was here that Burk first observed his future alma mater's team in action.

It is not clear whether, at the time of his propitious trip to Poughkeepsie, Burk had any confidence he would soon be admitted to the University of Pennsylvania. As one of the founding colleges of the Association, Penn annually rowed at the IRA and was often a formidable competitor. Burk described his self-financed 1929 trip to Poughkeepsie to Peter Mallory in 2005:

> I happened to read about how well California had done in crew. I had never been to Poughkeepsie, scarcely knew where it was, but I found I could take the train to New York and get on the New York Central to Poughkeepsie.
>
> I arrived there and didn't have any place to stay because every good place was already filled up, so I asked some bum on the street, and he told me of an old, broken-down hotel where I could eat and sleep.
>
> It was 1929, and California was the big shot crew then. I wanted to see the time trials they were having, so I took the ferryboat across the river and went to the California Boathouse. There was nobody around except for the manager, and he showed me the shells and so forth. I found it all very interesting, and when the race came off, he and I dragged a railroad tie up against the side of the building, climbed up and watched the race from the roof . . .
>
> Later in the day, I went back to New York on the train. I stayed up the whole night and got home the next morning tired but knowing that I wanted to go out for rowing.

Burk reported he had two cents left when he reached home. He was just fifteen years old.

By going to observe rowing for himself, Burk was demonstrating what would become an enduring characteristic: his penchant for a detailed and solitary analysis of an athletic endeavor. Seeing and doing for himself, and making his own judgments, would become patterns unbroken in his life, and a source of his frequent successes.

After completing his senior year at Moorestown, Joe Burk enrolled at the University of Pennsylvania with a commitment to play football. However, rowing remained in the back of his mind.

In the autumn of 1930, when Joe Burk and his brother Paul entered Penn, the school's reputation in college football was quite different from what it is today. Penn now plays primarily in the elite but more anodyne Ivy League, but in Burk's era, Penn played a game closer to what we now think of as big-time college football.

Penn then battled ferocious opponents like Knute Rockne's Notre Dame, Wisconsin, and Ohio State, as well as national powerhouses such as California and Penn State. Burk was eager to test whether he could compete in such an environment.

In those days, all Penn's freshman football players played on a freshman team, with its own schedule. *The Daily Pennsylvanian* that fall reported that early "light" scrimmages pitted the varsity team against "the yearlings"—the freshman squad Burk joined. Freshmen games that year that were reported in the student newspaper were limited to three—and the freshman team amassed a 2–1 record.

When the season was over, Burk discovered that Penn's rowing team would be practicing through the winter in preparation for a spring season, and he realized he could try rowing and stay with football. Penn rowing coach Rusty Callow, who himself had played both sports at Washington, was open to athletes pursuing both sports. Burk joined the freshman crew and began to row on the Schuylkill River on warm days and in the tanks in the basement of Weightman Hall when the weather was too cold. Burk would have felt like his first year of college was much like his last year at Moorestown High—shifting from one sport to another and moving from strength to strength.

The current specialization of college athletes is a relatively recent development in college athletics. In the first half of the century, many athletes competed in multiple sports, and being a "five or six letter man"—an athlete who could earn a varsity letter in more than one sport—was the sign of true versatility.

On March 31 of Burk's freshman year, the nation's icon of college coaches, Knute Rockne, was killed in a plane crash in the Midwest. News reports of his untimely death provide hard evidence of how collegiate coaches were viewed at that time. The papers of America were full of the news of Rockne's death, and words of tribute from fellow coaches, including Burk's own rowing coach, Rusty Callow, who knew Rockne intimately. Callow was among the coaches quoted by *The Philadelphia Inquirer* in describing the impact of Rockne's death:

> Athletics has lost the most dynamic coach it ever had in any of its branches. Knute Rockne turned out real boys, worthwhile boys. He was no gymnasium coach or athlete, and his death is a sad blow to college athletics.

Also, in *The Inquirer* was a column on Rockne's death from the most well-known sports reporter in the first half of the twentieth century, Grantland Rice, who sought to capture the essence of Rockne's appeal:

> Knute Rockne could have been an outstanding figure in any career or profession he might have adopted. He had brains, ability, character and the vital qualities of leadership. He stuck to football because that was the game he loved and because it belonged to the type of younger men who were his kind.

In the era of Rockne, a college coach's job was often conceived of as part coach, part father figure. Coaches were supposed to—in Callow's words—"turn out real boys, worthwhile boys." If they did not, then, in Callow's words, they were just "gymnasium coaches"—a derogatory label for those coaches who viewed their jobs only as mere employment and not as a professional commitment to develop character through sports.

At the time of Rockne's death, most Americans viewed playing sports as a developmental step (at that point limited almost entirely to boys) in the maturation process that would produce good and productive citizens. Sports were almost never viewed as an end in themselves, except for those rare exceptions in which fan support had allowed professionalization, such as baseball. Some sports, including professional boxing and professional rowing, were viewed as corrupt or ultimately exploitative of the athletes involved. In boxing, the risk of permanent injury was high. In rowing, there was a deep history of throwing races to benefit gamblers. But judging by the tenor of contemporary sports reporting, college football and college rowing in Burk's era were admired by the American public.

As a result, the coaches who taught those sports were widely viewed as wise and deliberate counsellors of youth. Rockne had served as the pinnacle of that vision in the world of football. Men like Rusty Callow played the same role in rowing.

Rusty Callow would be the first great influence in Joe Burk's rowing. Callow himself sprang from the heart of Western rowing in America—the University of Washington.

Russell Stanley "Rusty" Callow was born in 1891, "one of eleven children born to pioneers who had settled in Mason County, Washington, in 1870. His father was a retired sea captain."[5] Before he could go to college, Rusty had to earn the money to do so. After high school, Rusty taught school in a one-room schoolhouse in Mason County, and worked as a lumberjack, the most lucrative work available in the State of Washington where the logging industry was then booming.

Then, as now, logging was an exceptionally hard and dangerous business. Lumberjacks of that era were muscular, mainly large, and had the strength and endurance for a full day of grueling physical exertion—attributes still honored today in the Pacific Northwest by local lumberjack contests of chopping, sawing, and log rolling.

In the expansive and largely untapped forests of the Northwest, lumberjacks were the equivalent of the American cowboys on the Great Plains. Instead of herding cattle, the lumberjacks felled and transported enormously long evergreens. That raw material, moved out of the wilderness by water or rail, was integral to the nation's growth. Lumberjacks worked hard, lived hard, and delighted in the fraternity and rough language of the logging camps.

By the fall of 1911, Callow had gathered enough money to enroll in the University of Washington, just east of his home in Mason County. Callow was then twenty years old, and no doubt carried himself with a maturity uncommon among his fellow freshmen. He played football and joined the rowing team, lettering in both. Every summer during college, he returned to the logging camps to work until classes resumed in the fall.

Callow the lumberjack had more than mere strength—he had the gifts of persuasion and leadership—skills he had honed during this pre-college days by teaching in the one-room schoolhouse in Macon County, Washington. This tradition of learning to teach before learning to coach would later be a key factor to his coaching success and, further, it conveyed a certain legitimacy to Callow as a person. Knute Rockne's obituary had made clear—"Rock" was a chemistry teacher before he was a coach. Callow followed that same path.

After college graduation in 1915, Callow established himself as a logging camp supervisor—known in the logging trade as a "Bull of the Woods." He worked in the Olympic Peninsula, which Mason County is a part of. He found success. He stayed with logging from 1915 through 1922.

Washington crew had stopped during much of World War One, and restarted only in the fall of 1921. The great success of the 1922 varsity led to the Washington coach Ed Leader being offered the head coaching job at Yale that fall. Leader accepted—and Washington was in dire need of a coach.

Rusty Callow agreed to leave logging and return to coach the Washington crew. He had been away from rowing for eight years and he relied heavily upon UW's resident board builder George Pocock, himself a past champion rower, for guidnace. He also asked Pocock to build a new shell for the Washington Varsity for the 1923 seasoand he relied heavily upon UW's resident board builder George Pocock, himself a past champion rower, for guidance. He also asked Pocock to build a new shell for the Washington Varsity for the 1923 season.

With Pocock's help, Callow brought success back to Washington rowing. Before long The University of Pennsylvania lured Callow to come to Philadelphia for triple the salary he earned in Seattle. Callow came.

Sometime during his career, Callow established connections with two organizations that give clues as to his spiritual leanings. He became a Free Mason and remained one all his life. The Masonic symbols of the Square and Compass, and the All-Seeing Eye are on his cemetery vault in Lake Forest Park, King County, Washington. Further, Callow at some point became an ordained minister. The details of the exact denomination have been lost to history.

Joe Burk, like Callow, a multi-sport athlete, must have been drawn to Callow as soon as he had contact with him through the Penn crew. One can imagine that the Quaker trained farm boy must have felt a certain affinity for the logging camp leader turned rowing coach.

Six days after the news of Rockne's death, the newspaper mentioned that Rusty Callow had held a practice of both the varsity and freshmen crews on Tuesday, April 7, but Joe Burk was not named as being in any of the freshman boats practicing.

This meant Burk was then in the third freshman boat—the lowest of the low. Burk was not deterred.

Any athlete naturally enjoys the sports in which he or she excels. It takes a different personality to humble themselves to learn something new and hang on despite starting at the bottom. Many would go back to what they know, to what comes easily. Joe Burk kept rowing. Perhaps it was the earnest humility given him by his Quaker schooling. In any event, he was confident enough to take the time to stay with the new sport.

At the beginning of his sophomore year, Joe Burk, even more physically formidable from his time in the rowing tanks and on the river, returned to the gridiron. Because of his size—at the age of just seventeen, he stood 6'2" and 200 pounds—Burk played at tackle. In the fall of 1931, Joe Burk received no individual mention in the newspapers, but the list of teams the Penn Varsity played was worthy of respect: Swarthmore, Franklin and Marshall, Lehigh, Wisconsin, Lafayette, Notre Dame, Georgia Tech, Cornell, and Navy.

The game against Notre Dame in South Bend resulted in five injured Penn players, and *The Inquirer* detailed the number of substitutions that would be made as a result.[6] Burk was not among those named as now starting. He must have sensed that his time would eventually come. Meanwhile, he likely welcomed what he saw in front of him: more experience, and more time on the field readying himself for opponents like Notre Dame. He looked forward to his junior year. There was more football to play.

Joe Burk's college schedule was remarkably full. Neither Burk nor his brother Paul lived on campus but instead commuted to Philadelphia from the farm each day. When his classes were finished, Burk would report for football practice and then board the bus for home. Somehow, he found time for studies, not to mention the almost endless cycle of farm chores. Burk's day simply started early and ended late.

Nonetheless, Joe somehow found enough room in his schedule to eventually join the Delta Upsilon fraternity, known informally at Penn at "DU." Delta Upsilon was established in 1834 at Williams College, and is the nation's sixth oldest men's fraternity, "and the first to be founded as non-secret." The goal of its founder was to "create a new, non-secret society that would welcome 'all good men and true.'"

Burk seems an unlikely candidate for fraternity membership as it is understood today. He possessed a solitary mien, lived a life of quiet stoicism at home, and maintained a close relationship with his family. But fraternity membership was very much the norm at Penn in those days, and DU's more liberal and inclusive philosophy would have had a natural appeal to one trained in Quaker values. Most early fraternity charters often included religious or racial restrictions on who could join, which had to be amended when the tenor of American college life changed. Delta Upsilon never had such restrictions. The present Delta Upsilon website celebrates that no revisions to their founding documents were ever required.

As the spring rowing season of 1932 progressed, Burk's work and effort began to pay off. Burk's success on the rowing team came not in a blaze of athletic glory, but incrementally. By March of 1932, he was rowing in the starboard power position, number five in Rusty Callow's third varsity boat.

Callow himself had gone through a similarly methodical progression—being at first just a big strong man in a boat to ultimately perfecting his stroke to become a big, strong, and almost technically perfect oarsman. Callow's placement of the young Burk acknowledged that while the man possessed great physical strength, he was as yet not a great technician.

Burk was deterred neither by his pride nor his inexperience—yet another personal strength that would help lay the foundation of his later successes. He made good progress during his sophomore season, and by May 6 had been promoted to the five-seat of the Junior Varsity—a substantial move upward for an oarsman's second season of rowing.

More progress soon came. By the May 21 race with Wisconsin and Marietta College in Ohio, Burk was sitting in the five-seat of the varsity. That day the boat won decisively. Burk's relentless improvement was evidence of his patience during the learning process. This resilience while experiencing the new and the sheer application of energy in so busy a life would remain his strengths throughout his rowing and coaching careers, and even into his retirement years. His emotional buoyancy and balance did not wane.

Burk protégé Reed Kindermann (Penn '69) maintains that Burk's successes were due in part to his willingness to eschew the usual undergraduate lifestyle and its attendant temptations, in part because of his decision to live at home, and in part because he was a man of simple habits and modest demeanor. Burk had no need to appear—to use the phrase then in vogue—as "a big man on campus," a modesty likely originating in his Quaker education. Instead, Burk found the process of athletic improvement so intrinsically enthralling that his focus could remain on that aspect of life, so he simply did not worry how he might appear to others.[7]

In later chapters, we will see that Burk, when he later coached rowing, would urge that same focus upon the task at hand. That coaching approach must have had its beginnings in Burk's own athletic experiences.

After the race in Ohio, Burk would occupy either the three- or five-seat in the Penn Varsity for the remainder of the 1932 season, as well as the next two seasons. And he would go on to be elected Captain of the Crew for his senior year.

Following his first varsity college season, Burk could not have missed the news that a number of oarsmen from the rowing clubs along Philadelphia's Boathouse Row had won places in the 1932 Olympic Trials. *The Philadelphia Inquirer* devoted half a sheet of the leading sports page with pictures of the Philadelphia oarsmen who would go to the Los Angeles Olympics: Penn ACs rowing association's Bill Miller would compete in the single, Pennsylvania Barge's oarsmen won the Olympic berth in the coxed pair, Undine's oarsmen the pair without cox, Penn AC's oarsmen the coxed and coxless fours, and the Bachelors Barge oarsmen, the double.

Burk had to have asked himself—*If they can do that, why can't I?*

In the fall of 1932, Burk switched back from rowing to football for the fall season. While Burk was listed as a possible replacement at center in early pre-season reports, he apparently was mainly viewed as a replacement tackle. How much he played was mentioned neither in the Philadelphia papers, nor in *The Daily Pennsylvanian*. The team went 4–2, with a win over traditional rival Cornell on Thanksgiving Day. A postseason celebratory luncheon at the Shriner's Club of Philadelphia was held on December 1, 1932.

An article on the Shriners' luncheon mentioned that two Penn players, one of them Joe Burk, were both recognized for their efforts, but both refused to make speeches, instead, simply making brief bows. This football luncheon was just the first of many occasions when Joe Burk chose silence over comment following a contentious sporting event. This reticence in Burk would be often repeated in future years, despite his growing fame.[8]

The 1933 spring rowing season opened with workouts on rowing machines then located at the bottom of Franklin Field. *The Philadelphia Inquirer*, in a "teaser" piece on January 6, 1933, showed a picture of eight Penn oarsmen on ancient rowing machinery with Rusty Callow in a suit overseeing his charges.

The Penn heavyweights would have only three races in 1933, as the whole Poughkeepsie Regatta was canceled because of the economic conditions of the Depression. Coach Callow was quoted as saying "It's just as well, I guess. With financial conditions as they are, it would be impossible for the institutions that usually enter the affair to do so this year. And without them Poughkeepsie would not be the representative event that it is. Somehow it would simply not seem like Poughkeepsie with so many institutions missing."

As of March 30, 1933, Coach Callow had not finalized his selection of the varsity heavyweight crew. While Burk was listed as the five-man, *The Inquirer* noted in its edition that day that Callow "was shifting his men about in an effort to develop a speedier shell." Most notable was the prior varsity stroke Dick Jordan, whom the paper called a "veteran Upper Darby oarsman," and who had been demoted from the varsity to the junior varisty, was reassigned to the varsity.

This 1933 season was Burk's first full year in the varsity, and one might consider whether Burk was surprised that Callow was uncertain about the correct boatings at that stage of the season. We will see that Burk would, in his own coaching years, strain to seek quantifiable measures of every oarsman's performance so as to reduce the risk of his bias as a coach affecting the selection of each member of each crew.

By this time, Callow himself had no doubt about Burk's contributions to the varsity boat. Callow had Seattle shell builder George Pocock make a special oar for Burk, with a larger blade surface, because of Burk's power through the water. The larger blade would allow Burk to pull a larger load and still finish his stroke at the same time as the other members of the crew.[9]

Penn rowed against Yale and Columbia in the Blackwell Cup at New Haven on May 6. Wind and rain reduced the number of spectators watching the event, but 5000 loyal fans boarded the observation train that ran along the side of the Housatonic River to follow each of the races. Penn led the varsity race from the beginning, rowing about 34 strokes a minute, but Yale just managed to push past Penn at the finish, sprinting at 40 strokes a minute.

Princeton beat the Penn varsity in the following Childs Cup in a close race.[10]

Navy came from behind to barely beat the Penn varsity in the Adams Cup on May 27.[11]

The financial depression limited the racing to just those three events.

Burk returned to the Penn football team for the fall season of his junior year. Burk again did not start in the varsity eleven as the football season commenced in 1933. The team played poorly against Franklin & Marshall on October 14 but managed to win 7–0. The following week, October 21, Penn lost to Dartmouth 14 to 7. Penn's Eddie Lewis scored Penn's only touchdown and had suffered a "slight" concussion during the game. He was deemed fit to play against the Navy the following week.[12]

In the week before the Navy game, *The Daily Pennsylvanian* had written an editorial criticizing the Penn student body for "not cooperating with the members of the football team in helping them keep in training." Members of the football team, including Burk, signed a letter sent to the paper refuting the paper's criticism, and asking that the letter be published, which it was Friday, October 27.

The signatories denied that the team broke training: "The members of the football team do not break training rules . . .", and they "follow a proper diet, keep proper hours, and observe proper habits. Those who live with the players do NOT encourage them to break training. . . ." Finally, the signatories said, "it strikes us that the person or persons responsible for the editorial did not show the proper Pennsylvania spirit by sniping from the rear."[13]

The day after the publication of the football team's letter, the Navy football team came to Franklin Field and hammered Penn 13-0. The Daily Pennsylvanian noted that Penn Harman inserted substitutes to attempt to stem the Navy tide, and Joe was put in the line. "For the Red and Blue, Captain . . . Engle and Joe Burk in the line were outstanding. Substitute Burk effectively plugged that hole in the right side of the line through which most of the Navy backs were making most of their gains."[14]

After the game, *The Philadelphia Inquirer* noted Burk by name, saying when he was substituted in the Navy game for "an underperforming tackle," he seemed destined to continue the role.[15]

On November 4, Penn hosted Lafayette at Franklin Field and defeated the visitors 16–7. *The Daily Pennsylvanian* lauded the team's play and mentioned Burk as shifting with the tackle of the other side of the Penn line when Lafayette punting, disturbing the kicker's form.[16]

On November 11, Penn hosted national football power Ohio State at Franklin Field. The visitors defeated Penn 20–7, but *The Daily Pennsylvanian* called Penn's performance "a Great Moral Victory," and "ranking with the most thrilling, the most spectacular football contested ever waged on the worn sward [sic] of Franklin Field." Forty five thousand spectators filled the stadium.[17] Burk was announced as the starting tackle for the all-important rematch with Ohio State in November.[18]

He emerged from that game with a "bunged" knee—not an unusual injury when the Penn team faced the far larger Ohio State team. *The Inquirer* noted that he was excused from practice the following week.

Penn faced its traditional football rival Cornell on Thanksgiving Day, November 30. Cornell bested the Quaker 11 by the score of 20 to 12. *The Daily Pennsylvanian* called the season "the worst . . . in many a moon," which must reflect the natural disappointment of losing to a traditional rival. Joe Burk was mentioned as one of the fourteen seniors who would be missed the following season.[19]

Most summaries of Burk's career in Penn football simply mention his having played for four years, which is of course correct. But his extraordinary rowing success has deflected from the fact that his path upward in football was quite gradual, and that he did not appear to start a football game for Penn until midway through his junior year. This slope of development shows a patient athlete in two different sports, not an immediate star who plays as soon as he joins a team. We will see later that Burk expected the same patience from the athletes he would later coach.

The start of the 1934 Penn heavyweight rowing season was covered by *The Daily Pennsylvanian* on the first page in its January 18, 1934, edition with an article entitled "Plans Discussed for 1934 Rowing Season at Premiere Meeting," which proclaimed, "200 crew men aspiring for positions in the varsity, jayvee, lightweight and freshmen boats reported yesterday at the season's first rowing meeting."

Coach Callow outlined that the preliminary schedule included only three races, the Childs Cup, the Blackwell Cup, and the American Henley Regatta in Philadelphia. The reason for the limited schedule was financial. There were at that time limited funds, and the traditional Penn attendance at the Poughkeepsie Regatta was not currently in the budget because of the continuing Depression nationwide. Callow took a vote from all the attendees about "whether they would rather forego all the trips for all the crews in order that there might be a freshman and varsity eight at Poughkeepsie."

The majority there voted for the established schedule—which meant a trip to Poughkeepsie would remain in jeopardy unless more funds were found for the trip and traiditonal extended stay in Poughkeepsie to practice. The newspaper commented that the vote might well have eliminated the possibility of Pennsylvania going to the championship "on account of so many institutions feeling the hard times."[20]

Penn sent its varsity and freshmen heavyweight and the varsity lightweight crews to the Concourse-Plaza Hotel in the Bronx the Friday night before the Blackwell Cup in New York, "in order to obtain as much rest as possible before the first major regatta." The budget did not allow for the jayvee heavyweights to be included in the this early arrival, and they had to take a bus to New York City before the race.[21] As waw then the traditional at Penn, Coach Callow named Joe Burk as the Captain of the team the night before the team left for New York.

In the one and three-quarter mile varsity race, Penn, who averaged 170 pounds per man (with Burk at 195), lead the heavier Yale crew (180 pounds per man) by half a length after a quarter mile, but Yale rowed through the Penn crew and won by one length, with Columbia coming in third several lengths behind. Yale also won the JV and lightweight races, but the Penn frosh beat their Yale counterparts. Columbia crews trailed in all races.[22]

Credit Associated Press Photo, Print from the Collection of Thomas Weil, Esq.

Penn next rowed Princeton and Columbia on May 12 for the Childs Cup, held at Princeton, again at a mile and three-quarters. The lighter Penn varsity stayed close to Princeton in the early going, but lost by two lengths at the finish.

On May 26, Penn's varsity won the Adams Cup against Navy and Harvard, covering the one mile and 5/16th Henley distance in record time.[23]

Penn somehow found funds to travel to the IRA Championship at Poughkeepsie, which would be the rowing season climax in June. Penn's presence triggered the usual press coverage, including a photo of Coach Callow and crew Captain Joe Burk, crouching on the Penn dock with the broad expanse of the Hudson River in the background.

The crew rowed a time trial on Tuesday, June 12 that triggered a head-line in the New York papers covering the event: *Penn Crew Looms as Dangerous Contender in Poughkeepsie Regatta*. The article outlined that both western powers Washington and California seemed strong, as did Cornell and Penn.

> Take the case of Penn. Here is unquestionable one of the lightest, if not the lightest, varsity eight ever attempting to win Poughkeepsie honors for the Quakers, averaging only about 170 pounds per man. Yet through grim determination and the flawless execution of stroking, as wrought by a really fine coach Rusty Callow, the Red and Blue men are really considered as potential winners. [24]

On race day on Saturday, June 16, the western rowing powers California and Washington pulled away from Navy, Cornell, and Penn. While Penn challenged the Western teams early, as the race developed Penn fell back, stayed locked in a tight race with Cornell for fourth place—which they barely missed.

The spectators numbered 75,000 people, spread along the expanse of the Hudson at Poughkeepsie.

GRADUATION AND LIFE AFTER COLLEGE

In June of 1934, Burk graduated from the Wharton School of Business at Penn with a degree in transportation. During his college career, he received varsity letters in both football and rowing. His name appeared regularly in the Philadelphia newspaper for his last two years in college. With his athletic renown and a degree from one of the nation's most prestigious business schools, Burk could expect to be offered many opportunities for well-paid employment and a chance for future advancement into the heights of the corporate world.

But Burk eschewed this lucrative path and instead made plans for the 1936 Olympics. Burk's move was in many ways a bold gamble. In those mid-Depression days, young men possessing newly minted Ivy League degrees were taking a risk placing their income earning years on hold for a long-shot possibility that, even if successful, would having limited economic value.

Why would Burk defer almost certain prosperity for an uncertain shot at an Olympic medal? Burk must have thought of Callow's own career arc. When the University of Washington came to Callow asking that he lead the Washington rowing team, Callow had been easily drawn back. The choice had kept Callow close to the sport he loved and in the midst of a struggle he loved: the quest to make boats go fast and to develop the character of the young men of Washington.

Burk never commented on his decision, but he must have been motivated by the sense he had more rowing to do—and he remained fascinated by the art and science of making boats go fast. Callow would be there to guide him, having promised to put together a Penn graduate boat in 1936. It is quite likely Callow himself urged Burk to stay in the sport, at least through 1936.

Burk must have reasoned the corporate world could be tried after 1936. Meanwhile, Joe knew his father would need help on the farm. So he returned to his old rhythms of life—he would farm and he would row. This quiet product of a Quaker School, this picker of apples from the fields of New Jersey, would set his sights on the Olympics.

But the effect of Burk's Wharton education on his rowing and later coaching has been underappreciated. His business training gave him a facility with numbers, and an eye for practically testing what led to success. Burk was, in the modern parlance, data driven.

Burk's daughter would later remember that he wished that his grandson Michael had taken more accounting courses at Penn, because Burk proclaimed, "Accounting is fascinating!" Burk was trained as a man of numbers, and he naturally sought to quantify in order to optimize. He would as a single sculler, and later as a coach attempt to improve rowing by focusing on measurement and quantification of results over time. Other oarsmen, other coaches might focus on what a rowing style looked like. Burk naturally focused more on measuring speed than critiquing style.

This approach would be apparent later in his own sculling, and in the way his Yale and Penn crews would later row.

Burk knew he had been fortunate to row for Rusty Callow. But Callow could not coach Burk for the next two years, so Burk—probably at Callow's suggestion—moved down Boathouse Row to Penn AC. Young Burk soon found he was blessed with another good coach. The Penn AC team in 1935 and 1936 was coached by Frank Muller, who had been for many years the sculling coach for John B. Kelly Sr., winner of Olympic gold medals in the single and double sculls in the 1920s.

As coach at Penn AC, Muller required all of his oarsmen to learn to scull—even if they never planned to race in anything except sweep boats. This was a major change for Burk, since his Penn experience had been only in eights. The change would forever alter Burk's own rowing focus.

Small boats—and particularly the single—taught their own lessons in balance and restraint, in feeling the boat's reaction to the oars. In an eight, the boats were so big they gave less feedback to an oarsman—the single, the pair (with one oar per rower), the double (with two), the four (with one oar each), and the quad (with two) were not so forgiving. Rowing those smaller boats improved an oarsman's rhythm and taught him to better sense the flow of the boat through the water.

We will see later in his letters to Pocock that Burk learned to constantly study the flow of the boat through the water. This study allowed him to adapt his whole technique to maximize the efficiency of his stroke. The process began with the two years of training with Muller.

Burk said of that first season in 1935: "I was teamed with a young fellow, Tony Gallagher. He was a strong young kid with no previous rowing experience. We made a good combination in the double and were undefeated. It was a good summer, and it prompted me to get a single built by George Pocock."[25]

Burk, the future sculling champion, was being formed. And Burk—who doubtless had absorbed Callow's respect for and reliance upon George Pocock—now began his own study, primarily via correspondence, under Pocock, who built shells in Seattle and served as an unofficial coach of coaches for the University of Washington rowing near his shop.

CHAPTER FOUR

A Sculler and His
Final Mentor

During his college years rowing for the University of Pennsylvania, Joe Burk had rowed solely in boats provided by the University for its student oarsmen. After his 1934 graduation, Joe had used the rowing and sculling boats of the Penn AC. In both teams, most of the boats and oars Burk had used were built by America's preeminent boatbuilder—a brilliant Englishman named George Yeomans Pocock.

After his successful 1935 season with Penn AC in the double sculls, Burk began to envision a possible path in single sculling and considered purchasing his own boat. He naturally turned to Pocock, who by then built most of the shells then used in America, from singles to eights.

It is impossible to overstate how important Burk's choice to work with Pocock was. Just as Callow had asked Pocock to build a new eight for the 1923 Washington crew, Burk now in 1936 asked Pocock to build him a single. Theirs would be an historic partnership.

George Pocock had grown up in a family of boatbuilders and watermen in England. The Pocock family's lives revolved around making boats and mastering the art of rowing them—first in working boats that acted as ferries for passengers or lighter boats for moving freight from large vessels to shore. Pocock's father was so accomplished as a boat builder and oarsman that he had been named the boatman for Eton College—the preparatory school of choice for the upper classes of England, and historically one of the finest producers of young oarsmen in the world.

Pocock and his brother, Dick, were themselves champion scullers early in the twentieth century, but their passion and their family livelihood was boatbuilding. Before 1910, they worked for their father in the Eton Boathouse, where they were in daily contact with those Eton students who chose to row.

It is impossible to overstate to the modern American reader how elite the rowing in Britain and at Eton in particular were in that era. Before the First World War, when a young George Pocock was training Eton boys to row, Britain held the reins of an empire that literally circled the globe. The phrase most proudly used in Britain was "The Sun Never Sets on the British Empire"—because literally, it did not. During the whole rotation of the earth, the sun always shone upon some part of the empire controlled by the British nation.

Then as now, Eton enjoyed one of the best fleets of rowing shells in the world, more than 700 boats, and the most advanced rowing training opportunities for young oarsmen. In an elegant example of paradox, many aristocratic sons were drawn to the mastery of the craft of rowing a boat. Their teachers were the sons of men of another social strata who had been goaded to row by economic necessity. While Eton boys had no economic need to row—they were drawn to the boats by a need to master an important and rewarding craft.

The act of rowing well has its intrinsic reward, which can only be appreciated by the experience of pulling the oar and feeling the boat respond. Those who first experienced rowing in Britain were the working men serving the commercial vessels that moved goods to and from ships in rivers all over Britain. That work was done by specialized small boats called wherries or lighter boats, and the men who rowed did it for much needed money rather than pleasure.

But the thrill of watching well-handled boats move over water had its own appeal, and racing between those who worked in boats gradually shifted to be more of a spectator event. What had begun as an economic necessity for the poor slowly transformed into an athletic endeavor with its own delight for whomever could master it. Over time, rowing became understood as a sport appropriate for the lessons of discipline, hardiness, and boat-handling skill it instilled.

This appreciation was not lost on the wealthy of Britain. In the 1800s, they sent their sons to Eton, to gain the advantages in life that would make them rich, powerful, or famous, or all three. The powers at Eton, judging that an active sports program featuring rowing would enable the sons of empire to develop the character traits leading to success, kept a huge fleet of boats and maintained them by hiring the best boatbuilders they could find. In the early part of the 20th Century, that man was Aaron Pocock, George Pocock's father.

Once they felt the earliest signs of progress in rowing, these sons of the aristocracy were eager to learn the lessons that could be taught only by those who had built and rowed a boat for a living. As one George Pocock biographer said, "[W]atermanship was a great equalizer."[26]

Among those Etonians the Pocock brothers, George and Dick, had informally coached was Anthony Eden, "scion of a centuries-old baronial family, who would leave Eton to join the Army in 1914 and rise to the rank of Brigade Major at the tender age of twenty. He went on to become a cabinet officer under Winston Churchill, and later Prime Minister."[27]

The Pocock family suffered a terrible blow when the senior Pocock lost his job at Eton in 1910 due to political rivalries at the school. He briefly left the boat business, but soon returned to itinerant boatbuilding wherever in England he could find work.

The Pocock sons, George and Dick, had been asked by Eton officials to stay on at the school, but the brothers loyally refused to remain at Eton if their father was excluded. By that decision, they were forced to face an uncertain future, and decide where their best chance of success might lie.

The boys first considered Australia, where gold and other precious minerals were being found. But a suitor of their sister told them of the wonderful wages being paid in western Canada. The suitor's brother was employed there, in British Columbia, where he was "making ten pounds a week sawing down trees."[28]

Such wages sounded like the legendary El Dorado to the hard-working young Pococks. Like many sons of the English working class of the time, they decided their opportunities would be best in the westernmost part of Canada. The Pocock brothers took their own boatbuilding skills to Vancouver, and there they began building incredibly fast, technically superior boats from the fine old-growth cedar found all over the Pacific Northwest.

On its surface, the Pocock brothers' emigration from England was just another story of two disenchanted and impecunious Brits seeking a better life in the New World, as so many of their contemporaries were doing. But their move, forced as it was, would act as "a brain drain" of rowing and boatbuilding knowledge—a loss which was to fetter British rowing fortunes for decades to come.

Many years later, the British Olympic champion Jack Beresford, who would win both Olympic and Henley honors for Britain, would later attribute the decline in British rowing fortunes to the Pococks' emigration. "We never should have let men like the Pococks get away from England," he proclaimed.[29]

Burk's impending purchase of a single from George Pocock facilitated what Pocock himself called "some of the best correspondence I had . . . [on boatbuilding] with Joe Burk who, after graduation from the University of Pennsylvania where he rowed four years under Rusty Callow, took up sculling in a single shell with the object of competing in the Diamond Sculls at Henley."[30]

Only part of that correspondence still exists—Burk's letters to Pocock, which were in the possession of Dr. Thomas Mendenhall, formerly professor of history at Yale, and later president of Smith College. Sadly, Pocock's letters to Burk did not survive. Joe Burk's son Roger reported that, upon his father's retirement from coaching at the University of Pennsylvania in the summer of 1969, Joe Burk disposed of a large portion of his archival material. The coach's impulse for a fresh start denies us the insights such material would now yield.

The letters from Burk to Pocock as they now exist are now all available online at http://www.rowinghistory.net/essays/joe-burk -letters.

As the 1935 rowing season was set to begin, Burk began to prepare in earnest for the challenges to come. Having used the sculling boats available at Penn AC, Burk knew he needed his own boat, and to gain the competitive edge he would require, only a boat by the master Pocock would do. What he could not have imagined was that a lifelong mentorship was about to begin.

In January, Burk sent Pocock his first inquiry about ordering a standard single shell with no specific modifications. In response to Burk's initial request, Pocock sent Burk a quote for a single of $225, which would be just under $5000 today.[31] On February 13, 1935, Burk wrote back to Pocock acknowledging receipt of the letter from February 1 and enclosing a check to Pocock for payment in full. The last sentence of Burk's letter read: "I am very sorry that I was delayed in answering your letter and hope that it has caused you no great inconvenience." The letterhead Burk used shows the name and return address of Burk's father:

PAUL H. BURK
Fruit Grower
Buttonwood Farm
Beverly, N.J.

Burk's apology for delaying his response to a letter that had likely reached him but a few days prior displays an uncommon measure of courtesy, and it perhaps touched the old master. A quiet and ever-polite man, George Pocock soon came to appreciate Burk's own old-fashioned promptness and fastidiousness in his business dealings.

Burk was a quick learner. By August 12, 1935, after Burk had rowed only a few months in his first single, he had satisfied himself that he could do better with different rigging specifications and decided to ask Pocock to build a second single, this time with some very specific modifications:

Dear Mr. Pocock,

I still have my shell in my possession but have been able to save enough money for a new one. There are several fellows that are anxious to buy the boat but do not have the necessary cash at the present time. Eventually, I guess, it will be sold and I still have hopes of selling it before the end of the rowing weather.

Do you suppose you could build me a shell and have it here by the beginning of November? The reason why I set this date is that I am very anxious to start some single sculling in the fall and coupled with this is the possibility of going south with my brother[32] about the middle of November. I might even be able to take my shell with me.

At any rate, I wish you would start work on it as soon as possible and I will send you a check whenever you would so desire.[33] Also, could the shell be shipped by water in order to save on the transportation charges? If so, what would be the cost by water, and by all rail?

There are several bits of information which I would like to give which may be of some help. First of all the track of my present shell seemed to be too short. With the foot stretchers[34] all the way out[35] I could still just touch the forward blocks of the track with the seat and furthermore, I couldn't come up the slide as far as I am used to. This, in turn, I believe led to the following conditions. At the end of the stroke there was not enough clearance to allow the oar handles to swing out to the side of my body. It was impossible to swing them to the side even if I had an extra-long "lay back." I thought it might help you to give you my leg measurements—it is almost exactly 36 inches inside measurement.[36] Next, the foot stretcher seems to be too flat. At the finish of the stroke they seemed to be tight. I think it would help, not only in comfort, but in leg-power to have them at a greater angle to the keel. More like this ╱ and not like this —. Use your own judgment.

In George Pocock's records, Burk's letter is followed by a bill of lading, date stamped 30 Sept. 1935, for transfer of an item identified only as "Mil Frt"—likely "Mill Freight" and Burk's second single—to the

Luckenbach Steamship Company, with a total transportation charge of $9.50.

What can we glean from Burk's suggested changes for this second boat? First, that Burk found it comfortable to compress his legs more fully than most oarsmen, and further, that the finish he found most comfortable was somewhat upright, since he was asking Pocock to make adjustments so his body would not be too far past vertical at the end of the stroke (what Burk called "lay back"). This would be the style that Burk himself would determine was the most efficient and it is the precise style we see in the footage from his triumphant Henley victory three years later in the Diamond Sculls.

This correspondence has been studied by Gregg Stone, 1977 through 1979 single sculler for the U.S. team, and coach of his daughter Gevvie Stone, U.S. silver medalist in the 2016 Rio Olympics. Gregg suspected that the first Pocock single was built with stock parts, and in that era "the Pocock slides were short. Most people were short."

Stone thought Burk's request that the foot angle to the hull of the boat be less acute "was quite astute, allowing more power," although he also thought the suggestion for the angle change could have come from Frank Muller, then coaching Burk.

In 1936, Joe switched back to Callow's College Boat Club. He rowed in two boat classes competing for an Olympic berth—both in the "graduate eight" coached by Callow, and in the single. Joe Burk thus had two chances of making the 1936 U.S. Olympic Team. The first chance came in the single, in which trials took place in Princeton on July 4, 1936. Burk was placed in the second heat of what was called the Single Sculls National Championship and Olympic TryOuts. Three entrants were in this second heat, and only the winner would advance. Unlike heat and final formats in later years, at these Trials, if a competitor lost his heat, there was no second chance race, what we now called a *repechage*—a French word meaning literally "fish out," or "rescue."

The Union Boat Club entrant in the heat, former Harvard oar Russell Sturgis Codman scratched from the event. That left Joe Burk, then 22, representing the College Boat Club, and Daniel H. Barrow Jr., representing PennAC. Barrow was 27 and had had a strong rowing career. He had been the seven-man of the Penn AC "Big Boat" of 1930, which had travelled to Europe and won the European Eight-Oared Championship against a powerful international field.

In the heat between Burk and Barrow, Barrow won in a time of 7 minutes, 53.5 seconds. Burk was less than four seconds behind in 7 minutes, 57 seconds, described by *The* Philadelphia Inquirer as one and a half lengths.[37] Both Gregg Stone and Rick Stehlik (1973 World Championship bronze medalist in the lightweight double and restorer of the Burk single at Penn) viewed the margin as small in a two-boat singles race.

There was evidence to support that optimistic view. In the races following Burk's loss to Barrow, no one who advanced from the others heats and opposed Barrow in the semis and final would stay as close to Barrow as Burk had done in his heat. While it might have been possible that Barrow eased up in the heat when he knew he would beat Burk, the closeness of the race could also be read to suggest that Joe Burk in 1936 *might* have been the second fastest sculler in America.

Burk did not again row against Barrow in the single that year. Barrow went on to Berlin and won the Olympic bronze medal. Burk doubtless took heart in the fact that he had been rowing that summer at a pace not terribly far from what was necessary to win an Olympic medal.[38] And Burk believed that hard work in future years might well close the gap Barrow then enjoyed.

Burk's second chance in 1936 for an Olympic spot was in the eight-oared shell, where he rowed five in the Penn graduate eight, a crew of three Penn graduates (Burk, Jordan, and Swift) and the remaining five from the 1936 Penn Varsity, all rowing under the banner of the College Boat Club, the original club name for Pennsylvania undergraduate oarsmen during the 1800s. He was probably given back the extra-large oar that Coach Rusty Callow had earlier had George Pocock make for him, so his stronger stroke would end in tandem with the other oarsmen.

In the Olympic Trials finals of the eight-oared shells, Penn led for three-quarters of the race, rowing at a higher stroke rate than the eventual winners, the University of Washington (now known forever as *The Boys in the Boat*). Penn surrendered the lead only in the last quarter of the race but was a full length down as the boats crossed the finish line.[39]

Washington would go on to win the gold medal in Berlin.

What Burk *had* won was an education in where he stood versus the world's best competition; one which he was soon to take, quite literally, home.

After the 1936 Olympic Trials, Burk chose to continue to train for the next Olympics, but he would compete exclusively in the single. He also soon moved the bulk of his training from the Schuylkill River to the Rancocas Creek that flowed by his father's farm. It would be on this water—where he was the only oarsman—that Burk would develop, with George Pocock's help, what would become his unique and world-beating sculling style.

CHAPTER FIVE

Alone on Rancocas Creek

urk must have been pleased when he read on January 13, 1937, of his former college coach Rusty Callow complimenting Burk's little brother Jim. "The younger Burk may well develop into as great an oarsman as his brother."[40]

In 1937, Joe Burk was embarking on a solitary quest—one without a coach, and without teammates, other than when he and his brother Jim sculled together. He was setting his whole life up around sculling. He had bought his own single, fully customized, from George Pocock and had constructed a rudimentary cart to push it across State Route 130 near the family farm to the small boat dock he had built along the Rancocas Creek.

He rowed frequently, but not every day, because the physical work on the farm was always long, and sometimes brutal, labor. No more travel to Philadelphia, and no more school work.

Only sculling and the farm.

The details of Burk's plan involved walking off a course of the Henley distance—precisely one mile and five sixteenths, and marking the course so he would know exactly when he crossed the line in each direction. The course he rowed can still be viewed from a present-day pier into Rancocas Creek at 626 Harrison Street in Riverside, New

THE BRITISH HENLEY THEIR DESTINATION

1939

Joe Burk wheels shell from Bridgeboro, N. J., home to truck, which will take it to New York. He sails tomorrow to defen Diamond Sculls title. The boat-barrow is Joe's idea—to carry shell back and forth to practice on Rancocas creek

Credit: Burk Family Scrapbook

Jersey. The bottom floor of the building is occupied by a restaurant called *The Best of the Wurst*. The pier is approximately the midpoint of the race course.[41]

It was on this course that Burk would train, comparing times upstream to the east with downstream to the west toward the Delaware River. He would average them to roughly determine his time in still water. He then took the known times from the courses on which he intended to race, such as Henley Regatta, and estimated the average speeds he would have to attain in order to win those events. His intent was to train himself so he could maintain the average pace needed to win the race.

Burk's approach to maintaining an average winning pace was a dramatic departure from the prominent racing strategy then being used. "In Joe's era in sculling," said Peter Mallory, "the standard method was to blast off the start at your fastest possible rate, to discourage your opponents, so they would lose heart and give up. Those

(downstream toward the Delaware River)

(upstream)

trailing would most frequently challenge no further and all would row to the finish line. Joe's approach was truly radical. When Joe would get behind early, but then not give up, the leader would panic late in the race when he saw Joe relentlessly cutting into his lead. That was one of Joe's innovations."[42]

Part of the innovation sprang from the fact that Burk's training was almost entirely done alone. Relatively few athletes training alone have been able to reach the heights of international competition.[43] Many outstanding modern rowers now say that the daily presence of strong competition alongside practice is key to making progress. Such an approach has been incorporated into many modern rowing teams. Today's U.S. Rowing Team candidates now tend, with their coaches' and mentors' approval, to train together in groups of elite sub-teams and consciously row together as often as possible.[44]

Joe Burk, having tried this approach from 1934 to 1936, decided instead to take the more monastic path. He would row by himself almost exclusively, and would race the clock.

Burk's original approach of first estimating the winning times at each race distance and then basing his training on setting the attainment of those times has a modern equivalent. Jurgen Grobler, the former East German rowing coach (1972–1990) who later coached at the UK's renowned Leander Boat Club and then the United Kingdom men's team (1991–2016), would each year predict the winning time of the boats in each event in which he was coaching, and base all training for the year on the goal of meeting or besting those times. This prediction technique for the upcoming year was standard coaching practice according to the former East German Coaching Manual.[45] In this regard, Burk seems to have anticipated modern coaching practice.

But Burk did not report use the modern practice of developing aerobic ability by rowing longer than race distances as less than race pace, and slowly building great speed over time. Once Burk had determined what his race speed goals were set, Burk told his son Roger that he limited his practice mainly to the practicing of rowing at as close to anticipated race speed as possible. Burk's own logs were discarded, so we can only use sources who interviewed Burk about his training during that time. Fortunately, we have two reliable sources.

Rowing historian Thomas Mendenhall interviewed Joe Burk in person about his sculling during 1937 to 1940, and is quoted in Peter Mallory's *The Sport of Rowing* as follows:

> Joe: "When I first attempted it, I could go only a short distance before fatigue set in. So, I decided to scull every stroke in this manner . . ."
>
> According to historian Mendenhall, "the outings began with short stretches to warm up with and then longer pieces at racing stroke, 36 the first year, then up to 38. Eventually he was sculling for twenty minutes at 40–42. Everything was directed to eliminate all wasted motion, anything that might reduce the rate of striking with the slide continuously moving. The speed on the recovery was the same as on the pull through."
>
> In Burk's words, "I gradually adjusted to it. However, I sculled at that high rate with the same technique throughout the entire workout. When it became rather easy, I increased the rate and worked on that, over and over again.
>
> "Gradually, my distance grew greater and greater. Finally, I was able to do a full course in their manner. It was not very fast for a short distance, but it was fast enough to win at the normal race distance . . . I was not worried when my opponent moved away a bit at the start of a mile and a quarter race."[46]
>
> The other source is Joe's son Roger Burk, who recalled when he and his father discussed the older man's sculling during the late thirties. ". . . [I] don't know how much low intensity work Dad did. He only told me about ten minute pieces at full power. Once he could hold a given stroke rate for ten minutes, he would work on a stroke rate a bit higher."
>
> "When Dad was training in the single, he never did anything but full power. And he used his stroke rate as a tachometer. And that's fine

if you are very honest about your stroke count telling you how fast you are going—if you're not starting to shorten up, or coming too fast up the slide. So he would start out training at 34. He is going to practice rowing at a 34, being certain that he was rowing his perfect 34 stroke. And then, when he was able to do that for ten minutes straight, he would go to 36, but then lower the time [i.e., increase the speed].

". . . So he would be practicing rowing at a certain rate when he could row at that rate for ten minutes, he would have confidence he could row the stroke for the full race. . . . Everything was sort of race specific . . . his heavy training periods were fall, winter and spring."[47]

When asked whether his father had incorporated any training in what was then called "the Washington style," long pieces of many miles at a low stroke, Roger Burk said no. His father concentrated all his energies on perfecting his sculling stroke at full power, and at the racing speeds he thought he needed to reach in order to win.

"His philosophy was, you learn to row at race pace by rowing at race pace. Dad thought that a ten-minute piece would give him a cushion, since most of his races would be seven to 8 minutes. He would be confident if he could scull at race speed for ten minutes . . ."

When asked whether Joe did any long pieces at a lower stroke in the winter, Roger replied, "He thought if you did that, you'd be practicing rowing at a power and a stroke rate that you would never use in a race." When asked, Roger was not clear how long the total time of Joe's sculling practices were, but said, "I bet that the amount of time between these race pieces was substantial. It was not so much a matter of beating yourself into shape, it was practice in rowing."

"While we did not discuss it in detail, he said that from time to time, he did shorter pieces, to make it a little bit harder, just to make the ten-minute pieces a little bit more comfortable to him. And of course, nothing was 500 meters, it was quarter miles. I never heard him talking about any (long distance) University of Washington type practice, it was all geared to specific racing course conditions. His long-distance stuff came much later in his rowing and coaching career . . . that was the Lydiard philosophy . . ." (See Chapter Twelve which covers when Burk adopted a different training approach from New Zealand distance running coach Arthur Lydiard.)

Roger said that his father normally rowed five days a week during this period. A *Time Magazine* article from July 1938 relates that Burk had rowed 3,000 miles "throughout last winter and summer." It is not clear whether this was a figure Burk himself gave the reporter, or whether the reporter made a guess that burnished the hero and the story. Three thousand miles is an average of just under 18.6 kilometers a day, rowing five days a week, about half the weekly training mileage roughly done by the major international teams do today. Most international teams today row much of their mileage at 70 or 80 percent of a race day pace.

Roger Burk had an interesting story about how international class rowers competing in the 1974–76 era viewed his father's training. Roger had, upon his return in 1972 from service in Vietnam, resumed training with an eye to the 1972 Olympic Singles Trials and located himself at the Long Beach Rowing Association. Roger trained with Tom McKibbon and John Van Blom among others. He later returned to Long Beach to attend civilian flight school and renewed his friendship with Van Blom, and his then wife Joan Lind Van Blom.

As she was training for the 1976 Olympics (where she would win the silver medal in a disfavored outer lane against the reigning East German champion), Joan asked Roger about his father's training regime, and Roger began to relay the story just above.

"She made me stop," recalled, smiling at the irony of the moment. "She knew that she could never get away with so little. And she didn't want to hear it, she didn't want the temptation to cut back her program. Because of all the summer farm work, [my Dad] actually did very little [in the racing season]. Just a few quarter mile pieces, presumably to maintain a feel for the boat and water. The real work was done in late Fall and early Spring."[48]

Roger recalled that Joan was then rowing morning doing multiple raced three-mile pieces to a nearby Island, and then another race back. She and her training partners would do weight work at noon, or some other gyms work, and then multiple 500-meter pieces in the late afternoon.

We are left with a fascinating historic record. While Burk had clearly effected a dramatic increase in his stroke rate versus the other scullers of his era, his total volume of work appears modest when measured by later standards.

However, we view the comparisons to today's rowing, historian Tom Mendenhall captures a Burk variance from the orthodoxy of the day: "He reasoned that the boat should move much faster with less effort once he had shortened the stroke at both ends and conditioned himself to row comfortably at a higher rating."

Burk himself was clear on this latter point—he was trying to stroke more quickly *not because it was harder, but because it was easier*. It was analogous to a runner shortening his stride and increasing his leg turnover instead of running in bounds with an excessively long stride.

From 1937 to 1940, Burk would develop and train himself into the best single sculler in the world—and did it alone on the banks of the Rancocas Creek, far from Boathouse Row and away from many of the oarsmen with whom he would compete. Burk was able to be honest enough with himself to submit to the relentless clock and to gauge his training result with the diligence and honesty of a scientist recording the results of a lab experiment. If he could beat the clock, he reasoned, he would beat his opponents.

Burk was confident working with the science and numbers of rowing and performance. His financial training at the Wharton School of Business at Penn and the quantification and measurement used there came naturally to him. His daughter Kathy would tell a story from the era when Joe's grandson Kevin McCaffery was studying at Penn, where he graduated in 2008. Burk thought his grandson got a fine education at Penn, but he repeatedly told Kathy he "wished Kevin and taken more accounting courses. Accounting is *interesting!*" he would tell his daughter.[49]

In 1937, Joe Burk's first racing season focusing solely on sculling could not have gone better. Since Callow no longer conducted a College Boat Club system after the 1936 Olympic Trials, Burk returned to enter events under the Penn AC banner, although he rarely sculled at the boathouse itself. But his first 1937 race, his ten-length victory at the American Henley in Philadelphia, suggested the dawn of a new era along Boathouse Row.

But Burk's win, when published, had to compete with a major headline of the day, the details of which will give the reader a sense of the era in which Burk's sculling breakthrough was occurring. The tragic passing of yet another victim of the zeppelin *Hindenburg*'s explosion was the page-one headline in *The Philadelphia Inquirer*, as was Justice Louis Brandeis' refusal to retire despite President Franklin Roosevelt's suggestion that justices should not sit beyond age 70. Such were the times in which Burk's sculling reign began.

Burk's sculling soon generated headlines again, when he won the People's Regatta (now called the Independence Day Regatta) in Philadelphia on July 5—again by ten lengths in what *The Inquirer* termed "a complete runaway."[50] Then, on July 31 at the Canadian Henley at St. Catherine's Ontario, Burk put his pacing theory firmly to the test, conceding to John Coulson of the Toronto Argonauts a lead of *six full lengths*, and then catching him in the final 550 yards. Coulson was so hard pressed in his attempt to hold off Burk that he rolled his single just past the finish line and was unconscious when pulled from the water by the referee's launch.[51]

Burk ideas about pacing and effort were obviously steering him to success. The typical race strategy of the era was to explode from the start floats and try to "break" your opponent. Joe was following an "even splits" strategy of hitting his target speed and then never slowing down, allowing him to sweep past an opponent (like Coulson) who went out at a pace faster than he could maintain to the finish.[52]

Burk thereafter won the U.S. single sculling championship in Buffalo in August. The newspaper article announcing Burk's victory reported that "the red-headed sculling giant" would remain in top form, "never breaking training, but continuing his regular practice work at his farm on the Rancocas Creek in New Jersey."[53]

But Burk was quick to attribute his success to something other than his new method of pacing. An AP wire story appeared on August 21, entitled *Joe Burk Attributes His Rise to Fame to Seattle Boat Builder*:

Joe Burk, Canadian and United States single sculling champion, attributes his rise to fame to a new stroke suggested to him by George Pocock, builder of his shell at Seattle.

"He told me at Poughkeepsie one year to eliminate the layback and finish vertically," said Burk. . . .,

"I found George's system worked for me," Burk continued. "I also got my hands away quicker to speed up the stroke. At St. Catherine's, Ontario . . . I held to a beat of 40; most scullers row only 28. Even Pocock thinks that's sufficient, but I found I could hit 40. At 40 strokes a minute you can scull past a lot of boats."

Indeed you can—if you are Joe Burk.

It is hard to overstate the high regard for Joe Burk his 1937 season had instilled in the rowing world. In an article about the Penn AC rowing team being assembled for 1938, the team was described as being "led by gigantic Joe Burk." Among the Club's plan was "a possible trip to England for Joe Burk to compete in the Diamond Sculls next summer."[54]

Henley Regatta's Diamond Sculls was the championship event for single sculls, historically attended by the world's preeminent scullers, and in that time was generally regarded as the World Championship for scullers, at least in non-Olympic years.

But in order to justify going to Henley, Burk had to continue his exceptional sculling success. In Burk's first race of the season, a Championship Single Sculls, held at the same time as the Penn Varsity was racing in the Childs Cup, drew only one opponent—Roger Bates of New England's Cambridge Boat Club. Burk beat Bates by over a minute, a decisive win.[55] Two weeks later, Burk won a race on the Harlem River in rough water by eight lengths.[56]

Such domination promptly sent Burk to Henley Royal Regatta. On that first international trip, he was accompanied by his parents as shown in the photo on Page 3.

Preceding Joe Burk to England was a letter from the head of Penn AC, Henry Penn Burke (no relation) addressed to "Mr. Jack Arlett,

Henley, England," dated June 6, 1938. A copy of the letter remains in the possession of the Burk family, and it shows the smallness of the rowing world, and the high regard the American rowing community held for the families of English watermen who then dominated the Henley rowing scene. The Arletts were as knowledgeable about rowing at Henley as any family in the United Kingdom. Jack Arlett had been born in Henley-on-Thames and placed second in the World's Professional Single sculls from 1912 until 1920. His son Henry Arlett would scull with Burk and assist him both in 1938 and the following year in 1939.[57]

The letter read:

Dear Mr. Arlett:

Your friend, Mr. Geo. Pocock of Seattle, Washington, advises me that you are the best man at Henley to give attention and advise [sic] to anyone planning to row on your famous course.

I have entered a young man name Joseph William Burk for the Diamond Sculls. He is sailing from New York on the Normandie on June 15th and will arrive in Henley about June 20th.

My advice to Burk is to see you immediately upon his arrival at Henley and I wish you would give him your attention and best advice which I know will be valuable to him in his competition.

Incidentally, Geo. Pocock built the boat and sculls which Burk will row. You will no doubt consider Burk's style very unorthodox but he has had remarkable success having won the Canadian and American Championships last year. In Canada he decisively defeated Coulson, Campbell, Miller, Reed and others.

He is an exceptionally strong man and is able to row his style which would exhaust the average man before he had gone half a mile.

What he will need is practice rowing and advice regarding the water conditions. Geo Pocock tells me you have a number of sons who could go sculling with Burk.

As an old professional waterman, you know about what is needed and I am sure from what Geo. Pocock tells me about you that Burk could not be in any better hands.

Thanking you to be on the lookout for him and give him your vest [sic] attention, I am,

Very truly yours,
Henry Penn Burke

Joe Burk was—in short—being handed off to the best local coaching available in Britain in that day.

Burk was never seriously challenged at Henley in 1938. His custom Pocock shell—classified as freight—was diverted to Cherbourg, France for obscure import-export reasons, rather than being landed with Burk and his parents at Portsmouth. But after much consternation and a few phone calls, the boat itself was soon in Henley and Burk quickly acclimated to the waters of the Thames.

Joe later admitted that the 1938 Henley field was not as strong as it could have been. Conflicts in Europe over Germany's rise, and Britain's opposition to that rise, meant that a number of talented scullers from Europe simply did not come to Henley, largely as a form of protest. Burk found his races before the final not difficult, and his victories were decisive. Burk said that because of this, he intended his performance in the final to include winning the race in as fast a time as possible, so that there would be no doubt of his abilities even if the field were less than robust.

Racing at Henley has always been a series of single elimination match races on a two-lane course. Less experienced or less confident crews have therefore placed great value in attempting to push to the maximum right from the start, to get ahead of the other crew. The advantage of such an approach is leading crew can see their opponents, and the trailing crew must look around to see how far they are behind. In the narrow two-lane Henley Reach, with no buoys separating the two shell from each other, it is an advantage to get ahead and move toward the center to have your wake affect the trailing competition, and washing down the competition with your puddles, and to be able to tactically respond to a move from your opponent.

In the Diamond Sculls finals, Burk's opponent, L. D. Habbitts, pushed quickly off the start in a vain attempt to discourage Burk. Burk

(Cont'd on next page)

Setting a new record of 8:02 in Diamond Sculls in 1938 Henley. Previous record was 8:10, set in 1905 by F.S. Kelly of Tasmania. Photo: Bushell

Source is OARSMAN magazine, July/August 1978

simply kept the pace he knew he had to achieve to win, and pulled smoothly past Habbitts to win by 100 yards, about 11 boat lengths—a mammoth margin.

Burk's time, rowed in favorable conditions, was a new course record which would stand for almost three decades.

There still exists today a thirty second video of Burk's phenomenal performance at Henley as he crossed the finish line in 1938. It is the starting segment of a video overview of the 1938 Henley Regatta. In it, one can observe that the fluid nature of Burk's stroke is remarkably similar to scullers racing internationally today, sitting upright and rowing at a rate near 40.[58] In 1938, Burk was truly ahead of his time.

Burk's daughter, Kathy Burk McCaffery, retains in her father's archives a record album containing the live radio broadcast from Henley on that day. The English announcer calls out the last few moments of the race and, as Burk is motioned to come over the broadcast area, the announcer fills the time as Burk rows toward him with a commentary of what he sees:

And Burk—who has just won this race—he is a tall, fine-looking fellow, fair hair and beautifully built, magnificent arms and legs

that power him over the course . . . he has a bit of weight on him,
he's a hundred and ninety-four pounds, you call it in America, and
Habbitts is more like a hundred and sixty-eight . . . so [*Burk*] *had*
weight on him there. But such a magnificent physique, it's not sur-
prising that he had earned everything in America and Canada,
and now the biggest sculling race in Great Britain, he deserves ev-
ery bit, and he deserves to crack the record by eight seconds, after it
stood for thirty-five years . . ."

[*The announcer read the time*] *8:02—won easily . . .* [*at*
Henley, the margin of victory is hoisted on a preprinted board—
when the margin is so large that the loser would be embarrassed
if it were quantified, the verdict given by the officials as "Easily."]

There is a pause, and a distinctly American voice is heard:

"Hello everybody back home. I must have had a couple of horse
shoes in the boat with me . . ."—a reference to being lucky—"Half
a dozen I guess . . . they still appreciate horses over here . . . Thank
you."

And then Burk is gone.

Such a brief and self-deprecatory reply at the moment of greatest
victory, when lesser men might be tempted to preen, was wholly in
keeping with Burk's character and his Quaker education. Lucky horse-
shoes, indeed.

Burk did admit later to his local newspaper in Camden, New Jersey that, "The competition wasn't so hot, because political troubles
affected the regatta. There were no scullers from Germany, Austria,
and Switzerland present. That's the reason I wanted to set the record,
to show 'em I had the stuff even if the going wasn't tough."

Upon his return to the States, Burk was given victory celebrations
in New York, and again in Philadelphia, and finally in his hometown of
Riverside, New Jersey, where he rode in a parade. Burk accepted these
repeating ceremonies of victory with an easy grace. He acknowledged
each celebration with modesty and afterward seemed unchanged by
the adulation. So began a public life of a man who likely had no need

Photo above shows Burk soon after the Henley final, raising his hand in victory. International News Photo – from the collection of Thomas Weil, Esq.

of one—but was accepting of what came with his considerable success. The Quaker teaching remained.

After his return to North America, Burk easily won the U.S. and Canadian titles again later in the summer. At year's end, his sculling dominance was clear.

Sometime during this time frame, and after Burk had won at least his first Diamond Sculls title, George Pocock had the opportunity to come east from Seattle and visited Burk and his parents at their farmhouse on Rancocas Creek. The Burks and their guest sat down to dinner, served by Burk's mother Marguerite. The main course was roast beef, and Pocock was surprised to see that Joe Burk—still weighing near two hundred pounds and training and farming daily—chose

from Burk Family Scrapbook

to eat only a very small piece of beef, though the serving platter was quite full.

Such restraint in eating struck Pocock as evidence of a powerful discipline, parts of which had already been revealed to him in his work with Burk. Over twenty years later, Pocock told Joe's son Roger Burk, then rowing out of the Pocock shop, about his father's apparent daily discipline. Ten years after that, Pocock told Bill Tytus about the incident when the two were trading stories about great scullers.[59] (As we will see later, Tytus would, in the 1960s, ask Burk if he could row from the Penn Boathouse, and would himself buy the Pocock business from Stan Pocock in the 1970s.)

In 1939, Joe Burk again trained at home on the Rancocas, but this year he frequently was joined by his younger brother Jim, who was then rowing for Rusty Callow at Penn, who also sculled with his older brother as time allowed.

The documentary record about Joe Burk still available in both newspapers and photos still in existence begins after the 1938 to change to the eye of a modern reader. After his first Henley win, Joe Burk is now a celebrity, and there are in the Burk family more pictures

From the Burk Family collection

whose quality and production values suggests there is more often a professional photographer around to intends to create a record of not only Joe Burk the champion, but Joe Burk *with* his younger brother Jim, who by then was rowing for Rusty Callow in the Penn crew.

While the photo just before this text might have been taken by a family member, the photo of Joe and Jim Burk just below looks posed—as if the photographer was seeking to display and prove that the two Burk oarsman were training in the snow, and were together using axes to cut away the ice from the edges of the Rancocas Creek to get to their winter training.

The following year, 1939, Burk again dominated domestic competition on his path to defend his Diamond Sculls title at Henley in July. On May 30, 1939, Burk won the New York Rowing Association Regatta on the Harlem River, again by ten lengths. He had only one opponent from the New York Athletic Club, who led briefly and faded dramatically in the second half of the race. Burk by that time was viewed as *so dominant*, few people even thought to enter a race against him.

At the Schuylkill Navy Regatta in mid-June, Burk rowed unopposed. No one felt it was worthwhile to row against the Henley record holder. The Burk triumph was complete when Joe's little brother Jim Burk won his own single sculls event in intermediate singles. The family rowing dynasty at that point seemed apt to grow.[60]

On June 21, 1939, Burk again headed to Henley. The races were plagued with frequent rain. The Regatta started on July 5. Burk's first heat was that day, and he drew Canadian N.D. Moffatt of the Toronto Argonauts. Moffatt challenged for the first half of the race, but Burk thereafter pulled away to win by four lengths. But the times were slow—the rain had increased the flow of the Thames down the course [Henley is rowed upstream], and Burk took ten minutes to cover what he had covered in just over eight minutes the year before.

In the final on July 8, Burk faced Roger Verey of Poland. The AP Wire story printed in the July 9 *The Inquirer* gave few details—saying only that, "Verey, who led by as much as a length and a half for the first half-mile, was seized with a cramp and twisted his wrist near the finish. For a moment it looked as though he had collapsed, but he recovered quickly and finished strongly."

These details were largely incorrect from Burk's point of view.

The truth is far more accidental. Burk did fall behind, but it was a fluke accident which was not reported in America. Whether this was intentional, or simply summary reporting on a deadline, we cannot now discern.

Burk later told Peter Mallory the full story. Burk had observed before the race that the wind that day was blowing as a quartering headwind, so that the boats would tend to be blown to the left as they went down the course. Burk had the left lane and would be pushed into the booms first unless he paid attention and kept correcting his course to work against the wind blowing him to his port side.

Burk had recognized the danger before the race, and he arranged for a friend to bicycle along the course and shout warnings if the wind drove Burk toward the booms. Coaches and authorized people could and did routinely follow crews on the left-hand side of the river along a towpath, so his friend arranged to be at the start and pedal along with the others following the race. Advising contestants was in 1939 permitted, but is now illegal. Although Burk's comments in Peter Mallory's book did not include the identity of the friend, Stan Pocock later revealed it was Harry Arlett, son of Jack Arlett, who had hosted Burk the year before in familiarizing him with the Henley course.

Jack Arlett did not count on the crowd of cyclists who wanted to follow the final of the Diamond Sculls, and he could not get ahead of them on the narrow towpath once the race started. Arlett was not close enough so Burk could hear Arlett's alarm as the wind began to push Burk's boat in precisely the manner Burk had feared—to the left of the course, and toward Burk's port sculling oar.

The Henley course—then as now—is lined by wooden booms held in place along the later parts of the course by wooden stakes driven into the edges of the course. Hitting those booms has doomed a number of Henley competitors over the years.

Burk's finals opponent Roger Verey was an able sculler. He had been the European singles champion in 1935 and part of the Polish

from Hear the Boat Sing, August 29, 2022

double sculls that won the bronze medal at the Berlin Olympics in 1936. He would be true competition for Burk.

Verey took an early lead, but Burk slowly reduced the margin, and by the halfway mark on the course, finally surged ahead. But the wind had blown Burk into the boom, and as Burk's port oar struck it, the oar was knocked out of Burk's hand. His boat was brought to a complete stop. Burk told Mallory what happened next:

> Luckily, I didn't capsize. My oar was turned up square at the time, and it was knocked out of my hands. I grabbed ahold of it, but at that time, Verey was back ahead of me.
>
> I thought, 'Boy! I'm really going to have to work now!' and I forgot all about pacing, just rowed as hard as I could.
>
> I finally caught up to him, maybe a quarter mile from the finish. I started to go back towards him, but it was just about all I could do to keep moving.

I knew he would look over at me, so as I began to go by, I turned my head and smiled at him as though there was nothing to it.

Immediately, he dropped back and that's the way I was lucky enough to win that second Henley victory.

What the newspapers don't tell you!

After the Henley victory, Burk rowed in the U.S. and Canadian Sculling Championships, and again won both without difficulty. He had remained undefeated since 1937 and seemed to many in the rowing world as simply unbeatable. Thirty-five straight victories seemed to prove the point.

But as the fall approached in 1939, events were moving in a direction that would change much of the world. Burk, the Henley champion, and Verey, the valiant runner up – would soon find their respective worlds changed.

On September 1, 1939, Poland, for whom Roger Verey had won a bronze medal at the Berlin Olympics, learned that Nazi troops had crossed the borders of the Second Republic. The whole of Poland was now at war.

On September 3, 1939, at the last regatta of Burk's season, he raced in the 48th Annual Middle States Regatta in Baltimore on a one-mile course along the Patapsco River. With Burk in the event were two other scullers, Allan Mowatt of Union Boat Club of Boston and Joe Angyal, a 145-pound lightweight sculler from Ravenswood Boat Club in Long Island, New York.[61] Angyal had won the lightweight quarter-mile dash at the start of the regatta, and Mowatt had won the quarter-mile dash in the open division.

Burk had raced Angyal two times before—beating him each time, first at the New York Regatta on the Harlem, and again on the Schuylkill at the American Henley Regatta.

A picture of the racecourse during a fours race printed in the *Baltimore Sun* shows rough water at the start of the race course. Burk, rowing 35 strokes a minute, was slightly ahead at the quarter mile. Burk raised his cadence near the half mile, and Angyal matched Burk's stroke rate. By the three-quarter mile mark, Angyal was ahead and pulling away. Near the finish, Burk sprinted, but his surge was matched by Angyal, who finished one and one-half lengths ahead.

Angyal lay back in his single, exhausted after the race, and the boat turned over. The *Baltimore Sun* reported: "Members of the judges' boat had to fish him from the river. Burk appeared fresh and strong after the finish."

Burk never made a public comment on what caused the outcome of the Baltimore race. He was equally silent about his many victories.

On September 6, three days after Burk's loss to Angyal, newspapers across the United States ran a United Press article dated September 5, 1939. *The Philadelphia Inquirer* ran the article in its sports section that the war in Poland might doom the 1940 Olympics. The International Olympic Committee had suspended preparation for the Games, and Avery Brundage, chair of the American Olympic Committee was quoted as saying, "Unless there is an immediate settlement of hostilities in Europe, there will be no 1940 Olympics."

The Olympic chance that Burk—and no doubt Verey—had each worked for since 1936 seemed to be slipping from their grasp.

Burk's only comment about his loss was private, in a letter to his mentor George Pocock dated September 22, 1939, which is available at the Friends of Rowing History website. It is important enough to be included almost in full here:

> Now for the post-mortems. I don't hesitate to discuss it because as much as I hate to be beaten, *I still regard it more as a matter of scientific interest than a catastrophe* (emphasis supplied). I feel sure you remember Joe Angyal of the Ravenswood Club. He is still using a shell that he bought from you several years ago. At the time, he wrote me and asked if my opinion about the one that I got gotten in the Spring before. He is a good sculler, George—the best in the States

right now. However to be frank I have beaten him rather handily twice in the past and am going to try to do it in the future. He hit the nail on the head exactly on all the things you mentioned . . .

Pocock had apparently heard through the rowing "grapevine" some aspects of Burk's loss, and apparently he had written to Burk listing what in Pocock's mind might have accounted for the unfortunate result. Judging from Burk's letter, the old master must have sensed the truth from across the continent.

> I drove down to Baltimore the morning of the race against Mr. Burke's [the Head of Penn AC] wishes and then instead of taking a room for the day at a hotel as he suggested, I spent my spare time out at the Arundel boathouse [sic] viewing the other races. Then I went out on the course without ever having been on it before and *almost missed my arch in the bridge and had to do a semi-circle to get back in the proper lane* [emphasis supplied; most scullers would have not expected to be competitive after this event], had very choppy water in the last quarter and couldn't sprint and then ended a perfect day when Angyal collapsed as he crossed the finish line and almost went into the briny deep. But these aren't excuses, George, they are just interesting observations. With all the advantages I have here, I ought to be able to win in spite of all these things and do not and will not feel satisfied until I can. In my mind the race was lost long before I headed toward Baltimore. It was lost right here on the Rancocas and I ought to be able to win such races and all but the real tough races in spite of all little disturbances. If you are fast enough and better enough in practice, the races take care of themselves.

Burk told Pocock he was soliciting advice about what to do in the winter to ready himself for the 1940 season from Rusty Callow and from the champion runner Glenn Cunningham. Callow had suggested a brief rest, and Pocock must have done so as well. Burk said he felt he should continue, but admitted that with Pocock and Callow saying rest, Burk admitted "there must be some good ground there." Burk explained his approach:

> I have compromised by telling Rusty I would do this as follows. There is no sense missing such good sculling weather as this [the fall weather of 1939 near Philadelhpia was favorable] and if by winter I find I am going from rotten to putrid, I shall take the jail sentence during the tough winter weather when it is the least desirable. I eat like I hate to suggest what and Morpheus [the Greek god of sleep] is working the full shift, and I am as goofy over the sport as ever, so what's left?

Burk listed for Pocock others that had suggested other approaches. Glenn Cunningham, then the top U.S. one mile runner and 1936 Olympic silver medalist at 1500 meters, had told him "time off is just so much time wasted." UPenn and 1936 U.S. Olympic track coach Lawson Robertson suggested cross training rather than more rowing. Burk remained unsure. He ended his letter to Pocock by saying: "I am sure of <u>nothing</u> these days."[62]

Over thirty years later, George Pocock would tell U.S. single sculler Bill Tytus, then based in Seattle, that it seemed anomalous that the only sculler to ever beat Joe Burk had been a lightweight.

1940

An International News Photo shows the first practice Joe Burk had on the water in January 1940. The picture, labelled as being on the Rancocas Creek near Burk's farm, was more likely taken in one of the two 500-meter sand pits adjacent to the creek that Burk used when the ice of the Rancocas was too thick. This picture shows Burk had cut away ice from part of pit, and he sits, bare legged with only a sweatshirt to warm him, ready to scull on the limited water ahead of him.

The brief story line attached to the photo says that Burk will concentrate on the single in 1940 with the goal of making the Olympics—but then the next sentence says he might also row the double with his younger brother Jim, said to have started sculling himself.

Credit: International News Photo. From the collection of
Thomas Weil, Esq.

On January 10, 1940, the Amateur Athletic Union declared Joe Burk
the winner of the 1939 James E. Sullivan Award as America's greatest
amateur athlete. *The Philadelphia Inquirer* put the banner headline at
the top of its sports page:

JOE BURK AWARDED SULLIVAN SPORTS TROPHY:
Fruit Farmer Hailed As Greatest Athlete:
Penn A.C. Sculler Called From Orchard to Get Word of Honor . . ."

The Inquirer's first sentence set the tone, which had the overwhelming
benefit of being true: "A sorrel-haired South Jersey fruit farmer yesterday was hailed as America's greatest amateur athlete."

The article recounted that Burk's unbeaten streak had been broken in the summer after Henley by Angyal in the race in Baltimore. The paper said Burk himself had never offered a reason, but the paper offered its own diagnosis: "the result of too much rowing." The paper further added that Burk was "not touching an oar this winter, and by spring he hopes to be back in his old form." The paper quoted Rusty Callow as saying Burk was "the strongest man I ever coached."

The article ended with a classic teaser—the possibility that Burk, having won all the amateur honors, might turn professional. "'Well,' Joe admitted, 'I have received an offer, but there's nothing definite. And anyway, I wouldn't do anything until the Olympic Games are formally cancelled. I don't suppose there is a chance of their being held . . . Still, I'm hoping . . .'"

The following day, in the same paper, a separate column entitled *Strictly Sports*, the columnist Cy Peterman reported that Burk gave more details about his options for continuing rowing—this time possibly as a professional:

"I suppose, if the offer is right, I could turn pro," he began. "And yet I wonder if it's the right move. Bob Pearce, the Australian, has been urging on me the prospects for several professional appearances, now that the Olympics seem more or less in the background. But I want to think it over, and I can say now that the offer must be good."

"The chances are," said Sculler Burk, who can see ahead, although his sport propels him backwards, "such a competition would only be good for a few showings and then, like the professional tennis, it is apt to draw no more at the gate. And I, Burk, love to row far too much to find myself permanently on the sidelines—"

"We should know about the Olympics definitely by April," he pointed out, "and I'll remain amateur until the summer."

On July 21, 1940, Joe Burk drew only two opponents in the Championship Senior Singles and the single sculling Olympic Tryouts in

Red Bank, New Jersey: Theophiel DuBois of Winnipeg Boat Club and Frank Silivio of New York Athletic Club. Why DuBois—presumably a Canadian—was allowed to enter the U.S. Olympic Trials was not explained.

Burk won the race by multiple lengths. The man who upset Joe the prior year in Baltimore, Joseph Angyil, did not choose to race Burk at the trials but raced that same day only in the lightweight singles category and in the lightweight one quarter mile dash—winning both.[63]

Burk's younger brother Jim rowed with his doubles partner, Howard McGillin of Penn AC, and they also won—making two Olympic athletes in the Burk family for the 1940 Olympics.

Joe Burk and his younger brother Jim thereafter received their Olympic team uniforms. Neither man ever got a chance to wear them at the Olympic Games. As the Second World War expanded, the 1940 Games were cancelled.

Joe Burk viewed the Games' cancellation as the end of his competitive amateur career. In the late summer of 1940, by letter to the Philadelphia Rowing Community, Joe Burk announced his retirement from amateur rowing in a document entitled *A Farewell To Oars*. In it, Burk thanked his college coach Rusty Callow, "He taught in such a way that rowing became a mode of living and there was no breaking away from it."

He also thanked his mentor and boatbuilder George Pocock, "It was he who convince me that a short stroke would fulfill my requirements . . . his brilliance as a sculling coach . . . was a glowing beacon in the darkness . . ."

Burk returned to farming along the Rancocas.

CHAPTER SIX

U.S. Navy PT Boat Service

*"I wish to have no connection with any ship that does not sail fast;
for I intend to go in harm's way."*

—*John Paul Jones*

T he Japanese attacked Pearl Harbor on December 7, 1941.
Like many Americans of war fighting age, Joe Burk had
spent much of 1941 wondering if America would join the wars
now spreading around the globe. Pearl Harbor gave the answer.

Joseph W. Burk joined the United States Navy as an enlisted man
in early 1942. Prior to his enlistment, government records showed
him as twenty-six years of age, and living on Garden State Highway,
in the city of Beverly, New Jersey. He was shown in the record as employed by his father, Paul Heber Burk.

Burk was immediately placed into the accelerated naval training
program at the Navy's Officer Candidate School, designed to produce
in assembly line fashion the vast number of young officers the U.S.
Navy suddenly needed for the coming war effort in both the Pacific

and European theaters of war. All graduates were commissioned as ensigns, the equivalent rank of a second lieutenant in the United States Army. Such officers in both branches were identified by the slang designation "ninety-day wonders," because the training program was designed to move that quickly—and the established officers and senior non-commissioned officers viewed these "wonders" as being, at least initially, of little practical value.

Burk's first posting was aboard a cruiser whose assignment in those early days of the War of the Atlantic was to conduct patrols up and down the American East Coast in the hope of deterring attacks on Allied shipping by German U-boats. Prior to America's entry into the war, the U.S. Navy had not developed any specific doctrine for anti-submarine warfare, and longer-range German U-boats operating out of occupied French ports were so successful in sinking ships traveling between the U.S. and England, that the German U-Boat Captains began to refer to this period as the *The Happy Time*.

Burk left little record of his thoughts about this period of his service, but given his attention to detail, one can only imagine his reaction to such a lack of preparedness. Whatever his reaction, we do know that he found the patrol duty monotonous, and applied for a transfer to the smaller Naval craft known as patrol torpedo boats, or PTs.

These plywood-hulled boats were few in number at the time of the Japanese attack on Pearl Harbor on December 7, 1941. On that day, there were only twenty-nine in the Pacific Theater. Formed into three squadrons, these approximately eighty-foot launches had been built by Elco in Bayonne, New Jersey, and were manned exclusively by volunteers. (Other PTs were later built by Higgins Industries in New Orleans, Louisiana.) The boats drew much favorable public attention from an American public eager for encouragement after the losses suffered at Pearl Harbor. In fact, early in the Japanese attack on Pearl Harbor, two sailors assigned to PT23, Torpedoman First Class George Huffman and Gunner's Mate First Class John "Joy" Van Zyll de Jong, shot down two Japanese torpedo planes with the boat's two twin .50 caliber machine guns.[64] More aggressive action from PTs thereafter would soon come, and Joe Burk would prove himself among the most aggressive and skillful PT boat officers of the war.

One historian of the PT boat service in this war noted, "Interestingly enough, while these small craft were designed as torpedo boats, this first action, involving only automatic weapons, was an omen of the ultimate employment these boats would find."[65]

The idea that such small, fast, and maneuverable boats were so highly effective must have provided a certain emotional salve to Americans dismayed by the pictures from Pearl Harbor of mighty American battleships bound at anchor and unable to swiftly respond to the swarm of Japanese planes attacking them from above. By the end of the war, Joe Burk would be among the most prolific of those officers engaged in the true employment of these wooden wonders—which was the sinking of barges containing Japanese troops and their supplies.

Burk's service in the Navy is detailed in official records, but also in a series of letter Burk wrote to his former Penn Varsity coxswain, Sidney R. Phelps. Phelps saved all the letters Burk sent to him during the war. The two remained lifelong friends, and years later, at Christmas, 1992, Phelps gave his old friend a scrapbook which included all the wartime letters Burk had written him, along with numerous newspaper articles about Burk's rowing career before the war and his naval service during the war. He told Burk, ". . . the letters you sent to me during your Pacific duty are great. These should surely be of interest to Kay, and Kathy and Roger as well. Surely [also] to your grandchildren in the years to come."

Phelps' letter also recalled:

> [It] brought back memories of Poughkeepsie when you and I would walk up the hill after practice because you said it strengthened your legs (the crews took the bus!). . . . Do you recall after winning the first Adams Cup at Annapolis, that you, I think, took Swifty's oar in as he ran ahead to take a shower because Frank Sunderland was waiting for him with

two dates to go into Washington. Our manager rushed to the shower and told him to put his rowing clothes back on—he was keeping the President waiting. FDR [then Assistant Secretary of the Navy] was to present the first Adams Cup to the winning crew.

Burk first wrote to Sid Phelps on February 13, 1943, on stationery printed specifically for the Motor Torpedo Boat Squadron Training Center, Melville, Rhode Island. He reported that he had finished up training in Boston:

> . . . at the end of November, 1942, I luckily was assigned to the fourth Naval District, which is principally Philadelphia. About 85% of the class was sent down to Miami for further training on sub-chasers. If I had been included I wouldn't have been able to get here [meaning in PT Boat training in Rhode Island]. Just one of those lucky breaks that I have always had.

But as usual, Burk's lucky break involved a little more than luck. Burk's daughter Kathy relayed that during one mealtime when Burk was among fellow trainees in Boston, an obviously new officer entered the Officers' Mess and seemed to be searching for a place to sit. Burk immediately got up, introduced himself to the stranger, and then introduced the stranger to each of Burk's fellow trainees who were at the table.

Only later did Burk learn that the newcomer he had befriended was the officer sent by higher headquarters to select candidates for the slots opening up in the rapidly expanding fleet of Navy PT Boats to be sent to the Pacific theater, each of which needed new commanding officers.

This brotherly courtesy given to a fellow officer surely singled Burk out in the selector's mind as an officer and a gentleman.[66]

Another factor weighing in Burk's favor as a candidate for a PT boat command was that the Navy had begun to appreciate how hard it was to serve on a PT boat when it was operating at full speed. The selection team was instructed to "chose as officers the biggest, toughest athletes . . . they could find."

A partial list of officers so selected—fifteen in all—is contained in the definitive history of the *PT Boats in World War Two* by Robert Bulkley. It includes college football all-Americans, professional football players, and Burk—the lone oarsman and Sullivan Award winner—plus several lacrosse players and swimmers. Burk, still a Penn lineman at heart, was particularly excited when he found out that Notre Dame's all-American guard Bernie Crimmins—whom Burk had followed during the 1941 football season—was moving straight from his position in Fighting Irish line to a Naval commission and a spot commanding a PT boat in the Pacific. Burk would for years after explain with enthusiasm the intentional inclusion of athletes in combat roles, and Crimmins was the name he always called out first.

Bulkley wryly remarks that, "Squadron 21's arrival [with all these athletes] was greeted with astonishment, not because of the size of its guns, but because of the size of its officers."[67] Crimmins would serve in Squadron 21 with Burk and would himself be awarded the Silver Star for his valor in combat.

It is characteristic of Burk that he never mentioned any of this in his letters to Phelps. The modesty urged by his Westfield Friends teachers still lingered.

Burk would have had another reason not to crow to his friend and boatmate about his good fortune. Phelps had written Burk previously to bemoan the fact that he had been found "not heavy enough for the Navy." Burk wrote back with the same earnest encouragement that so many oarsmen would later hear from Burk the coach: "Hope that you can make up those pounds and get in the Navy. You will be mighty happy. However, I can readily understand how Punch [Phelps' wife] feels . . ." The young Mrs. Phelps' fears were, of course, well-founded.

Modern readers might be surprised at learning of Phelps' impediment because today the service disqualifier is more likely to be too great a body mass, rather than the reverse. But Phelps was not alone in his problem. Film actor and future bomber pilot Jimmy Stewart was initially rejected from the Army Air Corps pilot training for being too slender. He eventually gained sufficient weight to be admitted and flew twenty combat missions over Germany as a pilot of a B-17, and years later even flew a B-52 mission over Vietnam as a brigadier general in the Air Force Reserve.

Indeed, as British historian Andrew Roberts notes in his history of the Second World War, by December 7, 1941, "the Great Depression had taken a physical toll on American manhood; even though the Army would accept just about anyone who was sane, over 5 feet tall, 105 pounds, possessing at least twelve teeth, and free of flat feet, venereal disease, and hernias, only 60 percent of candidates could qualify based on such criteria."[68]

While Burk was still at the Motor Torpedo Boat Training Center, he wrote a long letter to his former rowing mentor George Pocock in early March 1943. It turned out that Burk's return to wooden boats—in this case PTs rather than single shells—had left him nostalgic for his shell designs that the two of them had so often discussed, and also *full of new theories* about superior single design. Burk felt it was time to renew the discussion:

March 1, 1943

Dear George,

I have meant to say 'hello' to you for quite some time but just didn't quite get around to it before. Ever since I have been in this exceedingly interesting branch of the Navy, my attention has been thrust back to those sculling days. Naturally it's all because of that elusive little thing called speed is a prime factor [sic] in this type of craft [the PT boat] and I just can't help from comparing these little speedsters with racing shells. The power is <u>slightly different</u>, of course, and the weight displacement changed a bit but it seems to me that they are essentially alike on being displacement craft and not hydroplanes. I don't know whether you have seen any PTs underway or not, but if you haven't, you would be surprised at how little planing there is. For this reason, I think that the performance of one would be at least indicative of what you can expect in the other.

A short time ago I found out something that was exceedingly interesting, although it is undoubtedly "old stuff" to you. This was that in a displacement type boat there is the same leveling off of the resistance curve that you get with a hydroplane, only not nearly as pronounced. It flashed upon me that this was the very explanation for the reaction of that last single that you built for me [in 1939]. You may not remember it exactly. In 1938 we had one that was exceedingly good, as later results showed and as later changes in design brought out. In 1939, at my suggestion, you lengthened the next one and made it a bit narrower in the bow and fatter in the stern. This was to keep the stern up a bit higher because the '38 boat looked as though it was riding uphill while underway at full speed. It was a beautiful looking job and sculled mighty fine at a low rate but after a certain point which was somewhat below racing speed, it had the feeling of becoming ten or fifteen pounds heavier. This was just plain work to get it above that sub-racing point.

I think that the explanation lies fully or in part in the leveling off point of resistance . . . Apparently, on the first [1938] shell the level came at or on racing speed because with the short stroke at a high rate she pulled along very easy at racing speed and power did not seem to be as much of a factor as endurance. On the '39 shell it began to be heavy at the racing speed and the matter was obviously (or was it?) in having placed the leveling off of resistance at too low a figure or boat speed.

Now what I have wondered is whether a shorter, stubbier, wider and flatter shell would move that desirable point up a few notches and if a sculler could get some pretty good speed[.] I may be all wrong on this and entirely off the [point] but it has wandered about in my mind during the past few weeks and I was interested in what you thought about it.

I hardly expect to go back to sculling again because I doubt if there will be any Olympics for quite a stretch and that was the only thing left that I wanted. I could still scull against Bob Pearce after the war since he is still at it and is still without doubt the world's best, in spite of his age.

However, I get a big kick out of tennis and other amateur sports and do not care to permanently sacrifice my amateur standing for a few dollars I might make from a race or two with Bob. If I were going to coach, it would change the aspect but I thought that all over a couple of years ago and came to the conclusion that coaching rowing is one of the most precarious means of livelihood that there is and besides I am afraid that my interests in rowing was more active than passive anyhow.

In a month or so I may be getting out your way and if I do I shall try my best to drop in and see you at the shop. However, when I receive my orders and if Seattle is in my itinerary I'll write you and tell you. It is just a remote chance and a long shot at that.

My brother Jim is out in San Francisco on a minesweeper. It is only temporary duty and he doesn't know where his next stop will be. He would like to be sent [to PT training] but his chances, I am afraid, are slim. It's pretty hard to change from one branch to another and then being married is just about the final factor. [Jim had married in 1939.] It certainly would be great if he could make it because I know that he would be just as crazy over the duty as I am. After being down at Cape May, New Jersey on a patrol craft that could barely squeeze out 14 knots, I am fully appreciative of the quality of these magnificent crafts.

Hope you are well and that there is still something left in the shell game. Best regards.

Yours sincerely,
Joe Burk

A brief aside about Bob Pearce, a champion sculler who had turned professional. Bob Pearce, at the time of Burk's writing, was then thirty-seven years of age. Hailing from Sydney, Australia, Pearce was, like George Pocock, the son and grandson of watermen and carpenters. He started rowing at the age of six and left school before graduation to become a carpenter. Weighing over 200 pounds, and immensely strong, he had held the title of Australian Army Heavyweight Boxing Champion from 1923 until 1926. After discharge from the Army, he devoted himself solely to sculling. As part of his preparation, he sought to enter the Henley Royal Regatta, but like John B. Kelly Sr., was refused entry because as a carpenter he was considered a tradesman—and thus, in the eyes of the Regatta's Stewards, ineligible, since they viewed Henley as a venue available only to gentlemen.

Notwithstanding his rejection at Henley, Pearce won the 1928 Olympics for Australia in the single sculls. He struggled financially during the Great Depression and was only able to attend the 1930 Empire Games (then open to athletes from the former colonies of Great Britain, now called the Commonwealth Games) due to the sponsorship of friends. Pearce won the single sculls at the Games in Hamilton, Ontario.

After his victory, he was given a job as a salesman by Scottish whiskey distiller Lord Dewar. Thus, having shed his blue collar for a white one, Pearce was then allowed to enter the Henley Regatta, where he won the Diamond Sculls the following year, 1931.

Pearce again won the gold medal at the 1932 Olympic Games and in 1932 turned professional, racing until 1938 when he retired from professional sculling.[69]

As we learned in Chapter Five, Pearce had contacted Burk as the 1940 Olympics was being cancelled and proposed that Burk consider turning pro and rowing exhibition races against Pearce in Canada. Nothing had come of the proposal, but the idea of someday sculling again competitively remained in Burk's mind. At the time, Burk made clear to Pocock that he thought Pearce was the best in the world, notwithstanding his age.

As we will see later in Chapter Eight, after the war Burk would consider again the possibility of racing Pearce.

Burk's letter to Pocock shows he was still mulling ideas about rowing, even while engaged in learning about his own PT boat and its planing characteristics. It was characteristic of Burk that once he had become interested in a problem, he would continue to ruminate and consider how things operated long after others had simply moved on to other subjects. That ability to continue to mull a problem would become a characteristic of his coaching days.[70]

Ensign Joe Burk graduated from the Rhode Island training center sometime after March 1, 1943. He received orders to proceed to the East Coast with his assigned boat PT Boat 320 to be loaded on a larger vessel for transport to the eastern side of the Panama Canal.

Contrary to his older brother's prediction, the Navy soon granted Jim Burk's request for a transfer from mine sweeping off America's Pacific coast to the PT service. Ensign James Reber Burk finished PT Boat training in time to travel with his older brother on the same transport ship to the Panama Canal. Both men would command a PT Boat in the Pacific. As the youngest of three boys, Jim had eagerly followed his older brother, first to rowing and a seat in the Penn heavyweight crew in college, and now he had command of his own PT-346—transiting the Panama Canal and into the Pacific War.

There is an appealing symmetry to the young Burk following his older brother in rowing and then in the PT boat service, but the path would come at a price.

At the Panama Canal, the Navy transport vessel unloaded the PT boats, and the officers and their crews boarded their assigned boats, then piloted them through the Canal. Then as now the Canal consisted of a series of locks lifting up to the high point of a man-made lake fed by mountain runoff water, and from that lake the boats then transit across the Panamanian isthmus, eventually to be lowered through another series of locks into the Pacific. The transfer itself allowed the PT boat crews to have a sort of shake-down cruise with their vessels. The crews then reloaded their boats onto the transport ship on the Pacific side for final transport to their next destination of Brisbane, Australia.

For this group of PTs, the transport through the Canal came with athletic challenges—compliments of the Burk brothers. While the PT Boats were transiting the lake that lay between the lifting and lowering locks, the two Penn heavyweight crew letter winners arranged a rowboat race between their sailors. The existence of this competition would have been lost to history, except for two coincidences.

The first was that a sailor on one of the PT boats would later become a craftsman for George Pocock.[71] Pocock, who well remembered building the enlarged oar for Joe Burk and later building Burk's singles to Joe's specifications, was only too glad to hear, even after the war, the details of the Burks brothers' nurturing the athletic fire in their crews, even on the way to combat.

The second coincidence was that Joe's son Roger Burk would later attend the University of Washington and row there, also in his own Pocock single. Roger spent much time with Pocock at his shop. Pocock made a point of telling Roger the story of his father and uncle Jim both continuing their rowing traditions *en route* to war.

In Australia, Joe and Jim assumed full command of their respective boats, albeit in different squadrons. Joe commanded PT-320 in Squadron 21, and Jim PT-346 in Squadron 25.

A future President of the United States, John Fitzgerald Kennedy, preceded the Burk brothers into the Pacific War as the commander of PT-109.

On the evening of August 2, 1943, Kennedy and his crew were idling in a passage of water near the Solomon Islands when PT-109 was rammed and cut in two by the Japanese destroyer *Amagir*. Over the ensuing hours, Kennedy managed to lead the survivors in a long swim to the nearest island in the chain. There they hid from any Japanese troops that might follow up on the incident.

In the next days, Kennedy and other officers swam into the channel passage near the island in an attempt to contact friendly vessels passing. Though unsuccessful, they eventually made contact with local natives friendly to the Allied war effort, and Kennedy was able to carve a simple message on a coconut that the natives took to Naval forces nearby, resulting in the rescue of the survivors.

By the time they reached their battle stations, the Burk brothers and their crews would have heard the story of PT-109's sinking, and of the stirring story of the rescue of the crew.[72]

By at least as early as October 3, 1943, PT-320 had been unloaded from the transport vessel that had brought her from the western side of the Panama Canal to Australia, where she floated in port at Brisbane. PT-320 was loaded with four Mark XIV torpedoes. She was moored alongside other PT boats, all awaiting further transport to their assigned places in the war zone.

In port, each crew familiarized themselves with their boat and its equipment, anxiously awaiting orders to the war zones then active in the south Pacific Theater. PT-320's Squadron 21, along with Jim Burk's Squadron 25, were part of what was known as Task Group 70.1 Motor Torpedo Boat Seventh Fleet. The Task Group was its own operating unit within the whole Seventh Fleet, which was commanded by U.S. Navy Admiral Herbert H. Leary. Leary himself reported to General Douglas MacArthur, then stationed in Australia, and the Seventh Fleet came to be referred to informally as "MacArthur's Navy."[73]

U.S. Naval forces located east and north of the area assigned to MacArthur (who was based in Australia), came under the ultimate command of Admiral Chester A. Nimitz (based in Pearl Harbor), whose title was Commander In Chief, Pacific.[74]. The division of U.S. Navy forces in the Pacific into separate commands was ordered by the U.S. Joint Chiefs of Staff, which had the delicate job of managing the growing military buildup of force in the Pacific to oppose the Japanese—and managing the expectations of General MacArthur. MacArthur had played an early but unsuccessful role in the defense of the Philippines in 1941–1942 and had to been ordered by President Roosevelt to leave his doomed U.S. and Philippine forces on the island of Corregidor and escape to Australia. (He began his trip from Corregidor via PT Boat.)

This divided command structure would later play a part in a tragic "friendly fire" incident, which would involve Joe Burk's younger brother Jim and his PT-346.

By 11:45AM on October 20, 1943, the tow line by which the U.S.S. Trinity had towed PT-320 from Brisbane was released, and 320 made her way to her slip at a small circular bay named Kana Kopa, at the southeast end of Milne Bay, New Guinea, near the Island's southeast tip.

Naval historian Bulkley described what Burk and his crew found as they docked: "On the whole, it was a good site, as sites in New Guinea go, but for the first few months everyone ashore wallowed in apparently bottomless mud. One truck was actually *lost in the mud* of

Kana Kopa."[75] The Base itself was slated to become a repair center, but the lack of spare parts meant that many boats undergoing repairs were temporarily cannibalized of parts for service on other boats—and it was a continual struggle to keep a full complement of PTs out and running.

For the next two weeks, Burk and his crew conducted drills on all aspects of PT boat work: gunfire, torpedo runs, radar, night patrols, and high-speed maneuvers. At the end of that period, PT-320 was put in dry dock, and one propeller shaft repaired, and the center rudder straightened—proof that the routine operation of these powerful boats strained the equipment employed.

It is from this busy station, mired in mud and short of supplies, that the recently arrived Joe Burk sat down on November 9, 1943, and wrote a reply to a letter he had received from his former Penn Varsity coxswain Sid Phelps. The stationery Burk used had letterhead "JOSEPH W. BURK" in the first line, and "BURK FARM" in the second line, and in the third line the family farm's address of "BEVERLY, NEW JERSEY." Burk had drawn through the second and third lines, but as he was in a war zone, he did not disclose his location.

Burk's letter started:

Dear Sid,

Your most welcome letter of Sept. 8 rolled in the other day and it [is]great to hear from you. A lot has happened since the last time we wrote. I left the states [sic] on the first of July and since that time have seen a large part of the civilized world and most of the uncivilized. It has been wonderful and I feel very guilty for enjoying it all so much. I have command of my own PT and have a second officer and eleven swell kids under my care.

Burk related to Phelps that he had seen in theater "several Penn men you might recall." These included an upperclassman and Psi Upsilon managerial candidate for the football team who was then "chief pilot of a big old Liberator that is in the Army Air Transport Service . . ." along with another alumni, an ensign in the Naval Air Service as part of a repair and supply unit, a former coxswain "way above coxswain's weight," a Lieutenant [sic] in the Army Air Corps, younger Penn grad "a couple of years after us ... a wrestler and pretty good, too ... [now] a full [Naval] Lieutenant and ... the third ranking officer in our Squadron."

Burk also thanked Phelps for making him aware of a mutual friend stationed nearby, saying, "I intend to drop in and see him at my first opportunity. Probably find that he has shoved off by this time but it's well worth a try."

It is clear from the letter that while the author was in the geographical middle of a fight with a determined enemy, there also comes through in Burk's letter a sense of wonderment that so many mutual acquaintances have come to the same war. Burk's closing lines to Phelps makes clear the odd contrast between the adventure and the war risk:

> We are settled in a wild but beautiful spot. Looks just about like a cypress swamp down in South Carolina or Georgia. The trees abound with strange and beautiful birds while the stream is teeming with fish and more than an occasional crocodile. There are even wild pigeons and turkeys to hunt or a small amount of gold to pan in our spare time which we don't get. Life is interesting and exciting with a lot of stories—some amusing and some sad. Wouldn't have missed this for anything. If you ever get a chance to get into PT service, don't pass it up.

Burk ended his letter saying he was still an ensign, "having missed the last date of promotion by four days"—a gentle reference to the inevitably irrational regimentation of any military organization. He added a postscript that he saw a lot of Roger Hallowell, a former Harvard oarsman, "who is with another [PT] squadron. He was in "Cassedy's crew"—and as if the Pacific were full of oarsmen—"also Jack Carey of the Washington crew—'37 and '38."

While Burk's recitation paints a picture of a gay reacquaintance with old friends and rowing foes, what Burk had chosen not to tell Phelps was that their former Harvard rival Hallowell's PT-136 had

Skipper of a different kind of crew: New Guinea, 1943.

picture of Burk with his PT-320 crew, Burk is squatting in the right most of the first row, hands clasped. Photo on open page of OARSMAN magazine dated July/August, 1978, "Skipper of a different kind of crew, New Guinea, 1943."

two months before run so hard aground on an uncharted reef in enemy territory that Hallowell ordered his crew to abandon ship. To ensure the boat did not fall into Japanese hands, Hallowell's crew then destroyed the boat by gunfire and left her ablaze in enemy waters.

Burk and those with him were truly in harm's way.

By the time Burk reached Base 6, the Japanese Army had gone as far it would go in occupying the islands between Australia and Pearl Harbor. Japan's high-water mark had been reached, and naval battles like the Battle of Coral Sea had so reduced Japanese strength that these Japanese army bases were all but stranded, and desperate to preserve their own sources of supply.

At that point in the war, neither side had such dominance as to be able to attack the other continuously. The major naval forces warily eyed each other, each seeking an opportunity attack with favorable odds. Meanwhile, the job of the PTs in the Burk brothers' squadrons was to patrol at night, and hunt and sink any Japanese barges sending troops or supplies to the stranded Japanese bases. The U.S. plan was to starve the Japanese soldiers on the islands rather than attack them directly.

The Japanese forces, in turn, had given hostages to fortune—they had placed valuable land forces on these advance bases, and as the Allies advanced faster than expected, the Japanese could risk neither the great good of fully defending them, nor the great evil of abandoning them.

The result was a slow, grim series of nighttime conflicts in which the PTs would seek to find and destroy the primitive wooden barges loaded with Japanese soldiers, ammunition, and food. In turn, the Japanese navy and army would seek to sneak these barges safely past the PT's patrols by placing them under the guns of their own army's shore batteries, thus menacing any American PTs seeking to destroy the barges.

At that point, neither side had air superiority, so night conflicts were the norm.

The Burk brothers' war fundamentally was a gun battle. The accuracy of torpedoes fired from PTs at that time was poor. Moreover, the Japanese wooden barges sat high enough in the water that even those torpedoes running true were apt to pass beneath the barges' shallow hulls.

As American PTs tactics against barges evolved, torpedoes were rarely launched. PT skippers preferred, where possible, to add more guns to their boats. The result was that PT boats became—for their size—the most heavily armed Navy asset afloat in the Pacific.

The initial armament consisted of a Swiss-designed 20 mm Oerlikon cannon, and twin .50 caliber machine guns. Occasionally, a boat crew would add further firepower, such as the Swedish-designed Bofors 40 mm anti-aircraft cannon. More was always better.

In order to bring these guns into effective range, PT skippers had to make the same quick judgment regarding risk and reward that had governed the decisions of their predecessors during the era of Admiral Nelson. In that environment, and in Burk's, the officers who hewed most closely to Nelson's own admonition that, "No captain can do very wrong if he places his ship alongside that of the enemy," were most successful and rated most highly. Burk soon was practicing that technique.

Burk learned early that PT boat patrols for barges were most effective when done close to shore, which placed the PTs near any enemy gun emplacements defending the infantry on the occupied island, as one historian wrote:

> ... the PTs became more efficient barge-destroyers by installation of 40mm guns and a new and improved type of radar which greatly increased their ability to locate the enemy and aided in navigation as well. And finally, the PTs improved their tactics by patrolling close inshore, close enough to make sure that no barges could pass undetected between them and the beach, and to be able to see any barges that might be unloading at the beach. This doctrine ... [often] resulted in the loss of ... PTs by grounding on ... reefs. In fact, more PTs were lost through grounding in enemy waters than from any other single cause, but the risk was acceptable in view of the vastly greater amount of damage inflicted on the enemy. Danger to crews was reduced by having boat patrol in echelon formation, with the following boat or boats offshore than the lead boat. In this formation, even if the lead boat should go aground, a following boat probably would not, and would be able to tow the lead boat off the reef, or failing that, to rescue its crew.[76]

Burk and his crew encountered the enemy on the night of December 3–4, 1943, while Burk's PT patrolled with a second boat, PT-193, commanded by Lieutenant Junior Grade (jg) Cyrus Taylor, a rank one above Burk's. As the more senior officer, Taylor determined the action taken. Both PTs were patrolling when their radar showed possible vessels near the shore, and possibly a barge nearby. Without approaching more closely, Lieutenant Taylor ordered from his own Boat two torpedoes readied for fire, one set at a depth for a submarine and another at a depth for a small ship.

Taylor ordered the first torpedo fired, and in response, a Japanese cannon fired at "what seemed to be point blank range," according to Taylor's later report. Taylor could not determine whether the fire came from the beach or a ship.

Taylor said the return fire on the boats' first pass had prevented him from firing his second torpedo. An explosion was observed near the beach, but it was not possible to determine whether it was the torpedo fired. Both PTs returned gunfire and Taylor ordered the PTs to come about and leave the area. About a mile offshore, the PTs stopped and found they had received no damage. They then returned to the area but were prevented by Japanese gunfire from getting close enough to see if the torpedo had done any damage.

Burk was involved in two further actions, the first on the night of January 8, and the second on the night of January 10. In the space of these three and a half days in January 1944, Burk would solidify his reputation as what PT historian Bulkley would later describe as "one of the coolest boat captains in the business."[77]

On the night of January 8, Burk was designated as Officer in Tactical Command of PT-320 and PT-323, the latter under Ensign James F. Foran. As "Officer In Tactical Command", Burk directeding the actions of both PTs. Burk's own report of the action is description enough:

At 22:25 [January 8], four barges were sighted one mile off Mindiri, about one-quarter mile offshore and headed south. All barges were about 70–80 feet in length and one was definitely seen to be carrying troops. As the PTs closed for a port run, the troop-carrying barge opened fire with light machine-gun fire and a huge amount of rifle fire. On the first run three of the barges were sunk, one exploding when hit by the 323's 40 mm gun. The fourth barge made the beach but was destroyed by PT-320 on its second run. There was an explosion of what appeared to be ammunition on this barge. All barges had been loaded. The barges took no evasive tactics other than to head to the beach and to fire upon the PT-320 which was the lead boat.

The night had been busy, but Burk did not limit the night to those two runs past the enemy. The patrol continued, past midnight for three more hours.

At 0300 [January 9] three barges were sighted about ½ mile off the beach at Maragum, 4 miles north of Enke Point. By the time the 320 and 323 closed to attacking distance, the barges were ½ mile from the beach, proceeding very rapidly. They were close ashore when both PT's opened fire, and there was no doubt about all three barges having taken plenty of hits. One was definitely hit by a 40 mm. When the PT's returned immediately after the first run, none of the three were observed floating. However, three other barges were seen lined up on the beach ramps down and stern seaward. These barges were empty while the others were loaded. While destroying the three barges on the beach, a shore gun that seemed to be about 3 inch (sic) in size opened fire from a position 2½ miles north of Enke point.

Once again, after two passes and an exchange with the enemy, and more enemy damage done, Burk would now respond to the shore gun. The report continued:

Both boats proceeded to close in on the shore gun at high speed, firing .50 caliber, 20 and 40 mm shells. This caused the shore battery to cease firing at both PT's, and [the PTs] proceeded to finish the task of destroying the beached barges. All barges involved in this action were of 70 to 80 foot length.

Burk was not finished. The patrol continued:

At 0400, Pommern Bay, about 50 boxes of Japanese foodstuffs were sighted and after collecting 8 samples, the remainder were destroyed by light machine-gun fire and small arms (sic) fire.

The personnel of both boats acquitted themselves very well, especially in view of the fact that so much of the action took place while under return fire.

What was not included in the report was that both PTs had fired *all their ammunition*. Ensign Foran was heard to have said later, "If a plane had jumped us on the way home, we'd have had to thrown rocks at it."[78]

The senior officers reading Burk's reports cannot have missed the fact that the two-boat squad Burk led had conducted multiple attacks on the Japanese whenever and wherever they showed themselves that night. Ammunition usage was routinely measured, so the fact that Burk's patrol ended only when all the bullets were gone sent an unmistakable message.

Burk would fight by Admiral Nelson's admonition: "No captain can do very wrong if he places his ship alongside that of the enemy."

The following night, January 10, Burk had Lt. Commander N. Burt Davis on board as Officer in Tactical Command for a three-boat patrol group comprised of PTs 320, 127, and 326.

The stated purpose of the mission was to patrol the area between Reiss Point and Bunsen Point for barge traffic, and to destroy any found. But the likely intent of having Lt. Commander Davis aboard PT-320 was so Davis could see for himself whether Burk was the aggressive war fighter that Burk's own report on the January 8-9 attacks suggest he was.

At 22:05 on January 10, the PTs sighted three barges in the patrol area and immediately attacked. Burk's report is set forth here:

> All three [barges] were Type "A," and later proved to be laden with troops. The three PT's made one run and sank one and severely damaged the others. There was return fire from the barges, some of it being from 37 or 40 mm artillery pieces, the remainder being rifle fire. There was also some fire from the shore from a hand-loaded 37 or 40 mm. The lead barge veered toward the 320 which was the lead boat and opened fire at 75–100 yards.
>
> On the second run one barge was sunk while the third was very low in the stern and obviously sinking. It was decided

to try to board this barge and the PT 320 moved in to within 15 feet when it was seen that there were still almost fourteen men aboard and some floating in the water. The troops in the barge offered some pistol fire but they were silenced by the sub-machine guns and the bow 50 cal. MG 9 [sic] on the 320. The 320 was able to touch against the barge and just as it began to appear as though a boarding would be made, a tank in the engine room, of the stern of the barge burst and it quickly sank. There were nearly a dozen men floating in the water by this time and three attempts were made to pull one aboard but they all resisted and were dispoed of. The fourth attempt was successful and a Japanese soldier hauled aboard. The 326 also got one aboard but he died shortly after from wounds.

Burk also included a note praising his crew's conduct: "The crew behaved excellently and deserves praise in its successful attempt to land a prisoner."[79]

Some context is needed for a full understanding of what Burk's report quoted just above—written in the fact laden style required of naval officers. In this period of the war, Japanese combatants rarely surrendered. A captured Japanese prisoner meant the chance to gain valuable knowledge. Junior officers who could produce such results were worth everything to the Navy.

Burk's boat had been the first boat in—leading the first pass. PT 320 then turned and immediately led a second attack. Not content with disabling all opposing craft, Burk directed his own boat to touch one Japanese barge now drifting. This barge blew up in front of Burk and his crew. Burk now ordered his crew three times to attempt to take the floating Japanese prisoners. Those resisting were shot. On the third attempt, the sole prisoner who ceased to resist was taken aboard.

Junior officers who could be trusted to display such leadership were rare. One who demonstrated it in front of a superior officer was destined for recognition.

When the after-action reports reached the desk of Admiral Herbert Leary, commanding the Seventh Fleet, he forwarded them to

Admiral Ernest King, the most powerful officer in whole U.S. Navy and a member of the Joint Chiefs of Staff, with the tart comment: "The destruction of three enemy barges by PTs 127, 320, and 326 is noted with satisfaction."

Then, as now, the rules of war required sailors to refrain from harming enemy personnel who had surrendered. In the Pacific War, however, it was well known that Japanese troops often feigned injury or death in order to allow them to ambush Allied troops. Thus, in this theater of operations, it became routine for Allied troops to view any sign of resistance as justification to kill them. In this instance, those who continued resisting capture were killed in the water.

Burk's superiors found Burk's action laudable. He was promoted to lieutenant junior grade four days after the incident. And this would not be the last of Burk's exploits; he would repeat such actions as the war continued.

Nonetheless, the natural fatigue of war and his own fresh combat experiences must have influenced Joe Burk's response to a letter he had belatedly received from Sid Phelps. A somber mood pervaded the February 15, 1944, response Burk penned to his old friend:

Dear Sid,

Your missing letter of Dec. 11 finally made its belated appearance yesterday. Remember the one where you were sitting in front of the fireplace, listening to the [Coke] hour and Punch was trying to conjure up a drawing for a post-card (sic) and you were giving your right arm to be out patrolling with me. Distant fields look greenest, don't they?

When I read of such a cheery, homey atmosphere of domestic bliss and tranquility, I sometimes wonder if possibly I steered the wrong course. Especially after a night of being tossed around in a rough sea and getting half-drowned by torrential rain and salt spray, eventually coming back empty-handed—except for a dull headache and a snoot full of salt. Yes, Sid it's not all beer and skittles and I am only telling you this so that you won't feel too bad as you carry out your parental duties. Don't give up Punch and the kids before you have to because there are plenty of able-bodied guys to fight that can be spared more easily [than you].

Things are pretty ... alright at present. That is, they are not productive—not dull. The shore batteries are springing up like wildflowers and the nips are shoving their planes out at us all night. So far our old faithful guardian has done a herculean job but it remains to be seen if we can maintain our luck. These Japs are either awfully poor shots or we are mighty tough targets. Sometimes it reminds me of standing at a railroad station while the express train roars by. It shatters the tranquility of the tropical night where the weather is neither too hot or too cold and the moon is either a blessing or a [Burk drew a straight line], depending upon how you look at it.

Well, gotta get to work. We need a new propeller.

Sincerely,

Joe

Lt (jg) J.W. Burk, USNR

MTB Ron 21

Eleven days after Burk wrote Phelps, on February 26, 1944, T.C. Kincaid, Vice Admiral of the U.S. Navy, and Commander of the Seventh Fleet, awarded the Navy Cross, the nation's second highest award for valor in naval service, beneath only the Congressional Medal of Honor, to Joseph W. Burk. The citation read:

For extraordinary heroism and intrepidity in action against the enemy. During the period November, 1943, through January, 1944, you made twenty-one combat patrols, courageously and aggressively pursuing Japanese barges along the north coast of New Guinea and the west coast of New Britain. You have participated in the destruction of twenty-six enemy barges, time and again in the face of heavy and accurate fire and sustained a direct hit on your boat by an enemy three-inch shell. On January 8, 1944, in company with Motor Torpedo Boat 323, while engaged in attacking ten enemy barges, fire from heavy shore batteries were encountered. As Officer-in-Tactical Command, you left the barges and proceeded under the shore batteries, silenced them, and returned to press home the attack on the barges, completely destroying them. Two nights later, in company with Motor Torpedo Boats 326 and 327,[80] you successfully attacked and sank four[81] heavily laden barges. One hundred and sixty enemy troops are estimated to have been killed in this action which was bitterly resisted by the enemy, and one prisoner was taken. You have on two occasions successfully carried out secret missions far behind enemy lines. Your actions were in keeping with the highest traditions of the Navy of the United States.

No record exists of Burk's reaction to being awarded the Navy Cross. He never mentioned it unless asked. Within his personnel records at Penn is an informational form he filled out in the early 1960s as a member of the University staff. Under the section requesting "honors won," he left the line blank.

This behavior is the residue of Burk's Quaker training. Other war heroes with religious backgrounds such as fellow Pennsylvanian Smedley Butler, the Marine general known as the "Fighting Quaker," and Tennessee's Sergeant Alvin York, both Medal of Honors winners, were known for their modesty and deep religious backgrounds as much as for their wartime valor. Perhaps the bravest Americans are also our most spiritual.

As we shall see later in this book, Burk's habitual modesty would be deeply respected by his oarsmen, and would set the tone for their own behavior as young men.

By March, 1944, Burk's Squadron 21 was beginning to encounter fewer direct conflicts with the enemy, and more action in what might properly be called "mop up" operations. On March 14, Burk's PT-320 accompanied PT-369 to assist a Major McCarthy of Army intelligence in contacting natives about whether the islands of Pak, Baluan, and Tong still harbored Japanese soldiers. A wooden canoe used by the

A more relaxed Navy — 1944.

from OARSMAN magazine

Japanese on Tong Island was quietly taken and sunk by gunfire from the PTs.

Burk's own report takes an almost apologetic tone in accounting for the amount of ammunition expended in sinking the primitive Japanese vessel, "The boat was sturdily constructed of wood and after having capsized was an exceedingly difficult target to hit, hence the large amount of ammunition used."[82]

The level of risk seemed by that time to have waned, and the report smacks of anti-climax. But danger still lurked nearby.

In early March, Jim Burk's Squadron 25 moved their operations bases to Rein Bay on the north side of New Britain, moving closer to the line where forces under MacArthur would begin to overlap forces under the command of Admiral Nimitz. While the convergence of the allied waves of immense military force is certainly a cause for celebration, it can also be a time of great peril, as the two forces may not have established adequate communications between each other.

Joe Burk again wrote to his old friend Sid Phelps on April 26, 1944. Burk had apparently been sent an offer of homemade cookies from Sid's wife Punch, and Burk been late in responding:

I must have been thinking about the latest shore batteries or possibly a reef or two. Anyhow, I would be tickled pink to sample some of her culinary arts when, as, and if convenient to her. If you promise please not to put either yourself or herself out by doing so, I'll enclose a request in this letter. Remember now.

We are taking a rest at present after leaving the Admiralty Islands safe for democracy. From our viewpoint it wasn't very productive of tangible results because the Nips just let their men die in the trap and didn't try to send aid. However, we had a lot of fun in the landing operations and took a lot of risks that we shouldn't have. Wonder just how far one's luck is good for?

Joe Burk's luck would remain, but his younger brother's would not. Only two days after Joe wrote the letter quoted above, two PTs from Jim Burk's Squadron 21, PTs-350 and 347 were patrolling near Cape Pomas, New Britain. Their target was possible barge traffic supporting the Japanese garrison at Raboul. As they patrolled near the shore, PT-347 became stuck on a reef near the shore.

PT-350 attached a line to PT-347 and attempted for five hours to tow her off the reef. All efforts failed. PT-347 was stuck fast, and the approaching dawn began to make both boats visible.

As the light rose and the PT boats were exposed, two Marine Corsairs approached from the east. The Corsairs were that day the leading edge of Admiral Nimitz's command coming from the east, and they did not realize that the PTs they saw below them were from

MacArthur's command, moving from the west to east. The Marine pilots made the crucial error of judging the PTs to be Japanese.

The sailors on PT 347 "signaled 'S' and 'V' with their searchlight"—the signs they were taught would identify them as friendly. Three officers aboard frantically waved their arms and tried to raise the pilots on the radio. Both the 347 and 350 displayed the United States flags fore and aft. Furthermore, PT-350 dropped its towline to the stranded PT and started a 360 degree turn to the right—a maneuver the PT crew had been taught was the universal signal to United States forces that the boat was identifying itself as friendly.

It was all in vain. The Marine commander of the Corsairs later reported seeing "no recognition signals of any kind." No explanation was ever given for why the signal given by PT 350 was not recognized by the Marine pilots from the other command.

The Marines attacked.

Because the planes the Marines were flying had not been routinely used in MacArthur's command, no one on the PTs could be sure whether they were being attacked by friend or foe. The 350 radioman alerted headquarters: *Both 347 and 350 were being attacked.*

The 350 returned fire as the Corsairs flew overhead and brought down the second Corsair. That Marine pilot would not survive.

PT-350 started a return to base with half its crew dead or injured, numerous damages sustained, and its engine room leaking so badly that all four torpedoes and two depth charges had to be dumped overboard to lighten the boat to allow it limp home.

PT-347 had not suffered any personnel or material casualties but instead remained stuck on the reef.

Alerted to the attack, the Squadron 25 Commander Lt. Thompson raced aboard Jim Burk's PT-346 and the two officers headed out to render aid to both PT-347 and PT-350. On board Burk's boat was Chief Petty Officer John Frkovich, whose specialty was pharmacy.

PT-346 met the damaged PT-350 limping toward home and attempted to render aid. The officers of the 350 shouted that they were so badly damaged that if were to stop to receive aid they would sink.

The only possible action for 350 was continue to home since she could not float unless underway.

Jim Burk's rescue team headed to PT-347, still stuck on the reef.

Meanwhile, the surviving pilot in the Marine Corsair that had attacked the U.S. PTs had reported to his headquarters that a "Japanese" boat 120 feet in length had killed his wingman.

The American PTs were only 80 feet long.

In response, the Nimitz Command sent 22 planes in an attempt to finish off what they believed was the enemy but was in fact the lead elements of the MacArthur Command.

Lt. Thompson and Jim Burk reached the stranded PT-347, and tied PT-346 to it, and began trying to pull the sister boat free. Both officers soon spotted American planes overhead and assumed they were the friendly air cover which Thompson had routinely requested before heading out on the rescue mission. Thompson ordered that the efforts to refloat the 347 continue.

It was only when the planes began to peel off from formation and attack both PT-346 and PT-347 that the tragic error became clear to the rescuers. Both boats filled the airwaves with all the call signs they knew to warn off the planes. Nothing worked.

The plane attack would continue for well over an hour. But on the first run of the attack, Jim Burk led the officers of PT-346 in holding up a large American flag in addition to the ones hanging fore and aft from the endangered PTs. Chief Petty Officer Frkovich saw Burk get hit by machine gun fire almost immediately. He ran to Burk and saw that his legs had been shot away, the two bloody stumps separated from what had been his lower legs. He gave Burk morphine and applied tourniquets to the stumps.

Neither man had been wearing a life jacket, since the planes had not been identified as hostile, and 346's crew had not been called to general quarters. They thought they were safe. Frkovich found a single life jacket among the wreckage of the boat and attempted to put it on Jim Burk.

Burk ordered Frkovich to take the life jacket for himself and to abandon ship. Frkovich did as Burk ordered.

Photo of Jim Burk in Naval Uniform

Photo of Jim Burk and his PT 346 crew. Burk is the seated officer in the first row, holding the boat's dog mascot.

Frkovich, when rescued, was wearing the life jacket Jim Burk had given him.

Jim Burk's body would never be recovered.[83]

Word of this horrific tragedy had reached Joe Burk at least by the time he wrote Sid Phelps on May 8, 1944, while his brother Jim was still listed as "missing." But at that time, Joe Burk still held out hope:-

May 8, 1944

Dear Sid,

Glad to hear that you are going to be able to stay with Punch and kids a while longer. Hope that you don't have to go at all because among other things, someone has to pay for all of this 100 octane[84] and ammunition that we have been so busily expending.

You made a crack in your letter about being careful of the guy that shoots before he looks. That's what we call being trigger happy without vengeance. A whole flock of Marine pilots mistook my kid brother Jim and his PT for a Jap and gave him, his crew, and his boat a proper going over before blowing it clean out of the water. Two planes were shot down. That was just a week ago and Jim is still among those missing. We are hoping that he and the seven others were able to get ashore and head back for the front lines. It's a long, long way and we may not hear from them for some weeks if they ever did get to the beach.

We are pretty well accustomed to battle, murder, and sudden death but I am sure the folks at home aren't quite to that stage. It was a tough job to write to his sweet wife and to my mother. I only hope that I can cable some good news before those letters arrive.

The boys and I escaped a similar fate from a big old Liberator[85] one night who had four or five one-thousand-pound eggs to deliver. We were on a special mission and sitting dead in the water at the time. He was one of those so and so's that usually doesn't get the word and was just gliding in with his bomb bay doors open and licking his chops. By one chance in a hundred one of our own intelligence officers had taken the night off and for some fun had climbed aboard this particular bomber. He was half dozing in the rear as the pilot called to him to watch the sudden demise of two Jap boats.

He climbed forward and rubbed his eyes and mumbled, "Where are we?" When told that they were just coming in on so-and-so island, he broke into a sweat and told them to hold everything. The target was your truly and another, and he, of course, knew of our where-abouts. A pretty close call and it just shows that good luck and bad are usually pretty well distributed. I guess I drew heavily out of the Burk bank that night.

Am enclosing a photo of one of our boats. Doesn't happen to be mine, thought but it's nearly the same except for a dearth of guns.[86]

Sincerely,

Joe

On May 28, 1944, Joe again wrote to Sid Phelps:

May 28, 1944

Dear Sid, Punch, Danny, Linda and Pint,

I hasten to answer your kind letter of May 10. We are about ready to set forth on another wild spree and I know from past experience that mail may be weeks in getting back to a base post office. We are all as anxious as racehorses to get back in the harness again. For a month and a half now we have been over-hauling, painting and generally polishing our boats. It was fine for a short time but it has stretched out so long that we are counting the hours until we can get back in the shootin'. It will probably be our last chance before we head for home for a leave. I feel almost like the Ancient Mariner! Remember that part that reads, "The ship was cleared, the harbor cheered," or maybe it was vice versa. But that's the way I feel anyhow.

My only qualms are about my crew. My regular boys (swell kids) are down in Australia on leave and won't get back up un-til the show is really over. I decided to pass my leave up so that I wouldn't miss some of the stuff that I came out here for. My best gunner decided to stick with me and get a few cracks in too. We have a relief crew aboard and I think we'll do all right. We also have a new second and a new third officer and a new coat of paint.

Poor old Jim is still missing and it looks pretty dim for him and the seven others who were with him. He was wounded before the boat was blown up and it looks almost hopeless.[87] Miracles have happened in the past, though, and maybe this will be one of them. I certainly hope so for his wife's sake and our mother's sake. I have heard from them since they got the usual bare telegram from the Navy Dept. and they say that whether the final news is good or bad they will square their shoulders and face it. I knew my mother would be that way because she was well aware of what we were going into and never voiced anything but enthusiasm. She always said you must be able to take the bad news as well as the good, and believe me, she can.

Thanks so much for the offer of the camera. When we left home there were strict regulations that we could take no picture nor have any taken. It was all so absurd that we often wondered why. However, we have seen ample evidence by this time. However, we do have a squadron camera and can send pictures home that are passed upon. I will send you one at my first opportunity. One example of the way that things are sometimes overdone is a picture of Jim and his crew. Each boat in his squadron had its picture taken while in Panama.[88] The pictures were not delivered to them until about two or three weeks ago.[89] One of the officers gave me one of Jim and his crew, which I intended sending home. However to my disgust and amazement it was stamped "Confidential" which is the second highest classification that military secrets may hold. This means that it's a court martial offense to send it home or show it to other than authorized persons. Naturally there was a mistake made somewhere but it doesn't help me any.

Thanks for the crew picture and the one of General MacArthur. That wasn't my boat in the foreground but it was one belonging to our squadron. We took the General for a ride at the time of the invasion of the Admiralties. . . .

Regards to all of you.

Sincerely.

Joe

PS: I was in the picture but it would take a military picture interpreter to spot me.

PPS: Ma says that you do not need a written request to send pack-ages to anyone in the <u>naval</u> service. I know that lots come through for which there has been no request.

On June 27, 1944, Joe Burk wrote to Sid Phelps as follows:

Dear Sid,

Mail finally came through and it was a pleasure to find two letters from you. Glad to hear that Spring (sic) finally came up your way and all of that tree planting made me feel just a wee bit homesick. How well do I know what it means to plant evergreens and to carry water. Hope that leg of yours is okay by now and that you get the Purple Heart!

I don't believe that I have written you since we changed our home. Fortunately, there are no Jap snipers in this one and the only break in the calm and serenity of a veritable tropic paradise is air raids. This is truly the prettiest and most picturesque spot I have seen in the Pacific. However, since we moved in a lot of the picturesque quality has gone by the wayside. When we first came there was nothing but white, sandy beaches, overhanging coconut trees full of screaming beautiful birds and a few native huts on stilts that stuck out in the water and to which we tied up. There was no drinking water, no nothin'. The civilized world soon took the beauty out of it but then she also provided the vague approaches to the comfort of life. It's still a pretty spot though and no mosquitoes which means no malaria or dengue.

It feels great to be back patrolling again even if I have landed upon reefs twice. The first time wasn't so bad though we did have to wade around in the water far up in Jap territory in a not so beautiful moonlight. The second time was something else again. We were on [meaning stuck on the reef] for five hours with the tide apparently in a hurry to get out. Again it was up with the Japs but this time while we were struggling the cry went up from the look-out that there was something headed our way and "it looks big." What an embarrassing position! Fortunately, the "big thing" turned out to be a several Jap barge loads (sic) of troops and supplies. They

*must have been dreaming of geisha girls and cherry blossoms be-
cause they passed a little over a hundred yards away and didn't
know we were there until we turned the shootin' irons loose on them.*

   *Gosh, I guess they were surprised and probably thought, "That
boat must be almost on the reef in there." How true! How true!
Well, after our slight interruption we went back to our evening
swim fest but things were no longer the same. The Japs, through
necessity, had gone in for bathing too and now the water was con-
taminated. Mixed bathing was not our idea of the correct thing to
do so while we worked we had to post a few armed guards to pro-
tect our rights. The Japs were apparently pretty peeved about it all
and gave vent to their anger by hurling vile words in English. Just
where and how they picked them up I didn't know but they had
us in a bad spot because we knew none of theirs to hurl in return.
However, with them to urge us on we finally got loose from our too
friendly reef and limped through the floating debris of the barges
and headed for the barn. A nice night and a lot of good clean fun.
It's just little things like those that make you wonder every time you
start out, "What's it going to be tonight." Last night it was all three
engines conking under the shadow of some big coastal defense guns.
Nothing happened, though.*

Sincerely,
Joe

Burk's description in this letter of the contacts with the Japanese
seem to intentionally mimic a Buster Keaton movie—the presentation of the circumstances of alarm, and then an almost comic dis-
sipation of the danger by sheer luck rather than any action of the
combatants. The reader must wonder whether Burk found that way
of writing a way of making light of his peril to his old friend, or to
Burk himself.

   A nice night and a lot of good clean fun.

In early July, Joe Burk received orders that his tour of combat duty
was soon over, and he was sent stateside starting August 12, 1944,
for further orders. Burk left the war zone about July 30, en route to

New Jersey and the farm. As he awaited transport home to the States, he again wrote Sid Phelps, thanking him "from the bottom of my heart" for a gift whose specifics are now lost to history—likely more of Punch's famous cookies. His handwriting was larger, and his words more animated:

> *Very unexpectedly, I am now on my way home and awaiting transportation. It is about a month earlier than I expected and I can't say that I am a bit sorry. Our action was beginning to slacken off and when that happens I begin to think that I might as well be back in the States eating fresh vegetables and drinking untold gallons of milk.*
>
> *It has been a wonderful year out here, excluding Jim's unfortunate accident and I am thankful that I had the opportunity to get out here. Such an experience is one that one remembers all his life. What the next move will be, I am not sure. However, the task force commander gave me the very disquieting news, just as I said farewell, that he was asking them to send me out immediately after my leave time was up. That's not very comforting since my leave will only be 15 days and you know how that will fly.*
>
> *Nevertheless, as he said, there is a war to be won and far be it from me to begrudge a nice trip to the States and back.*
>
> *This will be my last letter for some time but will drop you a note when I get back in the land of opportunity.*
>
> *Again, many, many thanks for your extreme kindness in sending such a delectable and wonderful box.*
>
>

Sincerely,

Joe
>

In the months since he had been given assignments usually reserved for a more senior combat officer and had been named to exercise tactical command of multiple boats, Burk had begun working with a naval intelligence officer named Charlie Black. Charlie's job in the PTs was to aggregate intelligence on enemy movements and to help plan missions for the naval forces in the area, including the PTs of Burk's Squadron.

In that role, Charlie Black soon learned which PT officers could be trusted to successfully execute dangerous and/or sensitive missions, then bring their crews home alive.

Rowing champion and Navy Cross winner Joe Burk was at the top of that list. The two men worked closely together, and Black, for a time, served as Burk's executive officer. Black was deeply impressed by the quiet bravery and sheer competence Burk showed in a crisis.

When Black found out that Burk was being rotated home, he asked whether Burk would mind stopping in to visit Black's mother at the family home in San Francisco. If Burk would, Black would give him some letters to deliver, and asked Burk to reassure his mother that Charlie was okay.

Burk agreed.

Virtually all returning service men from the Pacific came back to the States through the Port of Oakland, just east of San Francisco. Just before he paid his call on Charlie Black's family, Burk had a chance encounter at a San Francisco barber shop with an old rowing acquaintance. Tom Bolles was a former University of Washington oarsman and assistant coach who was then the rowing coach at Harvard. Burk was awaiting a haircut when Bolles emerged from the barber's chair and, recognizing each other, they talked. Perhaps prophetically, Bolles inquired whether Burk had any interest in coaching rowing after the war.

Decades later, Burk recounted the story to Peter Mallory:

I was coming back after my tour of duty in the Navy, and my executive officer, Charles Black, had said to be sure to stop in and say hello to his folks in San Francisco.

Of course, coming out of the Pacific I was pretty grungy looking guy, with hair down over my ears and so forth, so I went to a barber shop to get a haircut.

There was a fellow on the chair there, and when the barber finished with him, I looked up, and it was Tom Bolles.

Bolles had brought his Harvard crew to Henley back in 1939, the second time I rowed there, and that's how I got to know him, and that's how I got into coaching. At that barber shop, he said to me, "What are you going to do when you get out of the Navy?"

I said "I really don't know," and he said he'd keep me in mind for any coaching jobs that came up.[90]

Burk, thus properly coiffed and cleaned so as to appear the officer and the gentleman, then called upon Mrs. Black at the family's apartment in downtown San Francisco.

Mrs. Black met Lieutenant Burk at the door and invited him in. Her son had written her that Burk would call upon her, and she was anxious to welcome the young man back to the States and to hear news of her son. Black had told his mother that Burk was a brave and gracious man.

Mrs. Black excused herself and went up to speak to her daughter, Kay, who was herself still in mourning for her late husband, an officer and Naval Academy oarsman, who had perished in the Pacific on the Submarine *Triton* (SS201) in March of 1943.

Katherine Black, known as "Kay," was born into one of the city's most prominent families. Her father, James B. Black, was the President of the Southern Pacific Railroad, and of Pacific Gas & Electric, a major utility serving a large portion of California. Apart from a short time living in Bronxville, New York, due to her father's business, Kay had lived the bulk of her life in California.

While living in New York, Kay had attended The Spence School, a private all-girls school founded in 1892 and located on the Upper East Side of New York City. Spence's motto, *Non Scholae Sed Viate Discimus*, or "We do not learn for school, but for life," was a declaration of purpose which applied easily to Kay Black. She was vivacious, smart, energetic, and disciplined. Her blond hair framed a classically beautiful face, and she was at ease in all manner of company.

Kay attended Mills College, a private college in Oakland, California,[91] and after one year of college, she married a 1942 graduate of the United States Naval Academy and a member of its Varsity crew, Cornelius Dion O'Sullivan, who hailed from Napa, California. The couple were wed in the Naval Academy Chapel at Annapolis.

https://usnamemorialhall.org/index.php/
Category:1942 (accessed 16 September 2023)

Dion came from a military family, and his father was then a general in the U.S. Army. In 1943, Dion was serving as a Lieutenant (j.g.) on the Navy Submarine *Triton* SS-201 when it was lost in the Pacific—most likely on March 15, 1943, off the Admiralty Islands.[92]

Kay Black O'Sullivan was not expecting to enjoy meeting Joe, but this man was a friend of her brother, and her mother was always particular about welcoming guests to the Black home. She came down to meet the visitor.

Joe Burk's daughter Kathy Burk McCaffery later described the scene:

> *My Mom married very young at eighteen. And Dion was in submarines. And he was sunk on his first mission, so she was a widow something like four months after being married—something like that. And so we laugh—when she met my dad, she was not looking for a husband, my dad had just come back to see my Granny Black and bring information about Charlie.*

And my Mom told me, "I was still grieving, it was a couple of years afterwards, but still grieving." And she didn't marry Dad until she was—she was twenty-four actually. So Dad came back [to the U.S. and paid a call] and my grandmother Black said to her daughter, "You can't be rude, you have to come down, this man was with Charlie serving in the south Pacific."

And Mom said, "I saw your dad, and besides having clean fingernails, he was the finest man I had ever seen."

Despite the eight-year age difference between them, Joe Burk had found a remarkable woman in San Francisco. Characteristically, he kept his own counsel about the experience, and after his visit, he proceeded to the East Coast and to his family at the farm on the Rancocas. But he would begin a long and heartfelt correspondence with Kay Black O'Sullivan.

On August 28, 1944, Burk wrote to Sid from his parents' address in Beverly, New Jersey:

Dear Sid,

It's home sweet home again and I must say that there is nothing that can even come close to equaling the thrill and pleasure of returning. I have only fifteen short days and thus far have been swamped with telephone calls and visitors. I haven't had half the time I need to do all of the necessary things that I must do before I shove off again. There are a thousand and one personal duties that I have to attend to and get straightened out and a few naval trips to make to Phila., Washington, etc. So it looks as though I may not be able to drive up to see you and Punch and the children in the immediate future.

However, my next station is Melville, R.I. and I may have a few weeks there before returning to the Pacific. If so, I may be able to arrange a little get-together during that interval. It just seems as though there are a hundred things to do and only a few weeks to take care of them.

*I had a wonderful trip back and the closer I got the more im-
patient I became to arrive home. They say that you are usually lost
and disappointed after the first couple days but it ain't so. New
Guinea and the war seems a lot farther than ten thousand miles
away and it's a great relief to be able to look a bright and shining
moon in the eye and know that it's not going to bring a hail of
bombs, or, what's worse, just the possibility of it.*

Regards,

Sincerely

Joe

On September 7, Burk was honored for his wartime exploits at a luncheon at the Pennsylvania Athletic Club. Speakers included John B.
Kelly Sr., his doubles partner and fellow Olympic Gold Medalist Paul
Costello, PennAC president William Harman and Henry Penn Burke,
President of the National Association of Amateur Oarsmen, who had
written the Arletts on Burk's behalf before his first Henley. Such was
the tenor of the times that Burk, receiving a gift of a travel case, said
he would plan on returning to Philadelphia with it to display "some
stickers of some Tokyo hotels" on it. One can imagine the applause
such a line would draw.[93]

Burk's easy relations with the Press had come to him before the
war as his athletic feats had become better and better known. As he
returned from the Pacific, he seemed to grasp intuitively that the
American public in mid-war needed heroes and good news, and he
had the poise to oblige.

On September 17, 1944, Burk wrote again to Sid Phelps, this time
from the Rhode Island PT Boat training center where he was awaiting orders because of a decision he had made since they had last
corresponded:

Dear Sid,

*Sorry that I can't give you any definite information about my
week-end (sic) status. All I know is that I am here temporarily and
that I may be walking out any day. I could have gotten a permanent*

spot here but knowing that I wouldn't be satisfied I asked to go out and see some more of the world. It was wonderful to get home—in fact that is only putting it very mildly. However, there is still a couple of wars to be won and I could never enjoy the life here in the States with the fires still raging at the front.

The only time that I can get away is from Saturday afternoon until Monday morning at 7 A.M. and that hardly seems like enough to make the trip to see you and do more than just a day of "hello and good-bye." If I am still here for a few weeks longer, though, I'll put in a chit for a couple of days off and then tie that on to a week-end. The only thing is that I don't know just when my orders will come through. I am anxious to get over to France before it closes up there and to do so I must get my orders in a hurry[94] The school and the Bureau have been exceptionally kind and cooperative and although my presence had been requested back where I came from, they may let me go across to Europe.

It was swell to hear your voice again and thanks ever so much for phoning. I'll let you know if I can get away. Regards to all.

Sincerely,

Joe

Burk wrote again a letter dated only Saturday morning, but apparently sent in an envelope postmarked in the United States. The letter read:

Saturday Morning

Dear Sid,

Got your letter this morning. I had been holding off writing to you until I found out just what the score was. Here's the dope at the present in all its confusing aspects.

Recently, a friend of mine in the Navy Dept. in Washington wrote that he was requesting my services in his department. It could be temporary duty of some three months and would involve travelling over a large part of the U.S. and visiting plants that were doing work for the Navy.

"This," I thought, "would be a great assignment and would

enable me to visit Sid Phelps and some of those other great guys who are doing such a grand job in supplying the armed forces!" So I wrote and told him okay but, unfortunately, just at that time my name was going through the Bureau for orders to go out to the Pacific. Yesterday, my Pacific orders came through but they are still working on the other angle and I won't know for several days just which set of orders will be final.

However, I'll let you know just where I go and I feel certain that if this temporary duty comes through I'll be up around the Syracuse area and be able to make that long awaited visit . . .

Best wishes and hope that I get the chance to get up to your plant.

Sincerely,
Joe

Burk's orders to return to the Pacific became final, and on November 7, 1944, he wrote Sid Phelps from San Francisco, using stationery from the Hotel Whitcomb, where he likely was staying. Burk's mood was upbeat, and he described himself as "waiting for transportation to the wide open stretches beyond" the Golden Gate. He said he had been assigned to Squadron 20 rather than Squadron 21 in which he had previously been serving, which he called "the old faithful 21." He said he welcomed the warm weather of the Pacific since the winters in Rhode Island were, in his view, colder than those in Philadelphia.

He commented on Penn football, which had not done that well recently, and he guessed Sid would get to Philadelphia for the Thanksgiving Day game at Penn[95]—he asked Sid to "please do a little cheering for me. I expect at that time I'll be gradually knifing through the deep blue seas somewhere."

While he had not yet made it back to the Pacific fighting, the tone of this letter begins a shift in Burk's writing. His letters begin to refer more to the future, and to the world he had known before the war—the athletic contests and the shared joys of things like watching football. Even though there was fighting left to do, both Burk and the Navy saw a turning of the tides. The worry over victory in the Pacific was slowly turning to confidence in the public mind.

With this newfound sense of pending victory, the press of both the U.S armed services and public newspapers began to focus upon the heroes of the war effort. In the scrapbook he later gifted to Burk, Sid Phelps pasted a clipping from an undated *Stars and Stripes* article entitled *Former Sculls Champ Sinking Jap Barges*, with a dateline of Philadelphia. The article began:

> When Joe Burk was sculling down the Schuylkill River no man could beat him. Now the Penn oarsman apparently is finding the Pacific Ocean just a bigger stretch of water in which to continue his conquests.
>
> Joe, operating a PT Boat, is leading the championship sweepstakes with 13 and one-half Jap landing barges scored on his official Navy tally. The 195-pound Ensign, who once took the Diamond Sculls title and the Sullivan Memorial Trophy as "America's outstanding amateur sportsman," seemingly finds a motor no hindrance to making a boat leap through the water . . .

The article outlined Burk's rowing success, emphasizing the high stroke rate he had effectively used. But the article then contrasted the efforts of the Japanese crews that had tried to row at the same high stroke against the University of Washington at the 1936 Olympics, who found themselves defeated—and according to the Washington coach, "reminding him of a flock of ailing ducks . . ."

This article is just one example of how war news was transformed into war propaganda as the possibility of total victory in World War II grew. As America's forces won more victories in the Pacific, the home front was filled with images of a hapless Japanese enemy who just two years before had seemed full of menace.

When Burk returned to the fight in the Pacific, he reported for duty with Squadron 20, stationed in the Philippines. There he learned that his old boat, PT-320, had been destroyed by a Japanese bomb dropped from an airplane on November 5, 1944, while anchored in San Pedro

Bay, near Leyte, Philippines. The two officers and twelve crew assigned to her were killed. Only one enlisted man survived. The boat was so thoroughly broken up by the bomb that the boat's radar—then a carefully guarded secret—was never found by navy divers, despite an exhaustive search.

Burk wrote Sid on January 12, 1945, that his trip to the States had been "a lucky break" vis-à-vis PT-320's destruction—had he not had leave, the bomb would likely have killed him. Burk wrote "[she] was a good boat and it's a shame the Japs had to get her but she had more than paid for herself."[96]

The rest of Burk's letter recounted whom Burk had seen out in the service in the Pacific:

> One of the officers of this well-run base here is Hugo Rutherford. You may remember Big John Rutherford from Princeton. Hugo is an older brother and the second in line of a famous Princeton rowing family. The oldest, Win, was single sculls champion of the U.S. in 1935.
>
> Incidentally, some time ago I met the brother of Bret Simmons, the captain of the Harvard frosh crew in our freshman year, as I recall. Also Rog Hallowell is out again but since we are temporarily in different areas I haven't seen him since back at Melville [Rhode Island station] last fall.
>
> Hope that your wood pile is standing up under the strain this winter and also that I can be helping you with it at this date next year.[97]

Burk next wrote Phelps on April 3, 1945, and for a man in the middle of what was still a shooting war, he seemed as balanced as if he were working out in the gym at Penn. He commented on the mail being held up as the forces moved from one location to another and reported that he had moved to yet another squadron that he preferred because Squadron 20 had been Higgins boats, vastly different from the Elco boats he had started with in Squadron 21. As if he were in peacetime, Joe chastised himself for not writing, but commented, "but goodness

I've been busy for the past month." Sid must have mentioned that his son Danny was praying for Joe's safety, for Joe wrote:

> We were lucky to get in a position where we had a lot of business and you can tell little Danny that he has been doing a lot of good for his Uncle Joe. We have had several narrow squeaks. On one occasion we came back with forty to fifty bullet holes in the boat—three of them in the gas tanks and our bilges full of 100 octane gas. Some of the boys in the boat got pretty well shot up but on the whole we were really lucky to get off as easily as we did. On another occasion, Radio Tokyo announced that we had been sunk by a plane. True it was much too close for comfort but that's all there was to it.

Burk described his new job as the officer in charge of planning operations:

> My job thus far has been that of operations officer. I live ashore, do not have a boat but make my patrols as OTC [Officer in Tactical Command] of a section. It gives me quite a variety and has produced some very very interesting evenings.
>
> I hated to leave Squadron 20—they were all fine fellows but these are even better and we have had a world of fun.[98]

Burk wrote to Phelps again on July 31, 1945, and in his letter mentioned that his team had "once again been luckily placed in an area where we could do 'business' with the little Japs." But he noticed a change as America and her allies drove hard toward the war's conclusion:

> This time we have had the additional support of just about anything we want. Never before have we had the luxury of continued help from fighters, bombers, photo "recco" planes and lots of other stuff. It's like suddenly striking it rich.
>
> The other day I went on a bombing mission with some of our friends and we had quite a time. The Japs didn't play fair

and sent up a lot more flak than we anticipated and had us wondering when our parachutes had last been tested. But all the planes got back and not too much damage was done. Most of it was due to our pride—to think that they objected to our mussing up their good stolen, landscape!

Burk was in a jolly mood. He mentioned that he had met the brother of his former opponent, Dan Barrow, who had won in the single in the 1936 Olympic Trials, and then the bronze medal in the Olympics in Berlin. "Strangely enough he was on a tanker that dished out 100 octane gas to our boats back in the days when we were in Milne Bay, New Guinea." Burk further mentioned that Barrow's brother had not been home since and had apparently been transferred to another ship refueling destroyers.

Burk waxed lyrical about the weather and the gardening Phelps must have been doing:

> Bet you are having a good time with your garden right now. My mother writes that they have been having an undue amount of rain and if you're getting those same clouds, I can imagine you have your hands full with the weeds. A garden is a wonderful experience, though, isn't it? Gives you both the appetite and the food and there's no pleasure quite comparable to that of raising your own food.

Burk's last comment about the pleasure of growing one's own food may seem strange to modern readers accustomed to a home with only a lawn, but it is worth remembering that the America of the 1940s was closer to the agrarian past of America where farmers grew much of their own food, and Burk's experience on his family's farm was that of a farmer who grew most if not all of his family's food, and did much of his own farm work by hand.

Until the war's end, Burk could only write to Sid about what he valued most but did not have. Burk led PT boats fueled by others, he ate food supplied by navy ships, he slept in buildings often built by the

Navy's Construction Battalions, and fought an enemy that was losing because it did not possess the equivalent support.

Burk was beginning to long for a return to a simpler life on the banks of the Rancocas.

In early August, as Burk's letter shown just above was en route to Sid Phelps, B-29 bombers of the 509th Composite Group dropped atom bombs on Hiroshima and Nagasaki. On August 14, Admiral Nimitz sent a message to all naval troops fighting in the Pacific theater: "Cease offensive operations against Japanese forces."[99]

Today we would consider Burk's references to "Japs" and "Nips" as harsh, and Admiral Nimitz and all who fought in the Pacific doubtless used the same language. However, on the following day, August 15, Nimitz sent a further message to all naval personnel in the Pacific:

> With the termination of hostilities against Japan, it is incumbent on all officers to conduct themselves with dignity and decorum in their treatment of the Japanese, and their public utterances in connection with the Japanese. The Japanese are still the same nation which initiated the war by treacherous attack on the Pacific Fleet, and which has subjected our brothers in arms who became prisoners of war to torture, starvation, and murder. However, *the use of insulting epithets in connection with the Japanese as a race or as individuals does not now become the officers of the United States Navy* [italics supplied]. Officers of the Pacific Fleet will take steps to require of all personnel under their command a high standard of conduct in this matter. Neither familiarity and open forgiveness nor abuse and vituperation should be permitted.[100]

Sadly, the letters between Joe Burk and Kay Black O'Sullivan—which were many—have been lost to history. But we know that Burk was released from active navy service sometime after the war's formal end in August 1945, and that by November 10, 1945, Joe and Kay were

a wedding photo of the Burks by Associated Press. The print is from the Collection of Thomas Weil, Esq.

married in San Francisco.[101] At the time of their wedding, Kay was listed as the vice president of the Junior League of San Francisco, a mainstay charitable organization still active in the city.

Kathy Burk McCaffery remembered her mother telling her about her father and how he was so different from her mother's first husband, Dion. Dion was a concert level violinist, artistic and expressive—and an enthusiastic dancer.

Joe Burk did not dance. He was quiet. He was not remotely musical. He sang in the shower, but off-key. But Kay often repeated to her daughter that memorable first impression upon meeting him, "This was the finest man I had ever seen."

CHAPTER SEVEN

The Business Executive Turns to Coaching

"Joe Burk had such athletic accomplishments. His rowing, his sculling, he played football at Penn. He was a primo athlete. I think it removed angst from his personality."

—*Steve Gladstone* [102]

"On a scale of one to ten, where a ten is a coach speaking constantly, Joe was a one."

—*Jeff Fuglested, Penn Oarsman, '67* [103]

Joe and Kay Burk started their married life in San Francisco at 945 Green Street, slightly west of Chinatown between Union and Broadway. Their early married life is a classic postwar baby boom story. Their harsh wartime experiences—for Joe as a warrior, for Kay as a war widow—had matured them more quickly than they might have in a more peaceful decade. On their wedding day, Kay was twenty-four, and Joe thirty-one.

During the war years, American men and women had endured not just sacrifice but major life adjustments. Good men like Dion O'Sullivan and Jim Burk had gone off to war and never returned. Others returned emotional shadows of their former selves. But more than a few, like Charlie Black and Joe Burk, returned to resume a somewhat normal life.

Women had not just stoked the nation's home fires but entered her factories and her offices—and in more than a few cases, ended up as war widows like Kay.

Taken as a group, those who survived forged ahead as if their most important goal was to normalize—to marry, settle down in some semblance of their pre-war plans, and live the American dream. And this, of course, meant children.

The Burks' first steps in marriage hewed closer to the bride's prior life than the groom's as they first took up residence in Kay's hometown of San Francisco. This was quite a change from Joe Burk's plan to return to the family farm on the Rancocas—which is what he told the Philadelphia press during his leave in Philadelphia.

In October 1944, the University of Pennsylvania's *Gazette* had included a piece on Burk's trip home from his service in the Pacific. The article featured a picture taken from the *Philadelphia Evening Bulletin* of Burk eating an apple in front of one of his family's trees on the family's farm, and stated that, "Joe expects after the war to give up rowing and settle down to the family apple orchard."[104] But all this was before Joe felt comfortable telling people he had just met Kay, and that he might soon have other plans.

As the two began to learn more about each other, their life goals as a couple shifted. By 1946, Burk was employed by the American Can Company, located on Third Avenue in San Francisco.[105] At this stage of his life, Burk began to see what a life as a corporate executive would entail. He could see from his father-in-law's experience that the wealth provided by climbing the rungs of corporate America would certainly provide security for his new bride. American Can was a first step, and Burk, with his Wharton Business School degree, would have been able to chart with fair accuracy where that comfortable path would lead.

But the experiences of war had left many American soldiers wary of "usual" choices in careers. Those who had survived the war had come to place a priority on day-to-day happiness and the personal fulfillment that had so often been denied them as combatants in the war. Deferred gratification—and watching fellow soldiers die—had sharpened most veterans' judgment about how they wished to spend each day of what could be, after all, a short life.

Burk began to consider those sorts of choices and the world of rowing reasserted its pull upon him. Burk's son Roger reports that, during his time working at American Can, Burk began to realize that working in an office environment brought him little satisfaction—or inspiration.

Joe Burk's work on the family farm had been mainly self-directed and self-paced, and outside an office. His much-lauded rowing career had been much the same, and in the end, an entirely individual endeavor. The requirements of small-boat warfare in the Pacific had placed him in a leadership position, often many miles from a superior. He had been entrusted with the lives of young men who were given a job of killing other young men—and he had protected his boys with a skill and an ingenuity that the navy had deemed heroic. Small surprise, then, that the prospect of being confined to an office in a charcoal suit did not fill him with pleasure.

At some point during this period, he inquired at the University of California about a coaching job opening there but was not hired. Interestingly, he seems never to have mentioned the opportunity to his children. Both Roger and Kathy learned of this inquiry during the writing of this book, when Steve Gladstone noted that Burk had applied at Cal for a coaching job soon after the war.[106]

Burk's later description of the rowing connections that would eventually take him to Yale were more complex and multifaceted than simply running into Tom Bolles in a barbershop.

The war was over, and rowing people began to talk to rowing people about the sport's future. And soon enough, the talk on every oarsman's tongue was the question of Joe Burk. Would he return to rowing? Would he instead step up to coaching? The question was soon to be answered.

On October 9, 1946, Burk received a Western Union telegram

delivered to his home at 945 Green Street in San Francisco. It was from Allen "Skip" Walz, previously the coach of the Manhattan College crew. In the staccato tone of that era's telegrams, it read:

INTEND COACHING YALE.
RUSTY SAID YOU MIGHT HELP.
WIRE ME.

Reputations in the rowing community were enduring. Tom Bolles was not the only coach thinking that Joe Burk would make a good coach. Rusty Callow, then still the heavyweight coach at Penn, remembered his 1934 captain and star pupil and passed the word to Walz. Callow, ever a confident man—and keen judge of men—knew Burk could help reestablish the Yale rowing program after the war, which was Walz's assigned task. Callow's reputation and recommendation carried much weight.

It is worth noting that Callow was not recommending Burk because he was a duplicate of himself. Callow was a totally different personality with a quite different background. Callow had been a lumberjack, a product of the Pacific Northwest, a man from the woods, a big, bluff, talkative man—"a raconteur," as Steve Gladstone described him.

Burk was the opposite. A product of rural New Jersey, Burk was as quiet as Callow was loud; as reserved as his mentor had been expansive.

But each was fascinated with rowing. And there was a manly reliability about each. They were both the type who could lead others—men who could produce the *"worthwhile boys"*—the young men the nation needed to move forward after the war.

Skip Waltz was to some degree a version of Rusty Callow, but with an East Coast flavor and an early appreciation for the rapidly changing world of radio and television. A native New Yorker, Walz had come from a rowing family. His father taught at Manhattan College and coached the crew there.

The elder Walz, seeking the very best education for his son, sent him to The Hun School, a prestigious prep school in Princeton,

New Jersey. There Skip learned to row—as well as to play football and box.

Upon graduation from Hun, Skip enrolled at the University of Wisconsin, where he was a tackle on the freshman football team, just as Burk would be a tackle on the Penn frosh team the following year, 1931.

Walz might well have gone out for rowing at Wisconsin—the perennial Midwest rowing power—but he missed New York. He transferred home mid-freshman year. Since Wisconsin had great rowing and football teams, Walz had left behind great sporting opportunities at Wisconsin—but leave he did.

Skip Walz had been born in New York City—and he and his parents had always resided there. He came back and enrolled in Manhattan College, a private, Catholic, liberal arts university in the Bronx. It had been established in 1853 by the Brothers of the Christian School. The University's website described the tenor of the founding Christian Brothers:

> The Brothers were the bearers of an educational tradition that began in 17th century France with Saint John Baptist de La Salle, the Patron Saint of Teachers. The Lasallian tradition created a new type of school system and elevated the work of teaching school—treating it as a profession and a vocation. The Brothers were urged to go beyond rote memory to "touch the hearts" of the student. Practical subjects were taught that would lead to a useful role in society; religion was taught to impart a commitment to Christian ethics.[107]

Walz played football at the college, becoming the team captain in 1933, and continued to box, winning the prestigious Golden Gloves tournament while still in college. While Walz did not row for his college, he did row at the New York Athletic Club in addition to football and boxing.

Upon graduation, Skip Walz joined his ailing father in coaching the Manhattan College crew, and taught speech at the College. "Speech" as a subject is today called "Communications," and that better reflects what interested the younger Walz. Mass communications through print and radio, with television soon to be added, was fueling a growing consumer society, and New York City was the center of the new communications industry.

Skip Walz was an early sort of *Mad Men* figure, but with a good Catholic schoolboy's sensibility. He would make a demonstrative coach.

Upon his father's death in 1935, Walz became head coach of the Manhattan College crew.[108] During his five years of teaching and coaching at Manhattan, the younger Walz branched out into radio and early television broadcasting. He was the announcer for the first television broadcast of a National Football League game in 1939 between the Philadelphia Eagles and the Brooklyn Dodgers (yes—but not those Dodgers) at Ebbets Field. Walz later related that the quality of the TV picture was so low that when the sun set, the broadcast picture became so dark, that he was forced to continue the broadcast in the style of a radio show, describing the action as it happened. Having the heart of NYC trouper, that is exactly what Walz did, without prompting.[109]

As we shall see, Walz, while older than Burk by only a year, seemed to be a man embracing the elegant aspects of New York City in the latter part of the twentieth century—and always dressed as if he were ready to be on camera.

Walz made a strong impression as Manhattan College's coach of rowing. The Athletic Department of the University of Wisconsin took notice. In 1940, he was asked to return to Madison as the head crew coach. There, Walz managed the slender midwestern rowing budget given him by the administration with all the flare of a New York broadcaster. Stories are still told in Wisconsin of Walz sneaking crew and coaching personnel onto trains without paying fares to stretch the rowing budget as far as possible to keep his Badger oarsmen travelling.[110]

In 1942, Walz took a leave of absence from Wisconsin and, like Burk, served as a PT Boat commander during World War II. Details of his Naval Service have not been found, and Burk never mentioned to his family that Walz had been in the PT Boat service. Walz, as a football player, boxer, and rower would seem to fit the "athlete war-rior" model the PT service sought in 1942.

At the war's end, Walz returned to Wisconsin, coaching their var-sity to a dramatic victory at the first postwar Eastern Sprints in 1946. When Yale offered him the position of head rowing coach after the 1946 season, Walz once again left Madison for the East Coast and Yale, and soon contacted Burk at Callow's suggestion.

Burk quickly accepted the opportunity to move east and coach. While Kay undoubtedly remembered with fondness her time at Bronxville, just outside New York City, and her schooling at The Spence School in Manhattan, she could be forgiven if the sudden change brought about by her husband's new career left her somewhat staggered, since she has just given birth to her son Roger. However, neither of Burk's chil-dren recall any history of discord or hesitation between their parents as to the move to coaching.

The change brought enormous challenges. Joe and Kay Burk had just brought Roger into the world on September 27, 1946. The Yale offer came thirteen days later.

Burk promptly headed east. Leaving his wife and newborn child, Burk drove the family car across the country to New Haven, Connecti-cut. Kay and Roger followed in January by plane.

Roger Burk looks back with admiration on his mother's courage in taking an infant alone on such a long a flight in those days

For his part, Burk's drive must have been grueling. Today, using Interstate highways the trip of just under 3,000 miles would take at least forty-four hours. Since the Interstate Highway System did not exist in 1947 the trip would have been significantly longer on roads we would today consider small.

The young couple first found a residence at 45 Golden Drive, in Milford, Connecticut, just a few miles from the Yale Boathouse and the main Athletic Department offices on campus at New Haven. While the 45 Golden Drive address no longer exists, the home was modest, as would be expected a freshman coach's salary. They no doubt kept in the back their minds the dislocation that a quick change could bring, as they later helped others with similar transitions. Later, when Joe was coaching at Penn and the couple were settled in Philadelphia, they generously hosted Harry Parker when he was establishing himself in Philadelphia as a sculler, and later still, they put Ted Nash up at their house when he joined Penn as Burk's freshman coach. Nash fondly recalled first living with the Burk family while he searched for a modest apartment and then receiving a gift of furniture straight from the Burk home when he moved into the apartment they helped him find.

It was from the Milford, Connecticut address that Coach Burk wrote to his mentor George Pocock on January 12, 1947, and shared with him with an opportunity to return to rowing as a professional. The offer is little known to the rowing community. Burk wrote:

> *Dear George,*
>
> *I had a very interesting letter from Bob Pearce.[111] He said that the Canadian National Exhibition is very much interested in reviving the sculling championship race and it looks as though it certainly will be a program for the summer. With this in mind, I spoke to Bob Kiphuth[112] to see if there would be any objection if I entered it. He expressed the opinion that it would be acceptable to the university, so if possible, I am going to work on it.*
>
> *Last fall you said that you might possibly be able to squeeze me out a single when you built one for Jack Kelly. I am aware that that would be for a 185 lb. man but I think that I could safely train down to that weight. My rowing weight used to be 196 lbs. but I think that I could trim off 10 lbs. without any serious impairment of strength. The one thing that worries me is how soon I could get the shell. Do you think you could possibly get it finished to send east with the eights for Yale? I hesitate to make the request because I know how terribly busy you are, but my race will be, of course, a three-mile grind and I shall not have very much time to get ready for it.*
>
> *Dick [George Pocock's brother Dick had taken a job as the Yale boatman in 1923 when UW coach Ed Leader took the top job at Yale] has very kindly offered to let me use Jimmy's [Dick's son] for*

124

a work-out. However, there are a number of objections—one being that I dislike very much to borrow a shell and the other thing being that it is rigged quite differently and that I would have a tough time getting accustomed to it and later changing back again.[113]

Burk was indicating that he—just halfway through his first year of coaching—was, by early 1947, already considering reversing his 1940 retirement from competition. To a legion of Penn oarsmen who rarely, if ever, saw Burk show any doubt about *anything*, this human moment of uncertainty was rare. This turning point at which Burk so clearly missed his own sculling and racing evokes empathy in every heart that ever hefted a racing shell.

The remainder of the letter gives some hint as to the cause of Burk's interest in placing himself back in the boat: the difficulties inherent in restarting a rowing program when the whole society had so recently overhauled itself for just one endeavor—war.

Burk's letter continued:

Both Allen [Burk had not yet begun to call the head coach "Skip"] and I know exactly how you feel these days. We have so much to do and little time to do too much in one year but it's no fun to approach racing season [then just three months away] without a chance of winning and we just can't stand idly by and get beaten. It's a big job and very frankly that's half the fun. If it were just "cut and dried" we wouldn't be very interested in our work. Win, lose, or draw we are having a very interesting time trying to do what many say is impossible. You know, and you've often demonstrated it, that there is no such animal.

This remarkable letter is the closest evidence that Joe Burk ever had doubts about his decision to end his own rowing career, and the only evidence he ever considered a return to an earlier life of competitive rowing. It is perhaps reassuring to know that even Joe Burk did not achieve all without cost or doubt.

And it is also refreshing that Burk—who at first laments to his mentor at the "impossible" task of restarting the Yale rowing program, but then uses Pocock's own adage to assert that, "there is no such animal" as the impossible.

The 1947 Toronto Exhibition that Burk had heard about from Bob Pearce eventually took place but did not include a rowing event. The exposition itself was like a huge state fair in one of the United States—but for the Province of Ontario. In addition to the usual farming-oriented displays and events, sporting events had been added as the interest and the availability of athletes allowed. In 1947, there was a long-distance swimming race.

Burk was welcomed back to the rowing community with warmth. But Burk's new boss, Skip Walz, was essentially the opposite of Burk. Where Burk was quiet, Walz was a promoter, a doer, a man who enjoyed attention and took steps to get it to support the teams he coached. Burk coached quietly, Walz was emphatic. Walz's move to Yale was not only an effort on his part to get closer to New York City, but to use the proximity of Yale to New York to support his flamboyant promotional style of bringing Yale rowing to the New York headlines.

Yale's crews had reasonable results as of mid-season, but Harvard won the Eastern Sprints title.

On May 19, 1947, the Monday following the Sprints, the Connecticut-published *State Sports Journal* by Lou Black mentioned Allen Walz favorably, and reported on a tip undoubtedly given by the gregarious Walz:

Alan [sic] (Skip) Walz, Yale's new crew coach, has won himself a million friends since his arrival here . . . His frankness is amazing . . . Too bad his Blue oarsmen won't be able to halt Harvard's long dominance over Yale next month at New London . . . But, look out for Walz's Elis a year hence . . . Skip has his sights on the 1948 Olympics . . . The freshmen have been impressive and that's where a new coach concentrates.[114]

After the Eastern Sprints, the traditional members of the Intercollegiate Rowing Association continued with their traditional champion-

Walz and Burk in overcoats, Burk Family Collection

ship at Poughkeepsie, New York, on the same weekend the Harvard and Yale crews rowed against each other on the Thames River in Connecticut. Both Harvard and Yale—in a show of the financial strength and alumni support—had built on their respective locations along the Thames beautiful dormitories and cabins for their crews and coaches, as well as elegant boathouses for their team's shells along the river. Harvard's facility was named Red Top, so called for the bright red boathouse cupola. Yale's was known as Gales Ferry, the name of the village which hosted both camps.

It was to these historic training quarters that the crews of Harvard and Yale returned in 1947.[115] Burk brought his own single down from the Yale boathouse in Derby, Connecticut. He would scull along and across the broad width of the Thames when not coaching his freshman crew. His wife took a photograph of Burk in his boat in choppy waters—smiling serenely and sculling apparently effortlessly in the blue expanse of the wide river, which could be challenging for an oarsman in an eight, and positively dangerous for a single in rough

Joe Burk rowing at Gales Ferry, Burk Fmily Collection

weather. On the back of the photograph, in his wife Kay's handwriting, is the caption: *Sweetie at Gales Ferry.*[116]

At the Harvard-Yale dual race, the Yale Varsity lost by two lengths over four miles, the JV lost by one length over three miles. Just as the Connecticut *Sports Journal* had intimated (likely at Walz's intimation), Joe Burk's freshman crew won by two lengths over two miles.[117] There was promise for Yale's rowing future against Harvard.

In seeding stories with the press, Skip Walz was not limiting himself to the mode of a traditional Ivy League rowing coach—guarded and taciturn. Walz clearly wanted to influence the press covering rowing, and he made sure his plans—like his plans for the Olympics a year hence—would be mentioned to newsmen.

Walz's style of frequently feeding the press interesting stories may seem routine to modern readers, but the style of most coaches in the Ivy League in that era had been more reserved, perhaps because their Athletic Departments had expected it. To those coaches, any comment more than a bland *"We'll try to do our best"* risked appearing boastful, or not sufficiently thoughtful for an elite academic institution. This limitation was especially true for Yale and Harvard, who each valued comparisons against the other over all other measures of value.

For Ivy League rowing in that era—Ship Walz's counterpart—Harvard's Tom Bolles was the gold standard. Bolles was a tall quiet man, born in Minnesota and raised in Seattle, Washington. He rowed for Rusty Callow at Washington, graduated in 1926, and coached the freshmen at Washington for Coach Al Ulbrickson, now famous from *The Boys in the Boat*. Bolles later became assistant coach to Ulbrickson for the varsity, and his character was featured in *Boys in the Boat* movie. Bolles was a serious man, who took the trouble while he was coaching at Washington to take the courses necessary to receive his master's degree in history from UW in 1936. He became Head crew coach at Harvard in 1937, and in addition to his coaching duties took further graduate courses at Harvard.

Bolles was a stellar rowing coach, and his crews won at multiple Henley regattas, and most importantly, beat Yale 10 years out of 11. His style with reporters was a polite reserve.

This was the man against whom Skip Walz was measured by the Yale Athletic Department.

That reserved, that "no comment" style still has its adherents today, but both those covering the news and those making news now have powerful incentives to make an interesting story—mainly favorable to their side—come out.

Walz is an example of a coach with this voluble, modern style—the coach as promoter. Working the press was a major part of the process in his approach, and not mere duty. At the end of the 1947 season, Walz was confident enough that his varsity was improving. When he was informed of an invitation from the University of Washington to race in Seattle, he prevailed upon the Yale Athletic Department to fund the train travel west to race the best crews from all over the country. Walz's bet that his varsity would perform well against the best could well have backfired, especially since a trip west meant entering the territory of western rowing powers Washington and California.

The Yale Varsity crew departed for Seattle by train immediately after the conclusion of the race against Harvard at New London. The race to which they were travelling was the second annual Lake Washington Regatta.[118] The Regatta's supporters were hoping the contest would become an annual gathering of the best crews in the nation for a 2,000-meter race. While neither the Yale junior varsity or the freshman crews came along, Joe Burk accompanied Walz.

Film taken of the visiting crews at the 1947 invitational still exists and sets the tone of the contest as well as the high regard in which the crews and their coaches were held by the press and public.

Found on YouTube as "1947: Giants of the Galley, Washington Invitational 16 mm 16 HQ," it documents the race with a brief clip about Joe Burk attending the Regatta as the new Yale frosh coach.[119]

The race came off in exciting fashion—a fitting reminder that America, the ultimate victor emerging from World War II, was now putting some of its strongest young men to work—not as soldiers or sailors, but as oarsmen. Over 100,000 spectators were in attendance, including numerous pleasure craft motoring next to the course, and booms installed to limit the motorboat wakes on the course itself. The day was sunny, and the water generally flat. It would be a fast race, with twelve crews: Harvard, Yale, Washington, Cornell, Wisconsin, MIT, UCLA, Princeton, Cal, Syracuse, and Columbia—all starting abreast from stake boats spread at the bottom of the course.

Among the varsity oarsmen rowing that day are names which are known even today for victory on many future fields. To show how small the world of rowing was then—and remains today—a partial list of competitors and their place in rowing is shown below:

1. Frank Cunningham, Harvard stroke. Cunningham would move to Seattle and become a beloved coach and mentor in Lake Washington for many rowers—including Yale oar John Biglow who competed on the U.S. National Team in the eight in 1979 and in the single between 1981 and 1984. Cunningham would author, with Leslie Stillwell Storm, a book on sculling entitled *The Sculler At Ease*, which remains an essential sculling reference book.[120]

2. Robert G. Stone Jr., Harvard four man. Stone would become a leader in Harvard alumni affairs, senior fellow of the Harvard Corporation, and commodore of the New York Yacht Club, where his supreme sportsmanship during a contentious challenge by Australia to America's hold on the America's Cup is remembered today. His son Gregg Stone rowed at St. Paul's in 1970 and 1971 and Harvard from 1972 to 1975 and was America's single sculling champion in 1977 to 1979. Stone's daughter Jennifer Stone would row for Harvard-Radcliffe from 1976 to 1980. Robert Stone's granddaughter—the daughter of Gregg Stone and Lisa Hansen Stone, herself a 1976 Olympian—is Gevvie Stone, who rowed at Princeton and won a silver medal in the women's singles at the 2016 Rio Olympics.

3. The Cornell five-man, Peter Allsopp, would have two sons, Peter and Chris. Peter would row at Kent School in the 1960s and Chris would row at the University of Washington, scull on Pan Am and National Teams, and serve as Harry Parker's assistant coach for the U.S. 1984 Sculling Team.

4. Princeton six-man Peter V.W. Gardner would coach Princeton freshman crews for seven years and Dartmouth heavyweight crews for thirty-one years.

5. Pennsylvania's three-man, Charles F. Colgan Jr., would remain involved in rowing all his life, and his son Sean Colgan would row for Ted Nash at Pennsylvania in the 1970s and compete on multiple U.S. National Teams. Sean is currently a financial sponsor for England's most storied rowing club, Leander, as well as New Zealand Rowing, and is the author of *The Book of Ted*, a biographical compilation on Ted Nash, Burk's successor coach at Penn.

This list cannot be complete—it is only what the author knows from his own rowing background. Others familiar with rowing can undoubtedly add to the list.

Harvard won the great event, with Yale a close second, followed by Washington. The second-place finish for Yale coaches Walz and Burk showed that Yale had reestablished its rowing tradition after the war in fine style. There were a few public remarks that the high-stroking style of the Yale crew seemed an aberration from the norm, but the reaction to the race results seemed to be generally favorable. The future of the college's rowing—and of the nation after the war—was bright.

After the 1947 spring season, Burk received an offer from the Cornelius "Sonny" Vanderbilt Whitney, the father of Yale oarsman Harry Payne Whitney II to come to their Adirondack estate to personally coach young Whitney sculling on nearby Long Lake. Harry had been a member of Burk's 1947 freshman crew and now had an interest in concentrating on the single, at least in the off-season.

Burk accepted the offer, and he, Kay, and their infant son Roger were guests of the Whitneys for the rest of the summer at a separate cabin located on the estate.

It was there that Joe and Kay Burk first began to envision a possible retirement life. They were impressed by the serenity and isolation at the estate and began to imagine what type of retirement home they might establish for themselves that could mirror the rural relaxation they had enjoyed that summer. That "vision of life among the trees," as the Burks called it, while first imagined in the Adirondacks, would eventually take them to the steep green slopes of Montana.

But Burk did more than dream in the Adirondacks, he instilled in young Whitney his own fascination for sculling. After that summer of intense coaching, Harry Whitney would go on to compete in the U.S. Olympic Trials in double sculls the following summer in 1948.

It may seem odd for Burk, as an in-law of a wealthy Western family, to agree to be hired as a private coach for the scion of a prominent Eastern family. Neither Burk nor his wife and children seemed to find the arrangement uncomfortable. To Roger Burk, who recalled the event in an interview for this book, the arrangement seemed as matter of course. Burk's summer work is just another example among many in which the Burk family easily integrated into all strata of society without any sense of discomfort. The world of rowing in which Burk had begun was filled with examples of working-class folk being elevated into loftier positions—men like John B. Kelly Sr., or Canadian Bob Pearce—both of whom were initially barred from the Henley Regatta because of their backgrounds.

But by 1947, at least for some in rowing, strata did not seem to be determinative. As George Pocock had said, "Watermanship is a great equalizer."

Burk would coach the sons of many prominent families, from Philadelphia's Main Line and elsewhere. Joe and Kay would navigate all these worlds with equal ease, calling up the lines from Kipling's poem "If": "If you can walk with kings, nor lose the common touch, if all men count with you, but none too much."

As the fall of 1947 allowed the coaches to reflect and plan for the 1948 campaigns, it did not take long for the promoter Walz and the preacher Rusty Callow to get together to recast the traditional collegiate rowing season by agreeing to have their respective crews meet around New Year's Day in 1948 for a regatta to be held at Palm Beach, Florida. The northern press, knowing a number of their readers spent the Christmas holidays in Florida, soon announced that the Penn and Yale programs agreed to an exhibition race at Palm Beach, Florida, on the waters of Lake Worth near the Everglades Club. Florida newspapers likened the event to the intercollegiate clashes previously held on the Hudson River in New York. This race was billed locally as "Poughkeepsie by the Palms," and touted as the first time established collegiate crews had come to southern waters.

This post war era presented the opportunity to rowing communities to change old habits. The University of Washington's effort to promote an annual championship of crews from east and west was one example. Before the war, western crews had always to come east by train to race the best eastern crews at Poughkeepsie.

Walz and Callow probably saw the Florida experiment as a way to better prepare for the spring racing season, and to reward their crews with some training in the sunshine during the Christmas holidays.

Neither Walz nor Callow could be called shy men. Both knew that rowing's newspaper audiences were then located in the Northeast, so they picked a location that was familiar to the New York elite that wintered in Florida. "Poughkeepsie by the Palms" sought the fame and attendance now characteristic of postwar America and its booming economy.

Today, schools and colleges in colder climates often head south for early training in the winter. The states of Florida, Georgia, Tennessee, and South Carolina compete for the early spring business as established teams seek a more favorable training location. But this early trip south decades before such travel became common seems solely due to the promotional abilities of Callow and Walz.

The Yale and Pennsylvania crews not only boated eights as usual but also presaged a change to include small boats in college regattas by including both the coxed pair and singles competitions. John B. "Kel" Kelly Jr., son of Olympic sculling champion John B. Kelly, Sr., entered the singles for Penn. Harry Payne Whitney of Connecticut was one of two scullers for Yale.

In the January 3, 1948, race, the Yale Varsity defeated Penn by only a yard—which *The Miami Herald*'s Luther Evans said was "so close it was a shame anyone had to lose." Twenty thousand spectators witnessed the race along the 2,000-meter course on Lake Worth, which included spectators on 150 boats anchored along the course itself. In the single sculling contest, Penn's Jack Kelly, the then current Henley Diamond Sculls champion, easily defeated his two Yale opponents, Harry Whitney and Richard Krementz Jr. Yale's JV narrowly defeated Penn's second boat.

There was also a coxed pairs race, which Penn won. As a follow up to the "small world" of American rowing, the stroke in the Yale pair that day was one Craig Shealy from Stamford, Connecticut. Craig's son Al would be the stroke of the Harvard Varsity from 1973 to 1975, and the stroke of the 1974 U.S. World Champion eight. Al remembers his father telling him about Joe Burk—saying that Burk was so strong that "his single seemed to lift above the water" when Burk took a stroke.

The Herald article included a "Who's Who" section, which

mentioned that the then Secretary of Commerce Averill Harriman—who had rowed and coached crew at Yale as an undergraduate in the early 1900s—had served as the race referee, and that Florida Governor Millard Caldwell and his wife had been the guests aboard the yacht of shipping magnate Dan Taylor anchored by the course.[121]

The otherwise successful beginning of a new race tradition was marred by three of the Yale oarsmen being injured when the convertible in which they were riding home went into a fogbank just inside the city limits of Savannah, Georgia. One passenger suffered a concussion and fractured vertebra, and the driver suffered a gash on his leg.[122]

The 1948 spring rowing season began for Yale on the Severn River, where they defeated Navy and Columbia in varsity, JV, and freshman races of one and three-quarter miles.[123] Yale again swept the "Derby Day Races" against Pennsylvania and Columbia on May 10.[124]

Allen Walz was noted on May 15, 1948, as a contributor to an article in a magazine entitled "Boxing Must Be Banned," written by Andy O'Brian, appearing in the June edition of *Sportfolio Magazine*.[125] Walz was identified as a former Golden Gloves winner and the Yale crew coach.

The reader can only imagine what the Yale Athletic Department thought of Walz inserting himself into such articles on a controversial subject. Walz must have been betting on the truth of the old advertising adage "Any publicity is good publicity."

Yale's 1948 spring season was beset by illness. The Eastern Sprints were held in Cambridge, Massachusetts, that year, with *The New York Times* reporting that four of the Yale Varsity were suffering from influenza. Notwithstanding the illness, the varsity boat lost by a scant 1.2 seconds to the winner, Harvard. Then undefeated Cornell did not attend the Eastern Sprints, but rowed Wisconsin on the Badger's home water, Lake Mendota, and came from behind to beat their hosts.

Disappointment followed Yale's promising Sprints finish. The weekend following, the Yale Varsity also lost to Cornell at Ithaca by one second over a course of two miles, longer than the sprint distance of 2,000 meters by three-quarters of a mile. Cornell's stroke rate was lower than Yale's, leaving some to wonder whether the Yale stroke rate was not suitable for races longer than 2,000 meters.[126]

At the Harvard-Yale race, all three Yale boats lost. Allison Danzig of *The New York Times* noted that all the Yale crews were rowing higher stroke rates, sometimes approaching 40 per minute, but the Harvard crews were closer to 35 or 36 strokes.[127] Nonetheless, the Yale Varsity came within one and half seconds of Harvard, a slender margin. The JV and frosh boats lost but remained respectably close.

Never one to be easily discouraged, Walz assessed the Yale season and decided that the team had enough good oarsmen to enter a number of Olympic Trials in the small boats. It was a bold move, but Walz was a bold man, and he felt the team's results justified the effort.

At the 1948 Olympic Trials, Yale triumphed in the coxless pair and the four without cox. Yale crews finished second in the coxed pairs[128] and in the double sculls, which had been stroked by Harry Payne Whitney, whom Burk had privately coached the preceding summer.[129]

The New York Times reporter Allison Danzig commented on Yale's contesting the Olympic Trials in small boats, which were normally fought between out between club rowers, rather than collegians. The informal practice had been that U.S. college eights fought and won the eight oared races, and club rowers usually won the small boat spots. In a commentary entitled "Views on U.S. Rowing", published days before the Olympics, Danzig remarked that the U.S. rowing team had a greater share of collegians than normal in boats smaller than the eight:

> ... Heretofore the [rowing] clubs have provided the scullers and the fours and pairs. Now the lads from the campus are going to have a try at it in three of the events. They'd better make good, if only for Allen Walz's sake.
>
> Skip has been expounding that the college oarsmen can do a better job of it because they have more time to train and practice. To prove his point he made wholesale Yale entries in the Olympic tryouts, and Harvard, Princeton, Cornell and

Washington came in. The Elis [nickname for Yale oarsmen—Yale's founder was Eli Yale] made their coach look good by getting in the finals in five cases and winning two. Washington won another, the four with coxswain.[130]

Skip Walz was named an Olympic rowing coach for the 1948 Games.[131]

On July 5, 1948, Kathy Burk was born to Joe and Kay Burk.

The Yale coxed pair did not make the finals of the Olympics, and the coxless four was third in a three-boat final with Italy and Denmark,[132] coming away with the bronze medal.

However bold Walz may have seemed when he decided to enter the small boats trials, getting two boats on the Olympic team and one of them getting an Olympic medal showed he was a good judge of rowing ability.

For Yale, Cornell, Princeton, and Penn, the 1949 rowing season started on December 31, 1948, at what was billed in the Florida newspapers as "the Second Annual Regatta of the Palm Beaches." The printed Regatta Program, dated December 31, 1948, called the event simply "Palm Beach Regatta."

The crews came down early to acclimate, and the coaches, on a Saturday night before the race, went to a night club where the dancing girls employed there encouraged Callow, the ordained minister, to come to the dance floor. Two girls rolled up Callow's pants legs to show his socks and garters, and Callow himself rolled up his sleeves, and with his powerful arms swung one of the girls wildly while his surprised dance partner clung to the Bull of the Woods for her own safety.

The following day, Reverend Callow had been invited to give the sermon at a nearby church where the crews likely attended services. Many of the attendees complimented Callow on his sermon. One of the last attendees in line shook Callow's hand and said, "Reverend Callow, I'm very impressed by the breadth of your talents. I don't know *which you do better*, give a sermon or teach show girls how to dance."[133]

The newspaper reports showed Yale's Varsity sparkled in the

Palm Beach Regatta Program—Courtesy of Sean Colgan

sunshine by winning by one length. In the JV race, Cornell, who chose for the first time to travel to the southern regatta that year, won by less than a quarter of a length. No race was reported for freshmen crews, perhaps because the coaches thought it unwise to race the younger oarsmen so early in the season.[134]

In the picture on page 138 shows the cover of the December 1948

The Penn Varsity boat of 1949 before the race in Florida December 31, 1948—
Courtesy of Sean Colgan

Program with a shirtless eight rowing in preparation for the race—obscuring the identity of of the crew. The picture appearing on page 139 shows the Penn Vasiry boat just before the race in Florida.. Idenitifed are Charles Colgan at bow, James Heany as 2, John Apperger at 3, Al Lawn (who would coach the Penn lightweights the following year while a graduate student) is at 4, Al Tyler at 5, James "Moose" Erikson at 6, Larry Uslanger at 7, and J.B. Kelly Jr. at stroke, and Evan "Shorty" Hunt at cox.

At the 1949 Eastern Sprints, held at Lake Onondaga in Syracuse, Harvard swept the field, winning the varsity, JV, and freshman races. "Invincible Harvard maintained its supremacy over the East today . . ." read the news reports, and for the third successive year Yale was fourth in the varsity race, third in the JV, and Burk's freshman did not even make the six-boat final.[135]

This trend toward the negative could have comforted neither Yale supporters nor the Yale Athletic Department administration.

What remained for Walz and Burk was the annual Harvard-Yale race on the Thames at New London, Connecticut. A special preview of the contest, again written by Allison Danzig, appeared in *The New York Times* Sunday Magazine twelve days before the race, entitled "Nine Men and a Boat: Why varsity crews go through such ordeals baffles anyone who has never pulled a sweep."

The article struck chords familiar to those in the rowing world: the long workouts for a short season, with collective but no individual glory, and the expense of the shells and non-existent ticket sales. But the variation from the norm in the article was Walz, the outlier in a race almost mired in tradition. The article read:

Two years ago the New Haven institution hired Allen Walz to take over the aging Ed Leader's tasks. Walz in more ways than one is a maverick. He not only did not go to Washington [as did the majority of existing major college coaches] but he never pulled an oar in college. He came by way of Wisconsin from the sidewalks of New York . . . where his sports were boxing and football.

Alongside his coaching brethren, Walz is breezy—even brash. He literally talked his way into the silent profession . . . [at] . . . Manhattan College [with] Walz as its coach. From there he went in 1940 to Wisconsin, took time out for war service in 1942 and returned in 1946 when his crew won three big races, including the Poughkeepsie and Eastern Association sprints. That performance won him the job at Yale.

His arrival at New Haven was something akin to a squall. He was the talkingest rowing coach newspaper men can remember and he goes farther out of his way to arrange coverage for races than anyone before him at Yale or, for that matter, elsewhere. He sent chatty newsletters to alumni, informing them of what was going on in rowing and, in the process, drumming up support, financial and otherwise, for the sport. He plans to dredge and lengthen a canal close by the

Yale Bowl so his oarsmen won't have to travel to the Housa-tonic at Derby for their workouts.

Allen Walz had talked big—and Danzig's *The New York Times* arti-cle celebrated that apparent deviation from the norm of the solemn, tight-lipped rowing coach, perhaps best represented by Harvard's own Tom Bolles.

Danzig's piece was a delicious preview of the unexpected out-come. For this version of the Harvard-Yale contest, Walz's varsity came through with an unexpected upset of previously undefeated Harvard. The *Times* headline after the race below the fold on the front page read:

YALE CREW BREAKS RECORD TO BEAT HARVARD FIRST TIME IN 11 MEETINGS

. . . In one of the really stunning surprises of this oldest of intercollegiate rivalries, one of the lightest eight-oared crews boated by Yale humbled the pride of the East, the only varsity of its section that had remained undefeated, by one-third of a length . . .

In confounding expectations and ending Harvard's string of ten successive victories over the Blue, Allen Walz' thrice-beaten varsity, superbly stroked by 164-pound Richard Krementz of Camden, Maine, set a new upstream record for the 4-mile course of 19 minutes 52.8 seconds . . .

(Krementz had been the second Yale sculler behind Whitney in the 1948 Florida Regatta.)

After the varsity race, Allen Walz dove into the water fully clothed to swim to his varsity's boat to shake hands with each member of the crew. The victory had been preceded by the Yale JV beating its Har-vard counterpart, and Burk's freshman coming within two-thirds of a length of Harvard.

Danzig the reporter gave the context for Walz' delight and relief:

Of all the happy celebrants, none was more elated than the Yale coach. The fact that his contract expired with this race and that the victory possibly placed him in position to renew it may have been in his mind at that time, but more likely Walz was happy at the vindication of his methods, which had been so severely criticized for the high beat of his crews the past two years, during which . . . [Yale] had found little of sweetness in the uses of much adversity.

When Burk read this article, he must have recalled his own letter to George Pocock of 1943, remarking upon the lack of stability in the coaching profession. Burk had never been anything but supportive of Walz, but he could not have failed to sense his boss's conflict with the athletic administration at Yale.

Danzig ended his piece with the graceful tribute to Yale given by the losing Harvard coach Tom Bolles: "It was a great race. We lost to a better crew. I have no fault to find."

Danzig lauded Bolles's sportsmanship. "For a man who has had so little experience with defeat, Harvard's coach, whose record is matched by few, showed that he had no superior in meeting triumph and disaster and treating both just the same. No one better represents the spirit of this wonderful sport, which brings out the finest instincts in its neophytes, the true amateurs of them all."[136]

Joe Burk was offered the opportunity to coach rowing in Cuba during the summer of 1949. The details of the engagement and who arranged it are lost to history. Roger Burk was young, and his sister Kathy just born, and the Burk family archives indicate only that the family did indeed go to Cuba, but neither Roger nor Kathy have any memories of family discussions of the trip. At the time, the allegiance of Cuba was the subject of considerable competition between America and the USSR, the latter having opened an embassy for the first time in Havana in 1943, with future Soviet foreign minister Andrei Gromyko as its first ambassador.

In the 1950 Census, Joe and Kay Burk were living at 109 Franklin Road, Hamden, New Haven, Connecticut. Today that location is an apartment complex and located just up State Route 5 going north from New Haven towards Wallingford. It is likely that Burk had offices at the main Yale campus, and from there rode the team bus that would leave the main campus in the afternoons for the trip to Derby, where the Yale Boathouse still stands.

By the fall of 1949, doubtless because he had beaten Harvard for the first time in over a decade, Allen Walz had in hand a new contract with Yale. The Yale Athletic Department could hardly have jettisoned Walz after such an unexpected victory over its historic rival.

But the styles of the institution and the man did not mesh. Yale was Yale, a pillar of the Ivy League. While desiring victory, Yale preferred its victory delivered with a measure of reserve and understatement. Walz was a product of New York City, an energetic and talented man grasping the power of modern advertising and broadcasting. Reserve did not fit his personality.

At some point in the fall of 1949, as Yale practiced for the 1950 spring season, Allen Walz decided that he would hire a helicopter to allow him to fly above his crews and coach them from the air. At that time, helicopters were just coming into use, and were a potent symbol of technological advance, as well as a proud state product of Connecticut, where Igor Sikorsky had established his manufacturing facility in Stratford. The machines would soon play a major role in the evacuation of wounded in the Korean War, made famous by the flight scenes of the movie and TV series *M*A*S*H*.

Bills began to come through to the Yale Athletic Department— and the bills must have been large for such a new technology. Yale made discreet inquiries. A history of the Wisconsin crew program written by Bradley Taylor contains the following story:

> Wisconsin freshman coach Dick Tipple recalled being in his office when an administrator from Yale poked his head in with concerns about the budget.
>
> "Coach Walz leased a helicopter earlier this summer from

which he saw he can better observe and coach his crews," said the visitor uneasily. "As the whole thing is getting pretty expensive, I came to inquire if Wisconsin had ever supported such extravagances . . ."[137]

The Wisconsin head coach was not in that day. Coach Tipple told the Yale administrator that he, as the freshman coach, did not have visibility into budget matters. The man disappeared.

Whatever the Yale Athletic Department concerns, Walz's tenure continued into 1950. Yale again travelled over the Christmas and New Year's holiday, doubtless at prodigious cost, to meet Pennsylvania, still coached by Rusty Callow, in the Palm Beach races on January 2, 1950—which again drew near football-sized crowds.

Yale swept all the races, and publicity was good.

On April 22, at what was the historical start of Yale's spring season, Yale hosted Navy at Derby, and swept all three races—varsity, JV, and freshmen.

What came next has been little told in the rowing world. Walz chose to celebrate his use of helicopters as a coaching platform and got the finest publicity a modern ad man could want: an AP Wire story.

On Wednesday, May 10, 1950, *The Buffalo News* ran the story on its first sports page with the headline "Eli Coach Takes to the Air To Get New Angle on Oarsmen":

Yale's crew coach, Skip Walz, took to the air Tuesday in an effort to improve the work of his charges. In doing so, Walz completed a cycle. For years, coaches at Yale and elsewhere have watched their teams work from the same general level on which the teams were performing.

Not too long ago, Robert J. H. (Bob) Kiphuth, Yale and Olympic swimming coach, put on a diving helmet and went into the big Payne Whitney pool to watch his swimmers from below.

Tuesday, Walz hopped into a helicopter and got a bird's-eye view of what went on in the varsity's eight-oared shells—things usually hidden from the coach who follows the shells in a launch . . .

"I learned things from watching the boys from up above that I would never have spotted through trailing them in a motor launch. The whole pattern of the stroke is clearly evident, and the exact extent to which each man is powering the boat by the fullness of his sweep is clearly discernible."

"At the risk of seeming facetious," he said with a grin, "may I add that it opens up a new vista for rowing coaches."[138]

The effect of the article, doubtless arranged by Walz, was to blunt any criticism he might receive from the Yale Athletic Department for the helicopter rental expense by likening its use to the scientific underwater review of swimming strokes then being used by the Yale swim coach. Walz likely thought the Department dared no cut the helicopter without endangering the swimming underwater observation equipment.

Joe Burk never mentioned Walz's helicopter rental, but he no doubt watched and learned. Burk must have resolved that his future relations with college administrations were destined to be different.

In the 2000s, Burk did tell Peter Mallory the following story:

. . . Walz coached crew the way he had been coached football at NYU [Burk, like others, confused Manhattan College with NYU] with much swearing and yelling and shouting and really gave [the Yale crew] a rough time, so after I had been there four years, the athletic director told me they were pretty well fed up with Skippy and asked whether I would become head coach.

I said to him, "I wouldn't feel right to be moving up into the varsity job after having first been his Freshman Coach."

[The Yale administrator] asked me who I would recommend, and I told him Jim Rathschmidt. He was the Princeton Freshman Coach, and I knew from competing against him how beautifully his crews rowed and what a great job he did.[139]

At the 1950 Eastern Sprints, MIT, in a surprise win, beat Harvard, with Princeton third, then Penn, Syracuse—and Yale sixth. In the JV race, Yale was fourth, and in the freshman race, Yale was sixth.

In a preview article by *The New York Times* published on the Friday before the Harvard-Yale race on June 24, 1950, Allison Danzig nicely summarized the seasons of the respective crews—and as the year before, Harvard was the favorite and the far larger crew:

> ... [Harvard was] the winner in every race it has rowed this season except for its tenth-of-a-second defeat by M.I.T. in the Eastern Sprint Championships ... [and was thus] logically the choice over thrice-beaten Yale as it was a year ago ... Physical conditioning also is very much a factor, though that is not to say Harvard was not in shape. Allen (Skip) Walz puts almost primary emphasis upon the conditioning of his men, and that training paid off in carrying Yale [to victory the year before].
>
> [Yale] will be outweighed by a big margin—13 ½ pounds per man—and at 168 it stands as the one of the lightest varsities ever to wear the blue.[140]

In the event, mighty Harvard under Bolles, the nearly silent coach, swept all three races, the JV by two and a quarter-lengths and the freshman by two and a half-length. But the varsity race was close. Harvard led from the start and was ahead by open water, but in the last two miles the Yale crew closed at the end, forcing Harvard stroke Louis B. McCagg to raise the stroke rate to 40 at the finish to hold off the late Yale charge, with the distance between the crews at the finish being only 12 feet.[141]

CHAPTER EIGHT

To Stand in Rusty's Shoes

In early spring of 1949, Joe Burk's former coach Rusty Callow began to openly express his frustration with the progress of the rowing program at Penn. His comment was grave: "If something isn't done soon, crew will die out as a major sport at the University of Pennsylvania."[142] For a founding university of the Intercollegiate Rowing Association, this result seemed unthinkable.

There were several reasons for Callow's frustration. As the postwar boom made life easier for virtually all Americans, those fortunate enough to attend Ivy League colleges like Penn were lured away from many forms of hard physical labor—and rowing seemed to be one of them. The numbers and quality of oarsmen Callow was seeing at the Penn Boathouse seemed to sag. It is also likely that Callow the lumberjack missed other lumberjacks. Men of the East Coast, whose families had settled, in some cases, two centuries before the Callows reached the Washington Territory, had simply had a different life experience.

In 1955, Callow explained to *Sports Illustrated* that he had been lured away from Washington by Penn's offer to more than triple his salary, and that in hiring him Penn hoped to grasp the National Championship at the IRA. After all, Callow had brought Washington crews East and promptly won the IRA in 1923, 1924, came second in 1925, and then won again in 1926.[143]

Penn and Callow had both hoped that Callow could recreate in Philadelphia the IRA victories which seemed to flow effortlessly from the stock of tall sons of lumberjacks coming to Seattle to row under Callow. Pennsylvania, one of the three founding colleges of the Intercollegiate Rowing Association, had not won a varsity IRA race since 1900. The school hoped Callow could bring his luck to the East. But an IRA victory had eluded the former lumberman.

Thus disheartened by the talent available at Penn, Callow had to think that his chances of winning consistently in collegiate competition were better at Navy. And Navy wanted Callow. Navy's coach, Buck Walsh, was in ill health, and in an effort to preserve his legacy, Walsh personally asked Callow to join the program.

While the amount of Callow's Navy salary was not made public, it must have been plenty, and there was another nonmonetary incentive that the service academies offered prospective coaches of that era: a group of fit, motivated young men who were literally honing for battle and who fully expected their college life to be filled with physical challenge.

Today, the service academies are viewed more as a sports league unto themselves, and often a secondary one at that. But in the early 1950s, Army and Navy compared favorably with the major sporting powers of that day. The Army football team under Coach Red Blaik was a national power. Navy, too, had its share of all-American Football players.[144] In rowing, especially, the Naval Academy was traditionally held in high regard, and had won the IRA numerous times—and unlike Penn, its campus was located next to a long, desirable stretch of water. It could not have been lost on Rusty Callow that the waters of the Severn bore a certain resemblance to Lake Washington where Callow had first rowed and first coached.

In addition, Callow had never been able to bring his Penn crews to an ideal peak for the final race of the spring season—the Intercollegiate Rowing Association (IRA) Regatta. Part of the problem seemed to be the distance of the IRA races when compared to the rest of the regular collegiate races in that era. Most collegiate races in that day were between the Henley distance (1 mile and five sixteenths) and two miles.

But at the IRA, the varsity race was four miles long—and seemingly impossible for Penn to master. Callow felt that the distance was a handicap and believed that the Schuylkill's length of available practice water—three miles at most—meant his Penn crews were at a disadvantage against crews that could train without stopping.

At the University of Washington, Callow had coached the crews of his alma mater on long stretches of gloriously open water. Both as an oarsman and as a coach, he was accustomed to side-by-side practice racing at low cadences of about 20 strokes per minute, and for miles at a time. Callow felt those long, continuous stretches had been essential to his crews' development, and especially to their performance at the IRA championship.

Years later, Joe Burk commented that he thought Callow's decision to leave overlooked an obvious solution to the length problem in Philadelphia: simply turn the boat around and do it again. "I don't know why, but . . . [Rusty] didn't consider making several trips up and down the river," Burk remarked to Peter Mallory. "Every year we would spend two awful weeks at Poughkeepsie in vain attempts to build up stamina. I honestly think we were totally exhausted by our long, twice-a-day rows up there."[145]

To modern readers, Burk's observation seems to beg the question: If the solution was so obvious—why didn't Burk raise it to Callow?

The answer is that the 1930s era of American rowing, oarsmen were taught to listen and obey. It was the rare oarsman who asked questions, for fear of appearing to question the wisdom of the coach. Because rowing knowledge was not then widely dispersed, the traditional wisdom was that the coach was presumed right, and it was brash oarsmen who questioning the coach's approach. The fact that Burk—even when he was captain in 1934 did not feel comfortable approaching Callow about his thought about "just turn around and do it again" shows how powerful the tradition of "obey the coach" was at that time.

Coaches today—aided as they are by reams of scientific studies about when and how distance work and intensity are best interspersed—understand better the problem of introducing long rowing practices in the two weeks before the season's finale. Last minute surges of long, hard practices are generally avoided in favor of a tapering of practice.[146]

At the end of the 1950 season, Callow announced that he was accepting an offer from the United States Naval Academy to coach the Navy crews for the 1951 season. From now on, Callow would make his home in Navy's Hubbard Hall.

Because Callow was leaving on good terms with Penn, he was asked who he recommended as his replacement. Callow named Burk. Joe Burk was then offered the job of heavyweight crew coach at Penn in the midsummer of 1950. At that point in time, Walz remained at Yale.

Burk promptly accepted. In many ways, he was going home.

Both he and Callow would have moments of great success in their new roles. And Burk's crews would find that by the late 1960s, they would be rowing up and back the length of the Schuylkill—a full six miles—three times each weekday and four times on Saturday.

Burk bade farewell to his last freshman boat at Yale—the class of 1953—while Kay packed up the family and prepared herself for yet another change. The crew presented Burk with a silver stopwatch with the inscription:

Presented
To
Joe Burk
by his
1953
FRESHMAN CREW
June 23, 1950.[147]

A few years ago, this watch was rediscovered by Reed Kindermann and Rick Stehlik among Burk's personal effects as part of their larger effort to obtain and restore one of Burk's last singles. The meticulously restored boat now hangs from the ceiling of the Burk-Bergman Boathouse. In place of the regular wrist watch Burk had used in the 1930s, the stroke watch given him by his last Yale boat now hangs from the single's foot stretcher.

After Burk left Yale and just before the start of fall rowing practice, Allen Walz also decided on a different career path—away from rowing.

The *Yale Daily News* reported in September 1950:

Allen (Skip) Walz ended four stormy years as head coach of Yale crew last month to accept a position with a private concern in Brooklyn. He was replaced almost immediately by 36-year-old Jim Rathschimdt, freshman coach at Princeton.

Walz had been at odds, especially over finances, with some quarters of the Athletic Administration for some time, and his resignation created little surprise. It is presumed that when the right offer came along, Walz took the opportunity to step down. While here, Walz enjoyed moderate success; in 1949 his varsity boat defeated Harvard for the first time since 1935.[148]

Walz's new job was as a consultant on industrial relations with Arma Corporation of Brooklyn. He would later become vice president for public relations for Canada Dry Beverage Company, and later for Getty Oil.[149] Perhaps public relations of the 1950s variety better suited Walz's style.

An interesting side note to Burk's move from Yale to Penn was the fact that the first collegiate oarsman known to have been taught sculling by Burk, Harry Payne Whitney II, graduated from Yale in 1950. He would immediately follow Burk to Pennsylvania, where he would eventually receive a Master of Arts in Anthropology. It is interesting to note that while Whitney—scion of a wealthy family connected by both birth and marriage to the Vanderbilt and Harriman families— doubtless had his pick of universities, he chose Penn, where his only connection appears to have been Joe Burk.[150] There is no record of Whitney sculling from the Penn Boathouse—but who could be surprised if he had?

In the fall of 1950, Joe Burk at long last returned to the region of his birth and the river where he first learned to row—the Schuylkill. He came with his own vision of how to teach rowing and train young men to row fast. Burk's coaching style was quite different from Walz's. No swearing, yelling, or shouting.

What would remain in Burk's Penn crews would be a lean toward the high-stroking style that Walz and Burk had used at Yale, and that Burk had used in his own sculling.

It did not take long for Burk's new approach to be implemented. For the next two decades, Penn heavyweight oarsmen would become accustomed to a quiet but kind man, whose standards were exacting but fair. Many would find the experience among the most important in their lives.

On September 20, 1950, Penn's *The Daily Pennsylvanian* announced that Burk would "call meetings of all freshman candidates and varsity members for Monday in Houston Hall. Burk wishes to stress that no previous experience is necessary, and all who are interested in trying their hand at the sport are urged to turn out."[151]

The enthusiastic group that gathered in Houston Hall was so sizable that Burk was forced to cut down the squad by the second week in October because "it was impossible for me to give proper attention to such a large number of men."[152]

At winter approached, Burk made changes in the preseason training for his team, which included cancelling the collegiate events in West Palm Beach—the races in which both Allen Walz and Rusty Callow had taken such pleasure.

Burk the sculler, who chopped ice on the Rancocas to allow himself to row nearly year- round, may not have seen the value in travelling all the way to Florida for sunshine.

Whatever he truly felt, Burk publicized his reasons for opting out in nuanced language chosen to give offense neither to Walz nor Callow. Drawing from his observations of the effects on the Yale oarsmen, he told *The Daily Pennsylvanian,* "I find that the boys on the squad, particularly those who make the [Florida] trip, reach their physical and psychological peak at the Palm Beach races. When the regular season begins [in the late spring], it is an anti-climax."

Burk instead kept the team in Philadelphia—in the gym if the river froze over—while he assessed the individual weaknesses in each oarsman, and then prescribed the necessary weight lifting and calisthenics required to address them.

Thus, the West Palm Beach races—the brainchild of Rusty Callow and Allen Walz—were no more. There is no record that Yale objected. The likely reason was money. In fact, Yale soon found itself short on its travel budget, requiring alumni and oarsmen to make special contributions to allow Yale's crew to travel to Wisconsin for a regular season meeting.

Perhaps since he was in his first year as head coach, Burk did take pains to characterize his required sessions in the gym as in keeping with accepted standards. He told *The Daily Pennsylvanian* that his gym training system "is not an entirely new one, and is used by other coaches."

On November 30, 1950, Burk capped Penn's on-the-water practices with the traditional fall ending of interclass races in which each of the classes would form boats to compete in intra-squad "scrimmages." The sophomore class had entered two boats and both had come out on top against the other Penn classes. Burk noted the freshman boat did well, even though most were new to rowing, finishing only nine seconds behind the winners.

Burk followed his description of the races by announcing that further practices in the rowing tanks would be reduced to mainly those freshmen who need more technical practice. In general, "[t]he squad will do exercises designed to strengthen individual weaknesses and to prepare the men mentally and physically for the opening race in the spring."

Burk, over the years, would earn a reputation as an innovator. He would demonstrate flexibility in trying different approaches to coaching, rowing in eights and selecting who to seat in which boat. But his touchstone would remain a bias toward measurement of objective criteria. Burk's innovations were not a result of any particular intent on his part to innovate *per se*, but instead a natural outgrowth of Burk's own curiosity about, and focus upon, rowing—but not from the angle of rowing himself, which he had clearly mastered in the years 1937 to 1939—but from the angle of explaining to college oarsmen who were less talented than Burk.

When asked, as he often was, Burk freely admitted that "his standards were exacting."

He never relaxed them. While not all Penn oarsmen strictly followed every tenet of Burk's regime at every moment, they all took a certain pride in the fact that their coach was a stickler for training and would concede that his approach was likely the best one, based on his own fantastic results in the single.

These high standards, taken alongside the widely told stories of Burk's own heroism as an oarsman and as a naval commander, established in Burk's oarsmen the growing sense that however painful *their* experience at any one time might be, Burk himself had endured worse. His own silent example would be their constant inspiration.

Early on in his career at Penn, Kay and Joe established the tradition of inviting the whole heavyweight squad over to their house on weekends for games of croquet or soccer with Burk's children, followed by a barbeque, which would include ice cream but no beer. These events would allow the boys to learn more about their coach, his wife, and his growing children, to have time away from the campus, and to engage in fierce backyard competition.

These informal get-togethers reflected Burk's view of how to behave: no alcohol, no smoking, no bad language, not even any carbonated beverages. From the late forties through the late sixties, Penn oarsmen were discouraged from drinking Coca-Cola because Burk had concerns about the effect of the carbonation on his oarsmen's health and endurance.

The record of Penn rowing success in terms of wins and losses would vary during Burk's time coaching, with both slow and fast crews, with the tally reaching a crescendo in Burk's last three years. Burk's behavior throughout would remain unchanged. He would emphasize hard work, attention to good rowing, and to a sense of sportsmanship, for which Burk himself would always provide the best example.

Before the start of the spring rowing season in 1951, Penn announced that a key rowing prospect was coming the following year. Jack Guest Jr., the nineteen-year-old Canadian single sculls champion, committed to come row for Penn. Guest had won Canadian championships in the single, and the announcement reported that Burk would "replace Guest's father, a 1930 Diamond Sculls winner, as his coach."

This addition to Penn's crew was much needed, as John B. Kelly Jr. had graduated, and the pain of his loss was keenly felt. The article said Guest "will seek to replace the loss of Kelly . . . when he enters Penn next year."[153] While the traditional wisdom expressed among Burk's former Penn oarsmen is that Burk did not recruit oarsmen to Penn, Jack Guest was a major recruiting coup. Jack Guest Sr., Olympic silver medalist, Diamond Sculls winner and future Canada Hall of Famer clearly believed his son would be in skillful hands with Burk, winner of the '38 and '39 Diamonds.

The Penn crews were back on the water at the end of February, 1951, and their first race was against Princeton and Rutgers on Lake

Carnegie on April 21. A large contingent of Pennsylvania students made the trip north to cheer on their crew, and the Penn varsity won.

Penn faced Yale and Columbia for the Blackwell Cup on April 29, and the varsity was beaten by four feet on the Hudson.[154]

For the next race, Burk attempted to influence the conduct of students attending the Adams Cup races against Navy and Harvard in Philadelphia. In *The Daily Pennsylvanian* on May 9, 1951, Burk appealed to the Penn student body to restrain themselves at the annual "Skimmer Day"—a festival on the banks of the Schuylkill set for the following weekend when the gentlemen would wear straw hats known as "skimmers." Skimmer Day was such an elaborate production, it had its own program of the events for the weekend.

In past years, the event had become so rowdy with drunken fraternity antics that even the outgoing Rusty Callow had bemoaned the tradition. The banks of the river were often covered not with polite spectators, but with inebriated louts whose behavior brought no good reputation to the University. Beer cans found their way into the Schuylkill.

Burk's appeal was for the students to end the spectacle. "This is an appeal to the undergraduates of the University to prove that Skimmer Day can be conducted in a sane, yet festive manner," Burk warned. "It is purely a matter of exercising common sense and good judgment . . . If this is done, Skimmer Day will become an outstanding event among eastern collegiate activities. If it isn't, Skimmer Day is doomed and Pennsylvania has lost a wonderful opportunity for recognition."[155]

In anticipation of the event, *The Daily Pennsylvanian* got a supportive quote from Rusty Callow—now the visiting coach when Navy came to row on Skimmer Day—as saying, "Joe Burk, my successor, is one of the greatest oarsmen who ever lived, and is as expected doing a grand job coaching his alma mater's crews. The Pennsylvania oarsmen are a splendid group of boys and men. They are battlers and command my deepest respect."[156]

On May 14, the paper ran an article on Burk entitled, "Legendary Exploits of Joe Burk Could Make Him A Fiction Hero," in which his "muscular six-foot frame," was contrasted with his "ready smile and

The front cover of the Skimmer Day 1953 program

an air of informality about him until he steps into the Ben Franklin, the launch from which he directs the crews' activities." His war record and honors were often mentioned, but when asked about his war experience, Burk's only comment would be, "There were many times when it could have gone either way."[157]

With such war experience, it was not surprising that the Penn performance, sometimes good, sometimes less than hoped for, was borne by the former PT skipper with a philosophical stance—*sometimes it could go either way*.

Burk's crews travelled to Marietta, Ohio, for the IRAs, Penn's final race of the 1951 season, and the racing was marred by swift water conditions that limited all race to two miles, and wrecked hopes of success in many cases. Penn's freshmen were unable to row "after a mishap." Penn's JV finished sixth in an eight-boat field and the Navy JV sheared off the rudder of the Princeton JV, with neither boat able to finish. Penn's varsity finished fifth behind Wisconsin, Washington, Princeton, and California.

While Penn's 1951 heavyweight season had been mixed, Penn's 1951 lightweight crew, not formally part of Burk's responsibility as the heavyweight coach, had managed to achieve excellence just as the Penn Athletic Department had decided to withdraw its support from the program. According to the current Penn lightweight crew website, the University Athletic Department planned to discontinue lightweight rowing, "but an enthusiastic group of 14 oarsmen persuaded the University to modify its decision." The exact details of the "modification" are not stated.

What was reported is set forth here.

The Daily Pennsylvanian mentioned in its reporting of Penn lightweight 1951 racing results that the lightweights "were paying their own way" but did not elaborate how those payments were made. The lightweights did persuade Al Lawn, the 1950 heavyweight crew captain, to coach them on a volunteer basis while Lawn finished a master's degree at Penn.

No mention was made in newspapers of Joe Burk's opinion of the lightweight program. He was doubtless mindful that Skip Walz had battled the Yale authorities over financing and had ended his coaching career with the dispute unresolved. Burk, in his first full year as a Penn coach, could not have been eager to enter a fight with the Penn Athletic Department over finances.

Prior to 1951, Penn lightweight rowing had followed a schedule that had been set by tradition. Certain weekends were set for Cup races, and the Eastern Sprints included lightweight races that determined the Eastern champions. If Penn showed up for the races, there was no need to announce any change from the norm—so the lightweight crew showed up and the season simply kept going. The Penn equipment still existed, so the team, and most everyone else, simply kept acting as if the lightweight program were funded. Al Lawn showed up to coach, and Burk apparently provided him a launch. And thus, Penn's 1951 lightweight rowing schedule was executed—all with outstanding results.

Save for Penn's loss in the first race of the season to Yale, the varsity lightweight crew was undefeated in regular competition. But the effort was not without its moment of danger. On the eve of the Eastern Sprints, the lightweight varsity's boat was swamped and damaged, requiring extensive repairs. According to the Penn Rowing lightweight website,[158] "an MIT boatman worked through the night to repair the shell" of the opposing Penn team.[159] Due to the sportsmanship displayed by this unknown MIT boatman, the Penn Lightweight varsity won the Sprints championship the following day.

The example of one crew's support staff helping another at a major championship may seem quaint in today's "win at all costs" world, with its general lack of common courtesy, but such was the ethos of the 1950s.

The Lightweight varsity's success in the face of the Athletic Department's defunding created a perfect storm for the revenge of the underdog lightweights—and the rowing alumni took notice. Penn alum Crawford Clark Madeira—a leader in Philadelphia society, a veteran of the U.S. Army action against Pancho Villa in the 1916 Mexican campaign, and a former Penn oarsmen then still belonging to several prestigious boat clubs including University Barge and Bachelors Barge—took up the cause, leading a push by Penn rowing alumni to send the lightweights to Henley. And as a result, pressure was brought to bear on the Penn Athletic Department to reestablish the lightweight crew as a part of the Penn Athletic Department.

The Penn Lightweight crew and its volunteer coach Al Lawn left for London and the Thames Challenge Cup at Henley on June 25, 1951, via the Pan Am flight out of Idlewild airport in New York.[160] Joe Burk accompanied the team as an advisor. The U.S. State Department, learning of Penn's plans, arranged an additional race in Hamburg for the week following the English regatta.

The Penn crew had four military veterans aboard, including one with a metal plate in his head from war wounds, so the lightweights approached their international competition with the same mature and determined attitude that had allowed them to win domestic races. Their motto: "Press On Regardless."[161]

Penn lightweights had no trouble in their heats, advancing to the final. There they would get a chance to row against a heavyweight German crew that Burk viewed with some alarm as he had known of at least one of their oarsmen from the international rowing world before World War II. The Thames Cup at Henley was not limited to lightweight crews, so Penn knew a race against larger men was a certainty—one that the lean men of Penn likely viewed with relish, since they were that year the only lightweight crew at the Regatta.[162]

In the final, Penn won with a twist in tactics that fascinated *The Inquirer*'s John Webster of his column Sportscope:

> In this day of automatic gear shift and quick getaway, it shouldn't be surprising there was a push-button touch to the stirring triumph of Pennsylvania's 150-pound crew in the Thames Challenge Cup final of last week's English Henley Regatta. In this instance, a button was actually pressed . . . In the case of the Quaker blades, the pushing of the button was the call for top effort and greater speed. At a given point, the signal came from the riverbank and Al Lawn, who has been serving as volunteer coach of the lightweights while working for the master's degree he lately received at Pennsylvania. When Lawn, former Roman Catholic High and Penn heavyweight sweepswinger, gave the word, things happened. Coxswain Bob Robinson pressed a button and Pennsylvania, trailing [their opponent], went into high gear.
>
> From all accounts, the Red and Blue shell appeared power motored from that moment. It shot forward and spurted to a one-length victory over Florsheim-Russelsheim, the heavyweight German crew which is to meet Penn again this weekend at Hamburg, Germany. Penn's triumph came at the expense of husky opposition—the Germans, averaging 187 pounds, had a weight advantage of 37 pounds per man.[163]

On the first day of the races in Hamburg, Penn again faced the Florsheim-Russelsheim crew that they had beaten in the final race at Henley and defeated them again.

The second day, Penn lightweights beat a German rowing club Ruderverein of Kassel by one length. The race was rowed in the rain, and Penn covered the 2,000-meter course in 7:02—which the paper noted was slower than their time in the previous day's race.[164]

On November 1, 1951, *The Daily Pennsylvanian* reported *that, now under Burk's direction*, the Penn lightweight crew would alter their winter training: "The heroes of the Henley Regatta, often referred to as the 150-pound crew, will keep their muscles limber with daily workouts on the Schuylkill until they move indoors to Hutchison Gym shortly after Thanksgiving. In Fall workouts . . . the lightweights have been concentrating on fundamentals. When the 150's leave the river they will embark on a rigorous body-building program. Head crew coach Joe Burk, who holds to the theory that muscles win races, will put the men through specially devised exercises which include weightlifting, rope climbing and chin-ups."

The article continued: "Since Al Lawn, who coached the lightweights throughout last year's spectacular season, has been unable to volunteer his services this year, coach Joe Burk and freshman coach Dick Jordan have been sharing the 150 coaching burdens. As yet the University has made no move toward lending financial support to the 150-pounders. Since last year when the school considered dropping 150-pound rowing for lack of student support, the oarsmen have been paying their own way."[165]

The article did not clarify whether Burk had been authorized by the Athletic Department to coach the lightweight oarsmen. If he had been authorized, wouldn't the article have stated as much? If he had not, then by Burk's supporting the lightweight team, he risked being viewed by the Athletic Department as part of the rebellion. One can only conclude that his actions placed him in a delicate situation in his second year as Penn's head coach.

Penn's 1952 spring heavyweight season contained only modest

successes. The team won the Childs Cup and the Blackwell Cup, and the week before the Eastern Sprints, was seeded second behind Navy, but the Penn heavyweights did not live up to the pre-billing at the Sprints, finishing last in the finals, while Navy held off Harvard to remain unbeaten.[166]

Dick Jordan was Burk's freshman coach, and Burk asked him to do double duty—to coach not only the freshmen crew but also the lightweight crew, as time and circumstances permitted. How the practice schedules were juggled is not clear. But the problem of attending races posed a potential political dilemma, for the future of lightweight rowing was apparently still not finalized at the Athletic Department.

Burk and Jordan somehow finessed the question of practices— but the conflict in races could not be avoided. Penn's lightweight races were on a different schedule than the heavyweights, except for the Eastern Sprints. Burk had to choose which crew to leave on its own— and he made the conservative choice of leaving the lightweights to race alone, and Jordan always travelled with the heavyweights—since the Athletic Department had apparently paid for the latter and not the former.

The "Press On Regardless" motto of the lightweights prevailed again in 1952—and the Penn lightweights remained undefeated that season. Alumni funding again flowed in in recognition of the team's performance, and the lightweight varsity again went to Henley and successfully defended their Thames Cup championship. By the time of the Henley press announcements in June, Dick Jordan was identified as "Pennsylvania's lightweight crew rowing coach" without further explanation.[167]

For the heavyweights, on June 22, 1952, the IRA in Syracuse was an all-Navy show. Rusty Callow's varsity, JV, and freshmen heavyweight boats all won the finals, making the Academy's first sweep of the college championship. Navy's dominance was a tribute to Callow and his coaching acumen. He had taken a mid-range Navy program starting his first year in 1951, and by the second year had made the Midshipmen a dominant rowing power in an Olympic year.

At the eight-oared Olympic Trials, Navy was the favorite, but among the other entrants for the eight oared Olympic Trials were Cornell, California, Princeton, Stanford, Washington, Wisconsin, Harvard, and Yale. Buffalo's West Side Boat Club had also made an entry. Other entries were anticipated from Columbia and Detroit Boat Club.

The Olympic Trials in 1952 were held at Lake Quinsigamond in Worcester, Massachusetts. Rusty Callow's Navy Varsity was never seriously challenged and won by two and a half lengths over second-place Princeton. The eight would triumph at the Olympics in Helsinki and be forever after known as "The Admirals."

In December 1952, the *The Philadelphia Inquirer* published a picture from the Pennsylvania Varsity Boat Club's annual dinner honoring members of the unbeaten Penn 150-pound crew, which repeated its 1951 win at Henley. Also honored was Paul Strahlendorf, the Penn rigger who was retiring after seventeen years of keeping the Penn shells afloat, and Rusty Callow for his role as Navy's coach of their victorious Olympic crew.[168]

It was around this time in their marriage that Joe and Kay decided that their summers would be spent travelling back to the West Coast to visit Kay's parents and siblings, usually by car. Automobile travel had exploded after World War II, and consumers were lured with new models by the most prominent manufacturers who had retooled their facilities from making tanks, airplanes, and bombs to making the great American automobile.

Roger and Kathy Burk fondly remember their parents loading up their Pontiac Catalina Station Wagon to head west. Roger explained the routine:

> It was a time when there wasn't any summer rowing, and the last race for the Universities would be the IRA, in June. [Dad] would come back, about ten days later, we always had a Pontiac station wagon with the ersatz wood. He made a system, which he would fold the back seat down, put air

mattresses in the back, that would be his and Mom's sleeping quarters.

Then we would have a sheet of plywood that would go on the window level—that would be my sister's and my sleeping quarters, and the dog would sleep in the driver/passenger seat. We had a Coleman stove for cooking, and canvas water bags that hung on the front of the car that would be cooled by the air blowing over them, so we could take a shower at night.

It was at a time when you could drive across the country and just pull out into farmers' fields. Nothing you could do today. But the big thing was getting out into Ohio on the first day, because that's where the farmland started popping up, when we were growing up from '51 until '62.

And that is how [my parents] found Montana. They would always be looking for a they wanted to retire to, and we ended up camping just a quarter mile from the property they eventually bought.

And Grandmother and Grandpa Black had a weekend getaway between Monterey and Carmel—that was probably ten acres or so, with horses and just a beautiful place. We would spend a couple of months there. You cannot imagine a nicer place. When we were really small, we could go over to Carmel, which is really quite cold. But the Carmel River comes in and flows into the ocean a little bit south of Carmel. And in the summertime, it doesn't flow all the way, it forms sort of a little lagoon, and the water was warm there. My sister and I would swim there, snorkeling with masks and everything.

And as we got able to stand the colder water, then we would go over to the Carmel city beach, and [Dad] and I would jog on the beach from there, to warm up to go bodysurfing there in the real waves . . . He would usually work on the property in the morning, and Kathy, my mom and I would [go to town] because there wasn't any mail service there at the time.

"Do you have any mail for Black, Burk or Shiracki?"

Kathy Burk McCaffrey added:

> . . . [Jiro] Shiracki was Grandmother Black's cook, from San Francisco. They came down so my mom did not have to cook at the time for all of us. And Jiro, he was like family . . . I would hold him up for cookies in the kitchen and all that kind of stuff. But my Dad would say, "You know, Jiro . . . we love him so much . . . and he was from the nation we were fighting against . . ."
>
> Here my Dad had been taught to kill Japanese, and here was a guy he loves like a brother, who takes care of all of us, and Jiro was unique. He was with my grandmother for what . . . thirty years?

Roger confirmed—thirty years, but he continued:

> Dad after the war always felt a bit bad about it, he said. He mentioned one time that it was strange about war, "You do things that if you had done as a civilian, you'd be put away forever in jail, and yet you're a hero if you do it during war circumstances."
>
> And he had met some of the Japanese rowers from the Olympic Team in 1936, [the eight] after the war and liked them very much, and was laughing with them, because the word had been, they had rowed such a high stroke rate that they had all died of heart attacks.
>
> And he was laughing with them, "No, you guys are all supposed to be dead . . ."

Lest the reader think that all Burk trips in that era were as routine as Ozzie and Harriet TV shows, there were also stories of sudden alarm, as Roger remembered, "Everything worked well until one time we were in Iowa, of all places, and a cougar came out of the corn field, and was obviously after the dog. Of course, there were boxes and things outside of the car."

165

And Kathy added: "I slept through all of it—in the middle of the night we had to pack everything up—Mom held the flashlight on the cougar while Dad packed up the car, put all the stuff in the back and off we went."

"And the dog never made a peep," said Roger.

Both siblings confessed to a typical lack of interest in the scenery. Kathy said, "We unfortunately read comic books across the country."

Roger added, "Dad actually asked me one time whether we looked forward to the camping trips or not. My honest reply was it wasn't that we disliked them, they were what we had to do to get to Mesita," (the name of the Black family's summer home.)

"But my Mom would have grab bags," said Kathy, "and you would 'lose your grabs' if you were naughty in the back. So my Mom wrapped these little things—pink for me, blue for my brother . . . and we would stop at Dairy Queen. My Dad loved root-beer floats, and we would lose our DQ or our 'grabs' if we were not behaving."

Kathy concluded: "We have great memories—and it is at this age that we realize what an unusual childhood we had, because not many families have a whole summer off with their Dad. They'll take a trip somewhere for a few weeks or whatever, but this was three months. Every year."

The Burk summer trips would occupy all the summer and would serve as a way for the family to see huge parts of the country they would not otherwise have experienced had they stayed in either the confines of the East or West Coast. It was also a way of allowing Kay to stay close to her parents and her siblings. Kathy Burk recalled that for years, their Uncle Charlie would live a glamorous life of the well-connected bachelor. "For a while, the family didn't think he would ever get married," she said. But Charles Black finally met the childhood star Shirley Temple, and he was smitten. They married on December 16, 1950.

Roger and Kathy had already grown used to being the children of the James Sullivan award winner and war hero Joe Burk. They found being the niece and nephew of a movie star, and later American Ambassador of the United Nations, and other ambassadorial posts, was no big adjustment. *Aunt Shirley.*

All his oarsmen recall Burk's continual patience in his coaching style. His matter-of-fact and quiet manner conveyed his own confidence that he knew what was needed for good rowing, and that together the coach and team could make progress. Burk had a certain silent *gravitas*—which encouraged the oarsmen to take their task and themselves seriously. His own imposing physical presence, and the fresh knowledge of his war record, completed the picture. *This was a real man.*

One particular story has been told and retold. The earliest version comes from Fred Lane, six man of the 1954 junior varsity and the stroke of the 1955 and 1956 varsity crews.

Lane recounted to Peter Mallory that on the last day of practice before the Christmas break in 1953, that Burk decided to conduct a test.[169] "Joe wanted to be sure if we had a turnover, that we would survive in the water, so Joe said he was going to jump in. And Big Mouth here says, 'Ok, Joe. If you jump in, I'll will jump in too.'"

"And Joe jumped in. And everybody looked at me and several said 'Well?' So I jumped in, and at that moment," Lane laughed in recounting the moment, "I questioned my future ability to procreate."

"The experience was awful—there was ice on the dock and it was difficult to lift yourself up and over the edge of the dock. I had to be pulled from the water," Lane said years later. By contrast, Burk had swum out a significant distance, silently turned around, and pulled his huge frame up from the water. He wordlessly went upstairs to change into dry clothes.[170]

The oarsmen silently headed to the oar racks to get their oars and bring the boats down to the water. The silent example eliminated all complaint.

Burk's diving in was not mere bravado—the feat did have a practical basis.

Lane explained that when the weather got cold enough, ice would form opposite the Penn dock down near where the Schuylkill River gathers before the dam at the base of Boathouse Row. At those times, Burk or his boatman would go out in a launch and break up the ice so that oarsmen could go out to practice upstream. But Burk had to be absolutely sure that, should an accident occur in such conditions, that his boys could survive the cold long enough to either right the boat or be pulled into the coaching launch.

The story of Burk's jumping in the water has been retold so often, it is not clear whether there were multiple instances or just a natural variance in the retelling. However, many instances of icy swimming occurred, oarsmen of all eras often remarked that Burk seemed simply immune to cold. He rarely wore gloves in the launch, even though the temperatures were low and the wind was cold and constant. Some believed that eschewing gloves was another way for Burk to judge when it was too cold to continue practice, since he was feeling the same cold as the oarsmen who worked their oars barehanded.

Occasionally, a boat would be short a man due to sickness or a scheduling conflict. On those occasions, Burk would change back into the rowing gear he had used for his daily afternoon sculling, and take the place of the absent student, in effect having a second workout while his charges were having their first.

The 1954 rowing season gave early signals that the Penn Varsity might be rising in the intercollegiate rankings. Canadian sculling champion Jack Guest Jr. had finally arrived on Penn's campus.
The Philadelphia Inquirer remarked:

> When Joe Burk was an international sculler in the late 1930s, the friendships he made from the Rancocas Creek near Beverly, N.J. to Canada and even in England, were as pleasing as the victories which led to the Diamond Sculls championship. But even he did not realize that a friendship developed in Canada would be a key factor in Penn's successful 1954 rowing start.
>
> Coach Burk principally credits the superb stroke touch of Jack Guest Jr., towering 6'5" Canadian . . . for Saturday's victory over Princeton and Columbia in the Childs Cup classic on Lake Carnegie. . . . Saturday's victory, second fastest in the history of the 1 ¾ mile event, raises hopes for a banner Penn year.[171]

Penn did win the Blackwell Cup against Yale and Columbia in the last twenty strokes of a two-mile race to win by just about a quarter deck length ahead of Yale, with Columbia a length behind Yale. The freshman won by a length, the JV by three lengths, and the Penn lightweights by two lengths.[172]

The day before the Adams Cup race with Navy and Harvard, Penn's Varsity heavyweight crew and its coach got a warm preview article from New York's *Daily News*, under the headline *Quakers Seek Regatta Victory*, which emphasized that at least three of the crew were fighting physical challenges:

> A Canadian with a malformation of the lower spine; a 112-pound Massachusetts lad who still wears a brace as a reminder of polio, and a New Jersey husky who had to give up a brilliant basketball future because of a weak left eye—all are members of the unbeaten Penn crew which hopes to end one of sports' longest winning streaks today.
>
> ... With kids like Jack Guest Jr., Bernie Taradash and Bruce Crocco, in the shell, Penn certainly could make [Rusty] Callow's homecoming a sad one. The Navy coach directed Penn rowers for 23 years before sailing up the Severn.
>
> Guest is a former Canadian and U.S. singles sculling champion whose promising river career almost was cut short by a spinal condition. He was operated on for a malfunction of the spine and was incapacitated for some time. Although the lower part of his spine is stiff, he is doing a great job of setting the pace for the Penn Varsity.
>
> Taradash, 22-year-old Fall River, Mass., student whose back brace doesn't prevent him from being an exhuberant [sic] coxswain. Crocco, 6'4" number 7 man from Ridgewood, N.J., was one of the most promising basketball players in his state, but a very weak left eye deprived him of his best shot, a one hand push shot from the left.
>
> "Guest, plus a spirited attitude, makes the difference," Burk said. "I had a talk with my boys last Fall and told them

1954 looked like a very rough season unless they worked hard. So, we rowed all Winter on the river, with the exception of a few weeks when the water was frozen over. Other crews were indoors. That makes a difference. Tanks are a good substitute, but they're not the real thing."[173]

In the Adams Cup, Rusty Callow's midshipmen again won, but Burk's previously undefeated Varsity led Navy early, forcing the Middies to push through later in the race. Penn still finished second, beating previously undefeated Harvard by half a length, which must have cheered the Penn fraternity boys and their guests on what was Skimmer Day in Philadelphia.[174]

The following week at the Eastern Sprints, Navy again prevailed, with a surprisingly fast Yale crew second, Burk's Penn Varsity third, followed by Harvard, Cornell, and Wisconsin.[175]

On May 29, Burk's Penn Varsity beat Cornell at Ithaca over a race of two and one third miles, with Penn leading by almost six seconds, or one and a half lengths. Cornell won the earlier races in the frosh and jayvee categories.[176]

The day following Penn's victory over Cornell, Callow's Navy midshipmen continued their unbeaten streak at a totally new venue, winning the Newport Harbor Regatta in Newport Beach, California. They beat California by six seconds over 2,000 meters.[177] From a historical perspective, the pairing of Cal against Navy in California is reminiscent of Callow's earlier scheduling innovations with Walz in 1948–1950 for the trips to Florida. Like the Florida trip, the Cal-Navy race had had no prior history, and, by necessity, one Eastern rowing power versus a Western power meant that the race always carried a high travel cost that would grow difficult to bear. The Newport Harbor race would not be repeated.

At the IRA, Burk's Penn Varsity was not able to duplicate its Ithaca victory against Cornell, finishing seventh in the longer three-mile race, which Navy won, with Cornell second, followed by Washington, Wisconsin, California, and Columbia.[178]

The 1954 Penn heavyweight season showed Burk's patient coaching was beginning to pay dividends. His 1954 varsity had been competitive against the nation's best in the main season at race less than three miles—but the seventh place at the IRA showed that the Penn crew was not yet dominant at the longer race distances. There was promise—but there was still more work needed.

The varsity that would emerge the following year, 1955, would prove that Burk had developed into one of the best coaches in America.

CHAPTER NINE

An Exceptional Pupil

Harry Lambert Parker of Fitchburg, Massachusetts, joined the Penn rowing program as a lightweight oarsman in the fall of 1953. As with many lightweights, Parker was somewhat above the then-target weight of 150 pounds. As he learned the art of rowing, Parker realized that once the season drew near, he would need to manage his calorie intake so that he could make the designated weight. Years later, without complaint, he would only say that during his one-year Penn lightweight career, he "ate a lot of vegetables."[179]

Parker had been an able high school athlete at Fitchburg High School, competing on the basketball and baseball teams. He entered Penn on a Naval ROTC scholarship, the first in his family to attend college. His father was a carpenter and house builder, and his mother was a stenographer. It was not unusual for freshman to row in college without having previously rowed. Parker would prove himself to be among the most determined oarsmen Burk would ever coach.

As Joe Burk worked his way through the season, he had arranged for separate paid coaches for the lightweight squad, and he concentrated solely on the heavyweights. In the fall of 1954, Parker and another lightweight oarsman decided they wanted to row with the heavyweights. This was the first time Burk had had a lightweight ask to come row with the larger men. He agreed that the two could row with the heavyweights, but only in a pair together during the fall season.[180]

That winter, however, Burk eased the two lightweights into the squad. At that time, Burk had established a tradition of having a Friday race between the crews. While memories of the details of the system vary, all agree that the tradition involved the racing of a single distance (which might vary) between the crews practicing that day. The oarsmen of the fifties had the impression that Burk considered the results of those practice races in picking his boats for the spring racing season, but Burk did not then make clear the nature of the weight given to any particular result.

Such a coaching practice was within the normal ethos of the coach and athlete relationship of the era. The oarsmen were expected to listen, comply with the coach's instructions, and perform as best they could that day. Rowers in that era were like cavalrymen of the Britain's Light Brigade in Crimea—*it was not theirs to wonder why.*

Recollections of exactly how the system developed in the fall of 1954 differ. Some remember a playing card system where each of the oarsman's and coxswain's names were written on a card, and Burk himself would deal out separate piles of port oars, starboard oars, coxswain, and lanes, and then construct randomly the right number of eight-oared crews with a lane to race in that Friday. The first arriving of each boat would then arrange where each oarsman sat in the boat.

Others remember that the first two or three from the squad in the boathouse that day would select their crews from the cards of those rowing that day—which were placed on a table face up—so that each picker could evaluate each round who was then available for selection.

But all those recollecting the situation remembered that Harry Parker turned out to be a good picker—whether his selections were from face up cards for inclusion in his boat, or by placing those already in his boat in the best positions for their skill set.

In the mid-1950s, the outcome of these inter-squad races was known by those who participated in them, but no lists were kept of each oarsman's and coxswain's race achievement, and at that time no formal points were assigned for a particular result. It was assumed by Burk's oarsmen that part of Burk's judgment about who to put in which boat once the race season started might include race results, but Burk did not in those days tie himself to boating a varsity crew based on the Friday fall races.

In later years, Burk's crediting of race results would change, and become more formal and public.

Nick Paumgarten, the Penn Heavyweight Captain '67 recalled that Burk once confided to him that once the system changed to the first three to arrive at the boathouse picked the boats, that Harry Parker took pains to be among the first three, and that he was especially skilled in the *last* choices were made. The obviously great oarsmen were routinely selected first, but Burk thought Parker's skill was in making the more nuanced secondary choices—where good but not necessarily great oarsmen might perhaps make less of a contribution to a boat's speed—but perhaps not slow the boat down. In Burk's mind, Parker had a coach's eye for how to fill out a boat.[181]

Ken Drefuss, Penn '69 captain, had the impression that Harry's organized focus upon and success with picking boats under the system used was not fully appreciated by Burk when it was happening, but only later.

Paumgarten was convinced that Burk eventually changed the system and drew names blindly so that random chance, rather than a superior boat picker like Parker, would not skew the results.

In the ethos of the time, it was generally recognized with all college crews that the head coach was the first and final authority in deciding who rowed in the varsity, junior varsity, and third varsity boats. Most oarsmen felt their only job was to row and were surprised at the coach's involvment of oarsmen in the process of boat selection. The fact that Parker was "keeping his own black book" and thinking analytically suggested early on that Parker was a different sort of oarsman, already thinking like a coach.

Parker really was different. He seemed hyper-aware of the competitive circumstances at all times and took pains to follow Burk around the boathouse, observing his every move, sometimes even emulating his behaviors.

One observer later remarked of this period that whenever Parker was standing silently, hands in his pockets, and staring fixedly at the floor, that he was—consciously or unconsciously—imitating Burk's own contemplative manner.[182]

All who had known both men at that time agreed that Parker perceived Burk as a sort of father figure.

When Burk named the 1955 Varsity boat at the start of the spring season, Harry Parker was sitting in the two seat. The boat's complete lineup was as follows:

Bow	John Weiss
2	Harry Parker
3	Bart Fitzpatrick
4	Chuck Shaffer
5	Tom Friend
6	Frank Betts
7	Bruce Crocco
8	Fred Lane
C	J.L. "Fox" DeGurse[183]

1955 Penn stroke Fred Lane remembered Joe Burk's emphasis that season: the three-mile race at the IRA. "What I remember was that Joe was focused on one race in the '55 season—that was the three-mile IRA. That was his total objective. That's what Joe wanted to win. And all of our practices were based on the endurance necessary to win the IRA."[184]

Burk well remembered that his '54 varsity had beaten Cornell in their shorter dual race in Ithaca but had faded in the longer three mile race at the IRA. Burk was determined to address what he saw as a deficiency in his own training plan.

The 1955 crew was not large. "Overall, we were a fairly light crew," Lane recalled. "At the time, I was about 6'1" and 180 pounds. Joe worked us hard. By the end of the season, I was in the high 160s or 170, something like that."

Lane also recalls the specifics of Burk's training and evaluation methods that at the time were rarely mentioned in connection with Burk's coaching. "Joe would have pairs [within the practicing eights] race. The pairs' races would be a quarter mile." He further added that, "Unlike my freshman and sophomore years, in my junior year, we were on the river all winter. We never went inside. And I thought that was a very significant element of our success—because we had so much time on the water. The boat rigger was a guy named Wayne Neal, and he used to go out on the river and break up the ice so we could row. He would go out before we went out."

The 1955 crew proved to be a very fast boat—among the best Burk ever had. The boat was undefeated in the Childs, Blackwell, and Adams Cup races.

The biggest surprise in that string of preliminary races was the 1955 Adams Cup, awarded to the winner of the three-way race between the Navy, Harvard, and Penn. Before the 1955 race, the favorite was Rusty Callow's crews at the Naval Academy, who had continued an undefeated streak since the days of the 1952 Olympic-winning "Admirals".

But at the Adams Cup in May of 1955, the luck of Callow and the Navy finally turned. The civilians of the University of Pennsylvania, coached by former Lieutenant Burk of PT-320, got the best of both the Navy and Harvard crews. Afterwards, an article in *The Philadelphia Inquirer* emphasized that Burk had expected the good Penn performance he'd just witnessed:

Just about the least surprised man in the world when the University of Pennsylvania crew ended the U.S. Naval Academy's record string of 31 victories Saturday at Cambridge, Mass., was Joe Burk, the Penn coach.

In fact, Burk wasn't even astonished when the length and one-half victory came in the Adams Cup record time of 8:47.7 for the mile and three-quarters.

"The race went just about as we planned it," Burk said yesterday as he relaxed at his [Bala] Cynwyd home. "And the time was just about what we expected from our time trial Wednesday."

Burk made these observations with such casual modesty that a visitor was inclined to forget momentarily that the day before he had achieved his greatest coaching triumph. He had assembled a crew and planned the strategy that gave it victory—in the very same race in which he first had rowed with the Penn Varsity—over a [Navy] crew that hadn't lost since 1951.

Furthermore, the triumph had been gained over his former coach, Rusty Callow, who had brought international renown to Penn rowing for 23 years before moving to Navy and being succeeded by Burk.

The old coach commended his old star on a job well done with one sincere word, shouted across the River Charles as launches passed immediately after the race—"Congratulations!" [185]

Callow's was a generous gesture toward his former oarsman, and entirely in keeping with his character.

The fact that the Adams Cup race against Navy had turned out just as Burk said he had anticipated was not the product of bravado. It was an honest assessment of Burk's own expectation, based on the speed he had observed in practice and in time trials. Burk had developed this technique in his sculling days.

When Burk was developing his own speed in the single, Burk meticulously estimated the average speed that would be required to win and would then plan to achieve exactly that average speed—largely ignoring what pace his opponents chose. Adopting such an approach in rowing takes more moral courage than it does in sports like running. In running, the runner behind can keep his opponent in view and calm himself by being able to judge moment to moment how much more effort might improve his own chances of getting ahead.

In rowing, the position of the trailing competitor is reversed. An oarsman trailing cannot see his opponent(s)—and must disrupt his own rowing to turn to look for an opponent if he feels he must. It is the oarsmen of the leading boat who have an advantage. They can see their opponents and keep abreast of their progress, and if the opponent surges, the leaders can immediately respond.

Burk was confident enough to believe that if he computed correctly, he did not need to dissipate his own focus and energy on worrying about the exact location of his opponent. Instead, he could focus on his own speed and technique.

In rowing, fluid dynamics also favor even pacing. Because the water resistance on the hull of a shell increases exponentially with a linear increase speed, the greater the speed, the more energy is needed to accomplish it.

Burk accustomed his crews to rowing the required pace for victory—and to avoid surges until the very end of the race. Fred Lane remembered how Burk used the approach with the 1955 varsity. "Joe broke the race up into quarter mile segments, and he estimated what average speed was needed. Joe was always trying to get us to hit the mark . . ."

When Burk told the reporter the race had gone as anticipated, he meant literally that the speeds achieved in the Wednesday practice before the race gave him confidence for Saturday that the overall speed would be enough.

Before 1955, Penn heavyweights rowing under Joe Burk had found limited success at the Eastern Sprints. In 1951 and 1952, the Penn Varsity did not make the six-boat final, but in 1953, Penn made the finals, and by 1954 was third overall, a significant improvement.

After the Adams Cup win in 1955, Burk's varsity boat was deemed the favorite. That year the Sprints were held on the Potomac River. Burk's boys blew past their competition to win by a decisive margin.

The New York Times' Allison Danzig reported:

> Paced by Fred Lane, who took over as stroke when Jack Guest's back injury forced him out early in the season, Penn pulled even with Cornell a mile from the finish.

In the next quarter mile, with both crews at 32 strokes to the minute, Penn forged ahead by no more than a deck. Then the Red and Blue increased its margin to a half-length. With a quarter mile to go, Penn had three-quarters of a length advantage.

It was seen that it was Penn's race now. Both crews went up to 37 with their sprint, and Cornell could make no progress. There was almost a length and a quarter between the crews as Penn crossed the line.[186]

Experienced coaches will confirm that in all likelihood Penn did not increase their speed so much as Cornell likely slowed down. While there could have been greater effort expended at the end of the race, modern timing records show that times in the last 500 meters of a 2,000-meter course usually fall off rather than speed up.

The 1955 crew had at last achieved what Burk had demanded of himself: a steady and unaltering pace that achieved the best average speed over time. Smoothly pulling away from the Cornell crew demonstrated the Penn crew's newly honed ability to maintain the optimum speed over the distance. This unexpected triumph burnished the already high regard in which the Penn rowing alumni and Philadelphia's rowing community held Joe Burk.

The Penn alumni who financially supported the rowing program, again led then by Crawford Madeira, supported sending the crew to Henley after its great victory at the Sprints.[187] Plans were made and tickets purchased. Meanwhile, the crew prepared for its remaining regular season races, which included the traditional Cup race with Cornell in Ithaca followed by the Intercollegiate Rowing Association Regatta.

At Ithaca, Penn managed to beat Cornell at the longer race distance of two miles, but as seven-man Bruce Croco recalled, since Penn was "a sprint crew," the race was close.

Fred Lane remembered the scene at the last race of the season, the IRA, where the best of the East and West Coast crews would meet each other for a final championship over three miles at Syracuse.[188] Penn was picked as the favorite in the text of June 17, 1955, United Press photograph, widely publicized and showing Burk with coxswain

YP-061702-6/17/55-SYRACUSE,NY:Penn coach,Joe Burk,center,briefs Penn coxwain
John DeCurse,right,of Grosse Point,Mich.,and Stroke,Fred Lane,left,of Chicago,
Ill.,before they start on last practice run.Penn,picked as the favorite,will
row against 11 Other colleges 6/18 in the 53rd annual Intercollegiate Regatta
at Syracuse,New York.Penn last won the top college rowing event in 1900.
UNITED PRESS TELEPHOTO-pwh

United Press Telephoto credit, From the collection of Thomas Weil, Esq.

John DeCurse and stroke Fred Lane, shown in the photo directly above (United Press Photo, from the collection of Thomas Weil, Esq.).

Lane's parents had come from the family home in Chicago to watch this final contest. In Fred's view, the crew was ready, loose, and confident. After the race, Fred was surprised by his father's comment that his son's crew seemed "too cocky."

That father's sense proved correct.

Penn did not start well and found itself down by several lengths after a mile. The Penn crew began what Lane remembers as a long sprint from way out, and slowly climbed back into second, but Cornell finished a full ten seconds ahead. Penn barely beat Navy at the finish line by less than a second. [189]

There is no clear reason for the Penn Varsity's being beaten so soundly. Was the pace of the longer race unfamiliar to what Lane called "a sprint crew"?

The result might have occurred simply because Cornell—historically late to get back on the water in upstate New York and always fiercely competitive at the longer distance—had reached its peak late in the season when Penn's spirit was fading?

While Lane did not comment directly, it seems anomalous that in the year Burk was focusing his attention on the IRA, that the Penn '55 crew could not win the one race that had been the coach's focus for the year. It would be a dozen years before the coach's goal would be reached.

The very day *The Philadelphia Inquirer* article on Cornell's victory over Penn was published, the same reporter wrote a piece for the *New York Herald Tribune* news service announcing that the Penn crew would, indeed, be traveling, stating that, "with the co-sponsorship of the State Department [Penn] would send its varsity heavyweight eight oared shell to Germany as well as the Henley Regatta in London [sic] and in their tour it is it extremely likely that the Penns will meet the Soviets at least twice, maybe more times."[190]

It was also one of the first of many subtle hints that a new hand was feeding sports news to the papers—the U.S. State Department.

By 1955 the Cold War had settled like a shroud over the European continent. In the decade after the war ended, active hostilities had been replaced by a deepening fissure between Russia, its satellite states, and the West, and that fissure was negatively affecting that way amateur sports were conducted and viewed.

These looming tensions were brought to a peak on May 6, 1955, with NATO's inclusion of the newly reconstituted nation of West Germany, composed of sectors previously controlled by the U.S., Britain, and France, into NATO. This inclusion was perceived by the Soviet military as a serious threat. They responded eight days later, on May 14, with the formation of the Warsaw Pact, which formalized the Cold War fight between Communist nations of the East and democratic nations of the West.[191]

Burk's plans for Henley—conceived just after that Eastern Sprints victory in May—were abruptly reshaped by the governments of the United States and the United Kingdom into a celebration of NATO's expansion and would include a hastily arranged goodwill tour to West Germany for a friendly competition between NATO allies. It also recast the previously planned Russian crew's trip to Henley as a pointed opportunity to oppose a totalitarian domination of sport.

The Russian crews were coming to Henley to compete in an event that the Soviet diplomats themselves would have disparaged as a capitalist, aristocratic extension of England's class-based society. And the Soviet political goal was to humiliate the aristocrats at their own decadent festival with a display of socialist sports discipline.

Nothing in the U.S. rowing archives mention the State Department's influence on the sports calendar except a rapid expansion of sports competitions in Europe, but the postwar division between communism and capitalism had begun to color everything.[192]

Burk must have relished the chance to return to Henley a fourth time—the first two as the winner of the Diamond Sculls, the third time as adviser to the 1951 lightweight varsity, but now, in 1955, as the coach of his own heavyweight crew.

There were six entries for the Grand Challenge Cup—the fastest and most prestigious of the eight-oared events and contested at that time by some of the finest crews in the world. Columbia/Vancouver Rowing Club and the Thames Rowing Club were "selected" entries, meaning they were deemed fast enough to skip the opening round of heats.

The first round of heats on Thursday, June 29, pitted Jesus College, Cambridge, against the Russian crew, Club Krasnoe Znamia, USSR. The race was hard-fought the whole way and won by the Russian crew by a half-length. In the other opening heat, Penn pulled steadily away from London Rowing Club and led by two lengths at the mile by rowing a low 28 strokes a minute for an easy win.

In the second round, July 1, Penn steadily took a widening lead over the selected Thames Rowing Club. Penn's lead was as large as one and a half lengths at the mile, but a determined push by Thames cut this margin to two third of a length at the finish. In the second race, Russia started quickly over UBC/VRC and led by three quarters of a length within the first 40 strokes, but the Canadians steadily ate away at the Russian lead, passing them at the three quarter mile mark, and beating them by 1 and one quarter lengths at the finish.

Fred Lane remembered: "I do recall how disappointed I was that the Russian crew did not make the final, because I really wanted to row against the Russian crew. But they had been beaten by Vancouver, so we raced against Vancouver."[193]

The Grand Challenge Final was rowed Saturday, July 2. Henley Royal Regatta's formal history of the event contains a characteristically precise appreciation of the exciting final:

> Pennsylvania led by ⅔ length a the ¼ mile, but Vancouver gradually drew up and were only ¼ length behind at Fawley and a canvas[194] behind at the 1 ⅛ mile. Both spurted continuously from the Mile and Pennsylvania won a fine race.

Joe Burk's fourth trip to Henley had yielded a fourth victory—and in the most prestigious event for eight-oared shells.

In ways that neither Burk nor the other rowing experts could then predict, Penn's victory would mark an approaching high-water mark for American collegiate eight-oared rowing against international competitors. Only a year later, Yale's varsity crew would win the Olympic gold medal in the 1956 Games at Melbourne, Australia, but the Penn triumph at Henley and Yale's Olympic win a year later would be the best American college eight-oared rowing would produce in international competition for over a decade.

With this dramatic victory in hand, Penn left England for West Germany. Fred Lane remembered the trip: "The State Department wanted to improve relations with Germany and they provided funds for us to go to Germany and race. That's why we went. We had two races in each of the cities that we went to, one Saturday and one Sunday. The first one was Hamburg, the second was Essen, and the third one being Mannheim."[195]

The Penn boat rowed a stroke somewhat shorter than previous years, but one similar to the stroke Rusty Callow had trained the Navy crew to row. Many observers studied the apparently invincible team, and videos of their stroke were filmed and analyzed. One German rowing coach, Karl Adam, studied the Penn technique, and despaired of his teams ever being able to match the American performance.[196]

Penn's first stop in Germany was Hamberg, where they were slated to compete against two outstanding crews: the Hansa Boat Club of Hamburg[197] and the Germania-Hamberger Rowing Club[198]. As a further part of sporting outreach between the former enemies now turned allies, a British crew composed of members of the British Royal Air Force also competed.

This fine competition notwithstanding, Penn oarsmen won by a decisive margin—almost fifteen seconds ahead of Hansa and the British Royal Airforce. The Hansa crew led for the first 1,400 meters before Penn pulled through to win going away.[199]

Penn and Joe Burk would go on to triumph in every race during the German exhibitions.

The Penn crew split up after the racing in Germany was concluded. Joe Burk and Harry Parker flew back to the United States. Fred Lane and the remaining oarsmen rented transportation and toured parts of Europe with the Penn Director of Athletics Jerry Ford and his wife.

"That sojourn through Italy and Germany had a huge impact on my life," Lane recalls. "First of all, I'm Jewish—and being in Germany that close to the end of the war was—well, I had a very peculiar feeling about that. And the guy who led us around, a German who was assigned to us, had been a Messerschmidt pilot in the war.

"Hamburg was relatively untouched, bombing wise, because the Germans—Hamburg consists of two lakes, and the Germans had put up a fake bridge, over one of the lakes that was farther south of Hamburg. That's what the Air Force bombed the shit out of, so Hamburg was a beautiful old city . . . some of the tops of the buildings were gone, but basically the city was intact.

"Essen was gone. There was nothing there. One of the only things that was left standing was a synagogue—how that happened, I have no idea. It was a flattened area—still flattened [in 1955]—and I think the reason we were going through Germany—the State Department funded that trip—was to build up the relationship between the United States and Germany . . . at that time, ten years after the war.

"And in Essen, of course there you had the big manufacturing facilities during the war—that we bombed the hell out of—and I remember taking some walks up into the hills. I came upon a Jewish cemetery, still standing. I mean it hadn't been destroyed [by the bombing]."[200]

As most of his crew toured Europe, Burk flew across the Atlantic from London to meet his family in California. Along the way, he doubtless considered what the international trip meant for Penn's rowing future. The victories at Henley and in Germany, he believed, were signs the Penn Varsity was rowing near the Olympic level because at that time, the fastest American collegiate crew usually won the right to represent America at the Olympics.

The next year, 1956, would be an Olympic year. With five of Penn's eight oarsmen from the 1955 crew returning, Burk set his sights on the Olympic stage.

In that era, America's eight-oared crew was selected through trials every four years—and from 1920 onwards, American collegiate crews had triumphed in all but one of those Olympic quadrennials. A 1955 Penn Henley winner was a good start toward building an Olympic contender for 1956.

Fred Lane received some interesting advice from Joe Burk upon his return to Boathouse Row in the fall. "Joe told me that Harry Parker was gunning for my seat in the boat." The photo on page 187 shows a boating (date believed to be fall or spring 1955–6) with Harry Parker at stroke, and Fred Lane at four.[201]

It is unclear how Burk divined Parker's goal unless Parker himself had mentioned it to Burk. Lane himself was grateful to be told. "I think Joe was trying to motivate me," he explained. "And it worked—I stayed in the stroke seat for that next year."[202]

Given the fine results of the 1955 Penn crew, speculation within the rowing community continued to build regarding whether the Penn team that remained would make it to the 1956 Olympics in Melbourne, Australia. Similar speculation surrounded the 1952 Olympic champion crew from Navy, called back from duty assignments around the world to continue training under Callow's guidance in an attempt to repeat their triumph at Helsinki.

The feverish speculation made for good copy.

The Associated Press released an article by John Koenig Jr. which appeared in a number of papers across the United States on Sunday, April 1, 1956. *The Clarion-Ledger* of Jackson, Mississippi, used the

credit Basil L. Smith System, Philadelphia, from Burk Family Collection

headline "'Old College Try' Could Put Penn Crew in Olympic Games," to introduce the piece:

> If the veteran Pennsylvania crew—undefeated in sprint row-
> ing in America and Europe last year—is to represent the
> United States in the 1956 Olympic Games, it will be the 'old
> college try' that will turn the trick, Coach Joe Burk believes.
>
> The Quakers are working out daily on the Schuylkill River
> in Philadelphia's Fairmount Park and, with the aim of beating
> Navy, are intent not only on conditioning themselves, but of
> keeping up their "mental outlook."
>
> As Burk sees it, the Navy grads of the great years 1952–54
> at Annapolis, who are training for a comeback, will need more
> than their skill and conditioning of yesteryear.
>
> "A man reaches his physical peak at about 28," says Burk.
> "But as important as that is mental outlook . . ."

Although advancing no alibi, Burk said the Navy grads have the advantage for "they can practice all they want."

"The services are very good in encouraging athletes in their ranks," said Burk. "The old Navy crew has everything in its favor—except the one unknown—whether it will be able to keep up the enthusiasm of the undergraduates."

As for Penn, Burk—never one to blow his own horn—admits that he has a "good crew." Six of last year's varsity boat, including the coxswain, are back this year.

Their first real test will be against Rutgers on April 14. There will be one other dual regatta, with Wisconsin, and the annual Childs, Blackwell and Adams Cup regattas; the Eastern sprint championships, and the Intercollegiate Rowing Assn. Regatta, and Olympic tryouts in Syracuse.

"Right now we're equal to or better than we were at this time last year," said Burk.

It was the Penn crew that last year broke Navy's winning streak that soared above 30 victories spread over four seasons and including the Olympic title. In all, the Quakers won eight races in American collegiate competition in 1955 and eight in England and Germany. The European sweep included a victory in the famed Grand Challenge event at Henley-on-Thames. Penn was only the third American college crew to win that historic event.

Penn's only loss last year was to Cornell in the IRA Regatta. That was a three-mile event, not classed as a sprint.

Fortunate for the Quakers is the fact that the Olympics and all major races they will row are 2,000 meters or the Henley distance, a mile and $\frac{5}{16}$.

"The 2,000-meter race is again our best distance," said Burk. "This year we have as good a chance as anyone—and you can say we're not over-awed by Navy."

The Penn-Navy rivalry is a natural, for the Middies' coach, veteran Rusty Callow, also taught the Red and Blue for many years and was in fact Burk's coach while Burk rowed for Penn.

The international flavor also wears well at Penn, for Burk himself won the diamond sculls at Henley in 1938 and 1939 after his graduation.[203]

Indeed, the prospects of the Penn crew burned bright. On April 16, 1956, the Penn Varsity defeated Rutgers in a two mile race on the Raritan by a length and a half, and again the AP story was laudatory: "Joe Burk has a great crew," said Chuck Logg, the Rutgers Coach, "They are going to be very tough to beat."

Penn's coach was content: "On performance and time trials," said Burk, "the varsity is about in the same position or maybe a little better than last year's crew. They are not as smooth as last year's boatload and that crew was not a very smooth one. I'll say this—they're a bunch of alley cats. They'll give you a fight."[204]

On Wednesday, April 18, 1956, literally one day after the AP story touting the Penn Varsity appeared, Joe Burk conducted the usual intra-squad race between his touted varsity and his junior varsity.

To nearly everyone's shock, the junior varsity won. This result was an anomaly. Unlike the fall races when the squad was in mixed boats, if the right people had been picked for the Varsity, then the Varsity should win all the spring races.

Burk had to have been perplexed. His varsity, with five members from the 1955 Henley Champion crew, had failed to perform. Burk then made a fateful decision which he likely later regretted. He decided to let the JV—the winners of the intersquad practice—row as the varsity in the Childs Cup that Saturday.

In this topsy-turvy world, the junior varsity would be the first boat, and the varsity would become the second boat. *The Philadelphia Inquirer* found the move so noteworthy that it published a pre-race story under the headline *"Penn Displaces Varsity Crew For Childs Cup Race Tomorrow."*[205]

The paper reported the Wednesday intrasquad results and noted that this weekend's race would be the first time Bruce Croco, the former Varsity 7 man now in his third season, would not be in the Varsity.

On Saturday, April 21, Burk's changes went awry.

Princeton's Varsity prevailed over what the newspaper called "the promoted Penn Varsity," by two lengths in a two-mile race on the Harlem River. The article by Ed Sinclair—Special to both *The Inquirer* and the *Herald-Tribune* said: "On the basis of time trials held during the past year, Joe Burk, the Penn coach, decided to 'demote' the varsity to the junior varsity event and to 'promote' the jayvees to the varsity shell." (Why Sinclair incorrectly claimed that the change was due to multiple races was never explained.)

"Burk admitted just before the race that, 'I'm sure to be second guessed on this. But, if my new varsity is beaten, then my old varsity would have been beaten.'"

The "demoted" Varsity beat the Princeton JVs by "four yards of open water," or just over a length.[206]

In the following week, in which there was no reporting on any Penn intra-squad races, Burk reversed his decision and placed the original varsity back, and the "promoted" varsity resumed its place as the JV.

The results the following week were discouraging.

On April 28, at the Blackwell Cup, Yale decisively beat Penn—which changed the Olympic speculation. "Yale Crew Upsets Penn, Wins 25th Blackwell Cup," read the headline from *The Philadelphia Inquirer*. "Yale upset the University of Pennsylvania on the Schuylkill yesterday, creating a sensation by winning the 25 annual race for the Blackwell Cup by more than four lengths, virtually squelching Penn's Olympic hopes." The paper noted the Yale varsity had not been pressed in the later stages of the race.

The four-length defeat in the light headwind brought a sinking the hearts of the thousands of Penn rooters lining the banks—and in Burk himself."[207]

Neither Burk nor the Penn oarsmen could have then known that they had just lost to the Yale crew that would ultimately win the Gold Medal at the Olympics in Melbourne just months later.

Given Burk's unusual boating changes and disappointing race results, it must have been a challenge for both coach and crews to keep their collective poise. A ceremonial obligation for Burk the next night would not much improve matters.

All of Burk's grace was sorely needed the following evening, April 29, the same day *The Inquirer* reported Penn's upset by Yale. The same night the world read of Penn's latest 1956 rowing setback was, ironically, the banquet celebration of the 1955 crew's success the year before.

That evening, The United States Amateur Athletic Union, the governing body of amateur athletics connected with the larger Olympic movement, awarded the 1955 Penn Crew its annual award for excellence in amateur athletics. *The Philadelphia Inquirer* ran a photograph of Burk and Jack Kelly, the trophy presenter, with other luminaries.

The crushing irony was apparent to all those present that evening. It is a testament to the high regard that the rowing public had for Burk that no one has, in the sixty years since, expressly mentioned this unfortunate evening when Burk was forced to set aside his intense disappointment in his 1956 crew in order to receive the formal award honoring the accomplishments of the previous year.

Burk somehow met the challenge. He is shown in the picture smiling. Perhaps Burk had remembered the truth in the Rudyard Kipling poem that a man could "meet with triumph and disaster, and treat those two imposters just the same ."

That night Burk proved equal to the task set by the poet. And later in his life, he would have the chance to repeat this display of gentlemanly grace, and his oarsmen and the rowing world would take notice.

Daniel James Brown in *The Boys in the Boat* highlighted the uncertainty coaches must live with when he explained the concern California coach Ky Ebright expressed in 1934 when his Varsity began to lose to his freshman crew in 1934.[208] "The First" being "The Last"—(notwithstanding its biblical origins) when it happens in a coaching environment is an embarrassing refutation of the presumed wisdom of the coach, which can in turn fatally undermine the confidence of the whole enterprise.[209]

Father does not always know best.

Burk had always tried to assess his squad's progress using the same objective tools he had used to measure his own progress in the single. He measured whatever he thought was measurable and relevant.

Sometimes—as in the example of the reversed varsities—the results clouded the view rather than clarified it. What can a good scientist do when the race data does not reflect what is expected from the measurements taken in practice?

There was no clear answer. The only way forward was to try again.

Almost all Penn oarsmen from all eras seemed to accept and appreciate that Burk's intent was to have a fair boat selection, and many remember the fall card system and practice races as symbolic of Burk's effort to treat all oarsmen fairly.

The remainder of the 1956 season was less than Burk had hoped. The varsity lost the Adams Cup[210] and the next week finished two and half lengths behind the top two crews at the Eastern Sprints.[211] And sadly, the IRA yielded a sixth-place finish over three miles.

As the season was nearing its end, Fred Lane asked his coach about whether the crew would be allowed to stay in Philadelphia after the last collegiate race and compete in the Olympic Trials. The shorter races seemed to favor the varsity's strengths, and the Olympic distance would be 2,000 meters—about a mile and a quarter.

No, Burk told him. The boat was not fast enough.

Lane was disappointed and suggested to his coach that with an upturn in fortune in the next weeks, perhaps the boat could work its way upward.

Burk was firm—the boat was not fast enough to go to the Olympic Trials. The decision would become characteristic of Joe Burk and his approach to competition—both as an oarsman and as a coach—expectations were to be based on solid facts, on data. Careful planning and measurement of progress against realistic standards was the Burk way. Hope and luck alone were not enough.

Penn did not go to the Olympic Trials in eights. The Yale crew that had beaten Penn so badly in the Blackwell Cup race won the trials, avenging their six-foot loss to Cornell at the Eastern Sprints. Burk must have viewed the race results as confirmation of his decision not to enter the trials. The Penn Varsity had been beaten by Yale and Cornell twice—once in Cup races, and once at the Sprints. Penn was simply not a contender for 1956.

The 1956 Yale crew, whose coach Jim Rathschmidt had been recommended to the Yale Athletic Department by Burk himself back in 1950, won the gold medal in the Melbourne Olympics. Not just the nation's fastest that year—Eli's men were the world's fastest.

Kathy Burk McCaffery remembers an instance sometime in this period when her father's crews were not doing very well, and she was by then old enough to sense the disappointment of an unsuccessful race day. She recalls an especially painful Penn loss at a home race.

Kathy came to her father after the race crying.

"What's wrong, honey?" her father asked.

"You all tried so hard, and you lost."

Her father held her and smiled, his voice even and upbeat "That means we just have to try harder, that's all."

That's all.

In Burk's mind, defeat did not define a character, it was merely a sign that more work was needed. He did not seem ever to mourn the cost of a losing effort. It was this resilience that allowed him to progress as an oarsman and allowed him as a coach to encourage progress in his team members when they most needed it.

Kathy Burk recalled another incident of parental self-control—this time with her mother—from that same time period. The event stuck in her mind as emblematic of her parents' restraint and self-control. Kathy's mother joined with other women in Philadelphia, many of them from the socially prominent Main Line, in large, organized luncheons where each woman would bring large and ornate casseroles. Kathy would sometimes accompany her mother to those luncheons.

Routinely, the other ladies of Kay's circle would, like Kay, prepare large and rich dishes. Kathy noticed that while all the other women would take generous samples of each of the servings on the table, Kay simply pick up a plate, produced from her handbag a hardboiled egg, and then sit the others and converse while all had lunch.

Kathy asked her mother after they had left the luncheon why her mother had only eaten a hardboiled egg. Her mother said, "I cannot control many things in my life, but I can control what I eat. So I do." Throughout her life, Kay Burk maintained a slender figure, and in her

The Burk Family afloat on a Penn launch in the early to mid 1950s.

later years would jog a few miles with her husband through the valleys in Montana.

Such lessons did not go unheeded in the Burk family. Both Kathy and her brother Roger to this day are trim and eat modest amounts of food at meals. The habit of self-control, seen in the 1930s by George Pocock at the Burk dinner table on the Rancocas, and by Kathy Burk at the ladies' luncheon in Philadelphia in the 1950s, remains unchanged in the Burk family.

On May 22, 1957, Rusty Callow, then in his last years as coach at the Naval Academy, was honored in his hometown of Shelton, Washington, by his fellow townsmen. Callow was Mason County's special guest at the town's annual Forest Festival, a celebration of the logging business then still active in the county. At the annual Queen's Dinner before the Festival, Callow addressed a crowd of 250 residents who had come out to honor their favorite son.

Callow was moved to talk to his neighbors about what he felt was a recent bad turn in the development of college athletes. The NCAA had recently announced a revision to its previous rulings about the offering of scholarships to college athletes. Past NCAA rulings—attempting to keep college athletics a strictly amateur affair—had prohibited the offering of things of value in exchange for students playing college sports—including scholarships. The Association's reasoning was that the offering of money, or scholarships, or both, would violate the spirit of amateurism that the NCAA viewed as essential for the good of college athletics.

The earlier prohibitions had often been observed in the breach. Scandals involving all manner of schemes to circumvent the rules by coaches, administrators, boosters, and athletes had made a mockery of those earlier rules.

To Callow, who had essentially postponed his college life until he could earn the money in logging camps and schoolhouses to attend UW, held a dim view on the recently announced rules change. The Olympia, Washington, newspaper, *The Olympian* reported portions of Callow's remarks under the headline "Callow Opens Forest Festival With Plea For Sports Honesty:"

"America today is too selfish, too intolerant, and these tendencies are more evident in the East than in the West which still retains some of the pioneering spirit."

Callow added that the nation today is not turning out great athletes in its colleges, simply because young men entering sports "have their hands out, looking for gifts and financial gain."

"We've got to stop turning out professional football teams in college or we're going to end college football, wiping it out like college baseball," Callow said. He expressed the belief that college football games would continue to attract large crowds if returned to an amateur basis. He noted that getting an education should be the primary purpose of students attending college.

"We need today men of moral courage who will not be bought. A good man has no price," he continued. "The hardships of pioneer life taught us to carry our duties and meet our responsibilities. Honesty is more valuable than money."[212]

As this book has been written, the NCAA has promulgated "the creation of a new subdivision in which schools would be required to compensate at least half of their athletes yearly with at least $30,000 each in a trust fund." For star college athletes, NCAA rule changes enacted July 1, 2021, allow them to be paid millions of dollars for the use of their name, image, and likeness in what are known as "NIL deals." [213]

Callow's statement—"A good man has no price."—now seems much changed.

CHAPTER TEN

The Master Sculler
and the Earnest
Student–1959–1960

In June of 1957, Harry Parker graduated from the University of Pennsylvania with a BA in Philosophy. Following graduation, he began his Navy service obligation which was what he owed for his NROTC scholarship. His father died the year after Parker graduated, and his father's obituary mentioned that Harry was then serving in the Navy at the Boston Naval Yards.

At that time, the U.S. Armed Forces were beginning a program to encourage athletes with strong backgrounds to seek special duty assignments, which would allow them to train for international competitions—including the Olympic Games. By early 1959, Lieutenant (j.g.) Harry Parker was assigned duty in Philadelphia, where he was allowed to train at Vesper Boat Club, which then shared a dock with the University of Pennsylvania.

Parker's coach was Joe Burk.

When Harry Parker initially moved back to Philadelphia from his assignment at the Boston Naval Yards, he stayed as a guest at the Burk home until he found his own accommodations. For Parker and the Burk family, this was a reversion to normal. While many a Penn oarsman had been welcomed at the Burk house, Harry was the only one who ever spent the night—often whole weekends—with the family.

Parker obtained a single shell from Pocock, and he and Joe Burk began to scull together each day. Anyone on Boathouse Row in 1959 and 1960 would see Joe Burk out sculling every day that the Penn crew had practice, and often when it didn't. Peter Mallory coaxed from Harry Parker the admission that he and Burk rowed against one another on competitive terms, but stories from those on Boathouse Row today contend that either (1) Burk always had the better of the contest, or (2) Burk had the better of the contest until just before Parker left for the Olympic Trials, when the two had rowed on roughly equal terms.

In either case, the fact that Burk at forty-five or forty-six could row roughly alongside a twenty-something U.S. Olympian indicates what a dominant sculler Burk still was at that age. Had he been allowed to row in the 1940 Olympics, or had he given in to the temptation in1947 to row as a professional against Bob Pearce, or alternatively rowed as an amateur in 1948 for the Olympics, he probably would have done very well. After all, Parker—as competitive as he was—was comparatively slight at 5'11" and about 175 pounds. Burk at that time was still a muscular 6'2", 195-pound man who still sculled daily when in Pennsylvania, or ran with his son Roger when in California.

Steve Gladstone pointed out that in the age in which Burk reached adulthood, it was deemed "normal" for men of working age not to pay attention to their health. "Joe was such a unique human being, I mean, Joe was a healthy human being *before people bothered to be healthy*. Joe would be my father's generation, and when those guys came back from World War Two, they were smoking up a storm, they were drinking up a storm, and Joe never did. I mean Joe was like a monk. Joe never did anything like that. He never put anything in his stomach that wasn't good. I don't know that Joe ever drank alcohol."[214]

The result was a stern sparring partner for the young Parker.

Some in the rowing community heard fascinating stories about the results of the two men racing. One was that after especially hard workouts, Parker would flop onto the dock at Vesper and lie motionless beside his boat, entirely spent, while Burk would dock at the Penn Boathouse adjacent, silently lift his own boat from the water, return it to the racks, then shower before coaching his own crew.

It is not now possible to perfectly separate myth and truth. The various rivalries that would spring up in the 1960s between Boston and Philadelphia—between Harvard, coached by Parker, and Vesper, and later between Harvard and Penn, the latter coached first by Burk and later by Ted Nash--were all so intense that each side might delight in one extreme stories about the other.

But this much can be confirmed—certainly the Burk-Parker practices were intense. Also clear was that by that time, Joe Burk had adjusted his sculling technique and lowered the stroke rate at which he raced against Parker. Joe told George Pocock that in later life, he found that he could row faster than he had when he competed by rowing at a rate closer to the norm for scullers—between 34 to 36 strokes a minute.

There are three stories from scullers still alive that are worth examining. First, Harvard oarsman Gregg Stone (Harvard '75), the U.S. National Champion single sculler for 1977 through 1979, took up sculling with Parker in the summer of 1974. Stone was surprised when Parker would start their practices by rowing away from the dock in great haste, leaving Stone to scramble to keep up enough to make the practice worthwhile. The move seemed needlessly competitive to Stone.

When Stone suggested that Parker begin the pieces even, and only after some warm-up, Parker responded, "That's how Joe Burk taught me."

The second story involves Bill Tytus, born in Seattle, who found himself in Philadelphia in the fall of 1966 in challenging circumstances, having been asked to leave Princeton in his freshman year. Tytus, an able sculler with his own single, who grew up around George Pocock and the Lake Washington Rowing Club, decided to continue his college effort at Temple University in Philadelphia.

"I wandered down to the Penn Boathouse and introduced myself to Joe. I realized I would probably be welcomed down there because

I had known Ted Nash quite well in Seattle for many years when Ted rowed for Stan Pocock at Lake Washington RC."

Burk readily agreed that Tytus could store his single at Penn and row there. Better still, during that fall and winter, whether at his request, or Burk's initiative, Tytus found himself assigned a playing card and was included in Penn eights workouts and the Friday races. As we shall see later, Woody Fisher, and perhaps others, had also been included in the card and racing system after graduation from Penn in 1962.

"I was included in the mix with everyone else, and it was great fun," Tytus said. He was deeply touched by Burk's hospitality and inclusion of him at a point when he was recovering from a poor start at Princeton.

"Joe kind of took me in . . . I was literally a boy . . . Joe was like an uncle . . . he felt fine commenting about my grungy appearance, and my habits, and all that kind of stuff."

"Occasionally I'd go sculling with Joe, and then he really revealed himself. Let's see, in 1966 and '67, I was 19 or 20—and he was . . . almost as old as my Dad. So he was an old man . . .OK? And we would go out sculling, and I don't know if I ever got past him, it was only once or twice."

Tytus would make the finals of the 1969 Diamond Sculls at Henley Regatta three years later.

The third story regarding Burk's sculling prowess involves Rick Stehlik of Malta Boat Club, who was in the lightweight double that won the bronze medal in the 1977 World Championships and the coach of the double that won a bronze medal in the 1978 World Championships. Stehlik remembered, in the late 1960s, rowing upstream from Boathouse Row, and as he passed under the Girard Avenue Bridge, he saw a sculler rapidly approaching him from behind. As Rick was approaching the Columbia Bridge, he realized that the sculler was gaining ground on him even more quickly.

Suddenly, the sculler turned to return to Boathouse Row. At that point, Stehlik could recognize it was Joe Burk, then aged fifty-four. Stehlik was duly impressed.

For Parker the sculler, training alongside Joe Burk paid its dividends, whatever the physical or mental cost. He went on to represent the United States at the 1959 Pan American Games, winning the gold medal.

Parker also competed in the Diamond Sculls at Henley in 1959. There, he became friendly with Harvard coach Tom Bolles and members of the Harvard Varsity Heavyweight and Lightweight eights competing respectively in the Grand Challenge and Thames Challenge Cups.

Parker reached the finals of the Diamonds that summer, where he was defeated by the Australian champion Stuart Mackenzie. Historian Peter Mallory noted that Mackenzie "toyed" with Parker down the course, surging and then slowing, in what some spectators thought was an unseemly act of dominance.[215]

We will hear more about Mackenzie and Burk in Chapter Eleven.

Parker came back to Philadelphia after Henley and continued his training each day with Burk to prepare for the 1960 Olympic Trials.

The 1960 U.S. Olympic Trials were held on Lake Onondaga at Syracuse. Parker's principal opponent for the Olympic berth was Dick Blieden, who rowed for Lake Washington Rowing Club, and was coached by Stan Pocock. Stan Pocock's LWRC team in 1960 was especially strong and would win the Olympic Trials in both coxed and coxless fours and coxed and coxless pairs. Blieden was the LWRC entry for the singles. Stan called Blieden "a world-class-sculler."

In the Trials finals, Blieden led Parker with only 250 meters to go when Blieden's diaphragm spasmed so strongly he could not breathe. His distress was so profound he simply had to stop rowing. Parker rowed past his stricken opponent to win the Olympic berth.

Stand Pocock felt badly for Blieden, and when Pocock was named the small boats coach for the U.S. rowing team, he made Blieden one of the small boat spares. Pocock's gesture was well intentioned, but Blieden's presence on the team put Parker in an awkward position.[216]

Lyman Perry, stroke of the 1960 Navy crew, then representing the U.S. in the eights, remembers Parker going to and from practice with little interaction with other U.S. Olympic team members. "I have a clear memory of poor old Harry Parker coming down to the boat dock.

I made a point of trying to befriend Harry, and carry his oars down, being alongside him when he came to the dock.

"I felt sorry for him because he was not paid much attention—by anybody."[217]

The complexion of U.S. collegiate eight-oared rowing changed forever at the Olympics of 1960. The Naval Academy Varsity, which sought to emulate the 1952 "Admirals," lost in its first heat to Canada by one length. *The New York Times* reminded readers that the U.S. had won every eight-oared event in the Olympics since 1920.[218]

Navy managed to reach the final through the *repechage* but faced tough competition in the final.

The *New York Times* shared the news on page one of its September 4 edition:

America's traditional Olympic supremacy came to an end in another sport today as Germany's famous Ditmarsia Keil-Ratzeburger eight-oared crew won the gold medal in the second fastest time ever made in the quadrennial games.

Leading all the way over a 2,000-meter course on Lake Albano, beneath the summer palace of Pope John XXIII, the high-stroking Germans gave up the lead momentarily to Canada at 1,700 meters. They then came on at a blistering 45 beat and won by open water in 5 minutes 57.1 seconds.

It was the first time a German eight had ever won in the Olympics.

The United States Naval Academy crew, never better than fourth in the field of six, finished nearly three lengths back. It trailed Canada, Czechoslovakia and France, which finished in that order behind the winner. Italy was last.[219]

Since 1920, the United States had won the eight-oared championship eight times in succession, Navy crews triumphing in 1920 and 1952.

Although the middies' defeat today was not unexpected as they had been beaten by Canada in the heats and had to qualify for the final in the repechage . . . their failure to finish better than fifth came as a shock.

The *Times* notes that the overall U.S. rowing performance was the worst since the 1936 Berlin Olympics. Germany had won gold medals in three boat classes, and the Soviet Union in two, and then Communist Czechoslovakia one.

Harry Parker made the Olympic final in the singles and rowed well in mid-race, reaching third for a time, but faded toward the end and finished fifth of six finalists.

Only the coxless four from Lake Washington Rowing Club— whose two-man was Ted Nash—won a gold medal. A picture of the four on the dock receiving the gold medal appeared on the front page of *The New York Times*.

The New York Times reporter Allison Danzig also devoted a section to what seemed to him to be the equipment innovations brought by the Germans:

> The Germans use a spoon-shaped blade and they also have a novel rigging, the Nos. 4 and 5 oars pulling from the starboard side. They say they get hold of the water better with their unorthodox blades, and there is also less chance of washing out on a stroke. Having the two oarsmen coupled on the same side, they say, keeps the shell truer on course.
>
> They are an exceptionally high-stroking crew with a very short stroke. They scarcely go past the perpendicular or vertical, so little body swing is used.
>
> The Germans give the impression of using very little leg drive and doing all the work with their arms, though actually they use very strong leg drive. They maintain that the short, high stroke is less tiring and makes for more rhythm.
>
> They make a practice of opening around 44 strokes a minute and keeping the beat at 40 or better throughout the race. The rate of their beat at the finish depends upon how much they are extended. Usually they close around 40. [220]

Allison Danzig had—with his brief observations—started an ongoing public discussion about the "Ratzeburg methods" compared to what were then viewed as the U.S. orthodox methods. The discussion raged for decades, and in many ways has not been entirely extinguished.

Stan Pocock, as the U.S. small boats coach, had a chance to look at the German oars and boat at the Olympic venue, and was not impressed. Ratzeburg did not use the larger blade oars they had brought for the finals, and the Empacher boat they rowed in "was an old plywood bucket, heavy and hogged—['hogged' in this context means bent convex upward along its length]."[221]

Few were more qualified to critique boat design than the son of the esteemed George Pocock. Before the race, Stan had gone so far as to write to his father: "If the Germans, fortunate in having Karl Adam as their coach, win the eight—and it appears to me that they might—it won't be because of their boat."[222]

The day after the Olympic finals in Rome, Parker went back out to the boathouse where the U.S. boats were stored next to the racing course. He planned to row.

Parker was surprised to find that his single was gone from the boat rack. Some while later, he saw Ted Nash—who had the day before won the gold medal as the two-man of the Stan Pocock coached U.S. coxless four—*rowing Parker's single back to the dock.*

Parker was astonished. In his view, members of one crew did not appropriate the boat of another. Would an Olympic teammate do that to another teammate?

The bonds of being on the same Olympic team are sometimes slender. Of far longer standing are the bonds of the separate clubs where each team trains. Nash was then a product of Lake Washington Rowing Club, based in Seattle and deeply embedded in the University of Washington culture. Stan Pocock remembered that Nash would frequently train as Blieden's training partner in the single.[223]

While he was training for the Olympic team, Parker was a member of Vesper Boat Club, a Philadelphia-based club. The Lake Washington oarsmen might well have thought that save for his cramp attack near the finish of the Trials, Blieiden rather than Parker would have been the Olympic sculler.

Whatever good will that might have existed between Parker and Nash before that day vanished forever.

The incident was not widely known at the time, but, in later years, Parker related the incident to his Harvard lightweight coach.[224] The cool relationship between Nash and Parker was to influence the tenor of relations between those two renowned coaches throughout the coming era.

And Joe Burk would find himself in the position of being between Parker and Nash as soon as Nash was hired at Penn in 1965, as we will see later.

One must consider what had been the tenor of the relationships between competing coaches before 1960. The easy friendship between then Princeton heavyweight coach Delos C. "Dutch" Schoch and Joe Burk was representative of the norm of that time. Dutch had been an alternate for the 1936 University of Washington Varsity that won the Olympic gold medal at the Berlin Olympic Games in 1936, made famous by the book *The Boys in the Boat*.[225] He and Joe had known each other as competitors in the 1930s.

Dutch had served as an assistant crew coach for Princeton starting in 1938. Like Burk, he joined the Navy during World War II, serving throughout the war. He returned to Princeton as head crew coach starting 1946 until 1965, when a heart condition forced him to limit his coaching at Princeton to the golf team.[226] When Burk coached at Yale and then at Penn, their crews would oppose each other each year.

In those days, the courtesies of an earlier era prevailed among most rowing coaches. It was the tradition that each visiting rowing coach would be hosted for dinner at the home of home team's coach. Dutch's son, Fred Schoch (Washington Varsity '71–'73, silver medalist, '71 Pan Am Games), now the recently retired Director of the Head of the Charles Regatta, remembers attending dinner at the Burks' home in Philadelphia when the Princeton crew came to contest the Childs Cup. Young Schoch was impressed with the Burk's tradition of observing a moment of silent grace before dinner.

Fred also remembered the warm relationship between the families and especially between the two older men. "[Burk] was a very kind and gentle man and I know his crews adored him . . . Joe used to visit . . . [my parents] . . . in Princeton when Penn used to come to race on Lake Carnegie. It was a much more civil time between coaches then, and it was standard for the host coach to have dinner for the visiting coach the night before the race in their home! I guess you wouldn't see that today." [227]

CHAPTER ELEVEN

The Student Moves to Harvard

A fter the Rome Olympics, Harry Parker was looking for a job coaching crew. He initially applied for a position at the Naval Academy, but the job went to someone else.

Harvard's varsity coach Harvey Love was looking for a freshman coach for his heavyweights. Love had recently succeeded Tom Bolles as heavyweight coach when Bolles was promoted to the role of athletic director at Harvard.

Just as University of Washington graduates Rusty Callow and Tom Bolles had recommended Joe Burk, now Burk himself put in a good word for Parker at Harvard.

Burk would certainly have mentioned Parker's remarkable drive in going from Penn's lightweight crew to the heavyweight crew, his three years of rowing on the Penn Varsity, and his time as the U.S. sculler for the Pan Am Games and the 1960 Olympics. Bolles would himself have learned much about Parker when he trained with Bolles' crews at Henley in 1959.

If Burk had been asked about whether Parker had the passion to be a student of the sport, Burk would doubtless have mentioned

Harry's "black book" from his undergraduate days and his relentless study of what made crews go fast.

By fall 1960, Harry Parker was in place as the newly appointed freshman heavyweight coach at Newell Boathouse on the Charles River. At the time, Harvard's heavyweight rowing performance was beginning a decline from the more glorious days enjoyed when Bolles was coaching. Love and Parker faced a rebuilding period.

In 1962, the United States returned Germany's earlier hospitality in the 1950s, welcoming Karl Adam and his crew from Ratzeburg. Joe Burk and the University of Pennsylvania crew warmly greeted the German team when they visited the rowing mecca of Philadelphia. Burk and his family invited Adam and the Ratzeburg team to their house for a cookout, where one of the German oarsmen mistook a closed sliding glass door for an opening, creating quite a mighty Teutonic collision that alarmed the party. Fortunately, no one was hurt.

It was around this time that Karl Adam admitted to Joe that he had watched Burk's 1955 crew win at Hamburg in the summer seven years before and feared he would never be able to match the Quakers' performance.[228] According to his son, Roger, Burk himself was interested in the Germans' approach to training and was learning to read German at the time because it was clear to him that German rowing was on an upswing, and Burk wanted to understand their approach. He was still using the long, thin "pencil" blades that had been traditional in U.S. rowing for decades, and while he did not immediately adopt the use of German blades, he thought it prudent to keep an eye on international developments.

The year 1962 was, for many in United States rowing, a time of questioning the wisdom of traditional training methods and equipment, since the Germans had beaten the Navy crew at the 1960 Olympics, ending an unbeaten Olympic streak of forty years. The new oars and rigging and rowing styles of the crews that had bested the Navy crew at the Rome Olympics was shaking many coaches' confidence in their methods.

That American fascination with Ratzeburg would continue for the entire decade.

Steve Gladstone recalls that Burk was enough of a student of the history of international rowing he could draw tight parallels between what Ratzeburg was doing, the high stroking of earlier foreign crews, and his own sculling in the late 1930s.

"As far as Joe was concerned," said Gladstone, "there was nothing new under the sun when it came to what [Ratzeburg] was doing." Each move was little more than a tweak to or a variation of what others had found helpful in some earlier era.

Gladstone also drew his own parallel between Burk's even paced racing and that of three-time Olympic rowing medal winner Conn Findlay in the coxed pair with (1956, 1960, 1964). "Conn would figure out mathematically [what it took to win], and he would just travel up the course at one speed. There is no indication that people who employ that method speed up, other people simply slow down." [229]

Penn's varsity crew in 1962 was a remarkable group, filled with characters. Coxswain John Hartigan, at five feet and one inch tall, was the sparkplug of this talented team. Born with spina bifida, John weighed just over one hundred pounds, and walked with a pronounced gait, but spoke with a fiery spirit. Early in his time at Penn, Hartigan approached Burk about whether he could try out for coxswain of the crew.

Burk encouraged him, and Hartigan worked practices all year, learning his craft. In those days, the only amplification of a coxswain's voice came from a modest megaphone he wore. Coxswains who wanted to be heard were perpetually hoarse. Cold weather was no help to their condition.

As a result of heavy practice schedules, coxswains' voices were often strained, sometimes permanently, and some of Hartigan's fellow coxswains would choose to rest their voices and not always attend practice. Hartigan never skipped practices. He hammered through all of them—and yet saw no reward for his perseverance. If he did get in boats that raced in the spring, it was sporadic.

At the beginning of one fall season, Hartigan—not yet satisfied with the boats he was assigned to compared to his time on the water, in the cold, steering a boat while straining to be heard—approached Burk.

From the website boathouserowthebook.com.

Hartigan explained his concern. He had worked hard and thought he had done well. He asked Burk directly. What was his future? Then he ended it with a question to Burk, "So this season, shall I go out for football?" Such was the spark in John Hartigan.

He was Burk's varsity coxswain in 1962. After graduating, Hartigan would go on to cox countless successful boats during his time on the water, including Penn's 1968 Olympic coxed four that finished fifth at the Mexico City Olympics and the 1974 World Champion U.S. Lightweight Eight.

During the 1962 season, Joe had the pleasure of developing one of his very best crews. Burk's varsity that year was made up as follows:

Bow	Charles Eddy
2	Chandler Hovey
3	Ward Maier
4	Calvin Johnson
5	James Fitzgerald
6	Frank Shields
7	Fargo Thompson
8	Wood Fischer
Coxswain	John Hartigan

Early in the season, *The Philadelphia Inquirer* noted that the 1962 varsity was "the biggest, strongest crew Joe Burk's ever had," but was a "typical Burk crew—only three of his eight had pre-college rowing experience."[230]

Just before the Eastern Sprints on May 19, 1962, *The New York Times* declared Cornell the favorite for the varsity race, although reporter Allison Danzig noted that, "Cornell and Penn, two of the biggest crews, have shown the power to move the boat against a headwind in choppy water. Penn has been rowing at a higher stroke than any other eight and is more experienced at it, and higher stroking is in order for 2000 meters."[231]

In the event the following day, Penn and Yale tied for the Sprints Championship. Finish line judges could not determine a winner. Cornell was third.[232]

A shared victory for the Eastern Sprints Championships was enough for both the Penn and Yale crews to consider going on to row in the premier event for eights, the Grand Challenge Cup at the Henley Royal Regatta.[233]

After the Eastern Sprints, Penn travelled to Cornell to race a two-mile course on Lake Cayuga under windy and rough conditions.

The Ithaca, New York, crowd was excited by easy victories by Cornell's freshman and junior varsity crews.

In the varsity race, Penn jumped to an early lead at 38 strokes a minute under the guidance of Woody Fisher and John Hartigan, compared to Cornell's conservative 28–9 strokes a minute. By halfway, Cornell raised its stroke and began to eat into the Penn lead. Penn continued its torrid pace and managed to win the race by less than a second.[234]

The final race of the collegiate season, the IRA at Syracuse, loomed as the final hurdle, the long three miles, over twice the distance of the Sprints.

Around this time, Burk told the *Philadelphia Daily News* that Penn had been "pointing for" the IRA all year. He denied his crew had been limiting itself to preparation only for shorter races, explaining, "sometimes we've rowed up to sixteen miles in a day."[235]

Penn's preparations were apparently not enough. In the finals, Penn came in fifth, a distant four lengths behind Cornell, with Washington second, California third, and Wisconsin fourth.

Burk characteristically made no public comments about the IRA loss. But he must have been flummoxed to some extent. His crews were being judged in championship matches over two different distances—the Olympic or Henley distances, taking about 6.5 minutes to finish, and the IRA's three-mile distance, taking about seventeen minutes to finish. Try as they might, his best crews, the 1955 and 1962 Varsities could win at the shorter distance, but lagged at the longer.

The New York Times article commented, "It must have been a galling frustration for Joe Burk's fine crew after its splendid record at sprint distances (i.e., Henley or Olympic distances). It had hoped to score its first I.R.A. varsity victory since 1909."[236] [The year of Penn's last IRA win in the newspaper was a mistake—Penn's last IRA win had been in 1900.]

But Penn's earlier victories had been enough to earn it the right to go to Henley. But the poor finish IRA had to remain in the back of the minds of the 1962 Penn crew and their coach.

While he did not express it publicly during this period, Burk must have finally concluded that American college crews were faced with a dilemma. There was no way to resolve the inherent conflict in the two different styles of races American college crews faced. Each season, tradition had governed the length of races—from the Henley distance, to one and three-quarter miles for most early races, and then for varsity crews, races of three miles. Could the same training accommodate those varying distances?

Add to this diversity of race length the fact that every four years the Olympic distance was always 2,000 meters, or just short of one and one-quarter miles. Until 1960, U.S. college teams had managed to avoid specializing their racing at any particular distance and still put forward a college crew that could win the Olympics. The German victory in 1960 made every U.S. college coach begin to wonder if the U.S. approach could continue.

Both Penn and their fellow Sprint-victors Yale went to Henley, each with high hopes. Burk had been good friends with Yale coach Jim Rathschimdt since he had recommended his employment by Yale years before. Both schools were known at Henley and welcomed into the Grand Challenge Cup, reserved for the very fastest of eights.

In its first race, the Penn boat beat Thames Rowing Club to advance to the to the second round, but ominous news came from Yale's race on the same day against the Italian Moto Guzzi Club of Italy. Yale was thrashed by the Italian crew by two and one-half lengths. Since Penn had last tied Yale at the Eastern Sprints over 2,000 meters, the idea of facing a crew who had decisively beaten Yale the day before was chilling.[237]

Roger Burk remembers going to Henley with his father in 1962, where he witnessed another example of "the smallness" of the world of great rowers from many nations. Roger was accompanying his father, riding bicycles along the towpath at Henley and following selected races for the full length of the race except for the very last sections of the racecourse, where the towpath ended. Roger recalled that perennial

Australian sculling champion and 1956 Melborne Olympic Silver Medalist Stuart Mackenzie was that year contesting his last Diamond Sculls, which he would win for the sixth straight time. The group gathering along the towpath at the time included many of the old guards of the Henley Regatta, of which Burk, as a two-time Diamonds winner, was recognized as one of the most knowledgeable spectators.

Mackenzie was in those days known as what we would now call "a trash talker." Roger recalled Mackenzie that day before the start being talkative and informal, making remarks to his very experienced audience assembled at the starting line.

Joe Burk and his son had positioned themselves near the head of the cycling group and were listening to Mackenzie's familiar talk as all awaited the Starter's commands. Roger noticed that Ernie Arlett, known to Roger through his father, was on the bicycle positioned directly to Joe Burk's left, so that Burk was between Arlett and Mackenzie.

Ernie Arlett deserves a full introduction at this point, as he—like George Pocock—was a direct link back to the very beginnings of great English rowing, and later great American rowing.

G. Ernest Arlett was a native of Henley-on-Thames, born two years before Burk in 1912, the son and grandson of Thames watermen. In his youth, he had been a champion sculler and had plied the waters of the Thames at Henley, perhaps more than any other person gathered at the start that day.

After his sculling days, Arlett became the boatman for Radley School, a great English secondary school with a long rowing tradition, and for Leander Club in Henley, among other rowing programs.

Burk was not the only veteran of World War Two at the start line that day. Arlett had served as a soldier in the British Expeditionary Force, which fought Hitler's invading armies in France in 1940. Like many Tommies, he was awaiting evacuation at the port of Dunkirk, France, in May, 1940, as German panzers closed in on the port town. While most British Tommies waited interminably in lines running from the beach to the piers used to load soldiers, Arlett the waterman simply "commandeered a boat and rowed his fellow soldiers to a waiting British destroyer." [238]

Arlett had immigrated to the United States in 1957 and was the boatman at Rutgers in 1962. (He would go on be the sculling coach at Harvard in 1965, and go on to establish the Northeastern University rowing program later.)[239]

Arlett that day was not impressed with the trash talk coming from the Australian, who himself had just immigrated to Great Britain. He leaned forward just past Burk so that Mackenzie could hear his voice and called out: "I'd save your breath, Mackenzie. You're going to need it."

Arlett then leaned back so that he was hidden behind Joe Burk.

Mackenzie heard the comment and turned toward the shore. "None of your nonsense, Joe Burk!"

Roger smiled deeply as he related the story sixty-one years later. The world of rowing was small, the world of great rowing smaller still—and Joe Burk stood high in the ranks of that very smallest of circles.

Penn and Moto Guzzi faced off later in the semifinal of the Grand. The Italian eight blazed off the start with a stroke rate of 46, and Penn was simply left behind. Down the course, Penn was able to hold the Italians to no more than a one length lead, and then mounted a final challenge at the mile mark but were unable to pass.[240]

The physically strongest crew Joe Burk had ever had at Penn was out of the regatta before finals day. It was a hard blow.

The fact that neither Penn nor Yale were able to get the final of the Grand Challenge Cup, combined with Navy's 1960 Olympic loss to the German Ratzeburg crew renewed the discomfort among many in the U.S. collegiate rowing community. Burk was among those most concerned. He was quoted in *The Philadelphia Inquirer* about the Henley results: "This is a worrying outlook for American rowing. Very definitely U.S. crews are falling behind the [European] Continent."

In the same article, John B. "Jack" Kelly Jr. agreed: "I think that's generally true of college rowing. They are in a rut. Our colleges in general row too many long races instead of international distances. In Europe they don't row any of those long [two-three-four miles] races, except Oxford and Cambridge in England. They also row pairs and fours over there to prepare for the eights. Most of our college oarsmen have never sat in another boat except an eight."

Jack Kelly continued: "I think Joe [Burk] is a little more progressive than other college coaches. He uses a high stroke, like the Continental coaches. And I think our club (Vesper) is doing something radical. We've got a European coach [Hungarian Tibor Machan[241]] and I think we have the best eight in the country."

The article pointed out that the German crew in the Rome Olympics never dipped below 40 strokes a minute throughout the 2,000 meter Olympic final.

Kelly continued "We need to do something. We're not improving as fast as the rest of the world. Over there, they're willing to devote themselves to training. Our kids aren't. We have to woo our young kids away from fraternity parties or Atlantic City on weekends."[242]

All of the above was true. What had changed?

For the first half of the Twentieth Century, Olympic victories in the eight-oared event had become almost a constant to the American public—and in the past, that had been enough. Since rowing was introduced as an Olympic sport in 1900, the leading U.S. college team had duly won the U.S. Olympic Trials and then won the gold medal in the eights. The record was unbroken from 1921 through 1956. America had rarely had the same dominance in rowing in the smaller boats—and perhaps that seems acceptable to the average American, all collegiate rowing was done in eights, and collegiate rowing dominated the sport and headlines.

On January 14, 1963, Harvard head heavyweight rowing coach Harvey Love died unexpectedly of a heart attack at age 52. In 1934, Love had coxed the University of Washington Varsity coached by Tom Bolles while Burk was the varsity captain at Penn. After graduation, Love became the freshman heavyweight coach at UW, while Bolles moved up from the freshman coach's job to assist the varsity coach Al Ubrickson.

When Bolles was made head coach at Harvard, Love came east to be Bolles' freshman coach. Bolles was so successful as the Harvard heavyweight coach that he was promoted in 1951 to be Harvard's Director of Athletics—and Love had succeeded Bolles in the Head Coach's job.

The unexpected death caught Harvard and the rowing world by surprise. The immediate problem for Director Bolles was whether to advance the freshman coach, Parker, to the role of head coach or to take on a more experienced hand. The *Harvard Crimson* student paper mentioned former Harvard oar (and then current Rutgers coach) Bill Leavitt as a possible candidate, but noted he was already busy in New Jersey preparing for Rutgers' upcoming season.[243]

The death also caused surprise within the Burk household. Roger Burk said that the plan in his father's mind was that when Burk was ready to retire—which he viewed as within a few years—he would recommend to Penn that Harry Parker be named as his replacement. If Parker became the head coach at Harvard, to whom would Burk turn when he retired?

Burk promptly put in a good word for Parker with Bolles—the very man who had once approached Lieutenant Burk in San Francisco to suggest he return to rowing and coaching. Burk assured Bolles that Harry Parker was up to the task of leading Harvard as the head coach.

Burk's recommendation proved prescient. Harry Parker would soon bring in another golden era in Harvard rowing.

As the 1963 college season started, *The Philadelphia Inquirer* in its "Sportpourri" section noted:

> ...Only two oarsmen and the coxswain remain from last year's Penn heavyweight crew, which went to the semifinals of the Royal Henley Regatta in England. Coach Joe Burk, hoping to rebuild, is hampered by several losses among junior class candidates.[244]

The college season itself was marked by an extended visit from the 1960 Olympic champion West German Ratzeburg Rowing Club for a series of races in America in the spring of 1963. During that spring, their coach, Karl Adam, visited the Vesper Boat Club in Philadelphia and gave a talk to a group of American coaches eager to hear of his new training methods. Much of the discussion surrounded Adam's use of time prediction for final race speed by measuring speeds of practice runs over 500 meters and 1,000 meters.

On April 20, 1963, Ratzeburg's visiting eight raced Georgetown University and St. Joseph's College crews over a 2,000-meter course on the Potomac River. The Germans' winning margin was two lengths—an easy victory.[245]

On April 27, Harvard won its first race of the 1963 season against Rutgers and Brown by a length over Rutgers and four lengths over Brown. Harry Parker was then described by the Boston Globe as Harvard "acting head coach"[246]—a sign that his position at Harvard was tenuous.

On May 14, 1963, *The Philadelphia Inquirer* published a photo in its sports section of a presentation of a University of Pennsylvania banner to the visiting delegation from Germany led by the captain of the German crew, Karl von Groddeck, together with the German consul in Philadelphia, Dr. Edgar Reichal, Penn crew captain Frank Shields, and Joe Burk. While the German crew was in Philadelphia, Burk and Penn seemed to be their main hosts.

The Ratzeburg crew was invited to row in the Adams Cup in Philadelphia. Ratzeburg was pressed at the beginning by Penn, who at that time had won no races, but Ratzeburg drew ahead and won by one length ahead of Penn, followed by Harvard a half-length behind Penn. Navy was not a factor. The Ratzeburg captain admitted to the press that the cold winds had hindered his crew.

Nick Bancroft in the Harvard varsity that day told an interesting story about the impact of the German crew. When Harvard rowed up toward the start of the Adams Cup, "we rowed past them—they were just sitting there in their shell, and then we stopped. And then they rowed past us. A, they *had beards*, and B, they were rowing with one arm each, at a paddle, but one arm nonetheless, and they were looking over at us."

At the start, Bancroft said, "They started off at some amazing cadence. We weren't counting, but it seemed like they were rowing thirty-five chop strokes or something, and then they settled to a forty-five [strokes a minute]. And beat the hell out of us."

Nick recounted the differences he and his Harvard crewmates saw between themselves and the German crew: "They're older, they have a different style of rowing, they have different oars . . . the oars have different shapes . . . Who is this Karl Adam guy? Well, he's kind of a 'can-do' engineer, he's got mathematics, he's going to revolutionize rowing . . .

"We were impressed. We were all enthusiastic, and Harry [Parker] was willing to go along with us, but I think he was skeptical about it. Before the Sprints, we decided to use their style . . . what the heck, let's row their style and start off at a forty-five . . ." Harvard trained to that plan for the week between the Adams Cup and the Eastern Sprints.

Ratzeburg had also accepted an invitation to participate in the 1963 Eastern Sprints Championship. There were so many crews that morning heats were held, and only the two highest crews in each heat would advance to the finals.

Bancroft outlined how the heats went for Harvard. "So we get to the Sprints, and Tom Bolles was there . . . and we rowed like hell, and we did not qualify *at all* [for the finals]. I think for the first time in history . . . so we came into the dock. I remember Tom was there with Harry, and somewhere along the way I asked Tom, 'What did you think?'

"Tom said, 'Well, if your oars had actually gone into the water during the race, you might have done okay,' but he said, 'You were basically pulling an awful lot of air.'"[247]

Even the Germans also had a hard time in the headwinds that prevailed during the heats. They fell to Cornell's varsity, who was in their heat. One newspaper report said:

Coach Stork Sanford, who doesn't want to get too enthusiastic about his predominantly sophomore varsity, said that the spanking morning headwind was made to order for his new shell, Windjammer: "The strong headwind really killed off the high-stroking crews like Ratzeburg, Penn, Columbia

219

and Harvard." The last three didn't qualify for the final, and the Germans barely nipped Wisconsin for the qualifying spot back of Cornell.

While Germans rowed at 40 or 42 strokes a minute most of the way, Cornell was cruising along at 28 for most of the course. [248]

In the media, Coach Karl Adam explained the loss to the press by saying that, had Ratzeburg brought their own shell, the German team could have made adjustments to the outriggers to account for the heavier load on the oars created by the headwind. Instead, they had brought only their own oars and rowed in a borrowed American-made Pocock with fixed riggers, which did not allow adjustments.

Burk's Penn Varsity fared no better than Parker's Harvard Varsity. Neither made the seven-boat final.[249]

In the afternoon finals, the wind died, and the Ratzeburg crew could use their high- stroking style more effectively. They won by a length over Cornell, with Yale third, two and a half lengths back of Ratzeburg, followed by Princeton, Wisconsin, Brown, and Syracuse. *The Philadelphia Inquirer* quoted Karl Adam and the head of German Rowing at a later luncheon stating that America had a large number of good crews compared to Germany:

> Both Adam and the German Rowing Federation president, Dr. Walter Wulfing, emphasized at yesterday's rowing luncheon in New York, that the U.S. has many more good crews than Germany—"ten good eights to only one or two."
>
> "I hope Cornell will have a great chance in the 1964 Olympics," said Dr. Wulfing. "I am impressed with all the great discipline of your crews. If you elected an Olympic eight from the pick of all your crews, you might even be stronger."[250]

The last quoted remarks from Dr. Walter Wulfing started a dialogue between American coaches and rowers about how to best select crews of the U.S. Olympic and National Teams. Traditionalists had long held to the idea that an American Olympic eight was best picked by a trials system. Whoever won the trials won the right to represent the U.S.

Proponents of a national team system suggested that in the eights, the strongest boat would likely be a combination of the best of U.S. rowers from all sources brought together under one coach. Those proponents argued that no one college or club had all the best oarsmen—so why not pick the best eight men from all sources?

This debate would rage for almost another decade.

Dr. Wulfung's motives in his public comment were likely limited to the diplomatic gesture of complimenting West Germany's hosts and noting the richness of rowing talent in America (then a nation of 189 million when compared to West Germany's 58 million). What was left unsaid, but then obvious to all, was that America's economy had become the largest in the world. By comparison, West Germany was far smaller and was denied the benefit of the 17 million Germans stuck in East Germany laboring under Soviet domination. But his remarks did tend to crystalize for U.S. rowers and coaches the reality that smaller countries with fewer people could create eight-oared crews that could beat the best of the U.S collegiate crews. That rankled.

The mechanics of what Ratzeburg did to develop its eight were comparatively simple. The German coach Karl Adam picked rowers from all over Germany and brought them to Ratzeburg on weekends to row as an eight. During the work week, the oarsmen returned to their home clubs and rowed in singles, or other small boats—and then practiced together in the eight on weekends.

That method had produced the 1960 Olympic champions, and the subsequent West German crews that had visited America and beaten most of their opponents.

At the end of Harvard's 1963 season was the Yale race at New London, Connecticut. Just as Skip Walz had felt pressure before his 1949 race with Tom Bolles and the then-dominant Harvard crew—when his first season was almost completed, Harry Parker must have felt pressure as he travelled to Harvard's Red Top training quarters at the end of his first year as the "acting" head coach at Harvard. After Harvard had collapsed at the Sprints attempting to mimic Ratzeburg, Yale had at least managed third place at the Sprints, staying with their standard approach. They were thus heavily favored for the four-mile race against Harvard.[251]

Bancroft was clear that Parker and Bolles must have decided that it was time to go back to the style Harvard had used before. "Parker said, 'Let's go back to the old way.'" Bancroft reported.

The June 15 Harvard-Yale race day for the jayvee and varsity had to be postponed for a day due to rough weather. But the combination race and the freshmen race—both at two miles—did go off on Saturday before conditions worsened—and they signaled a growing trend toward a Harvard upset possibility in the Varsity race. The combination race was Harvard's by half a length after having fallen three lengths behind. 4 Harvard Crews Win by 16 ½ lengths..

The two remaining races, when they were finally rowed on Sunday, completed the clean sweep or Harvard, the varsity winning the four-mile race by a huge margin, eight lengths, and the jayvee the three-mile race by five lengths. *The Boston Globe* sub-headline crowed, "4 Harvard Crews Win by 16 ½ lengths."[252]

This upset Harvard victory at the 1963 Yale race was the beginning of a Harvard Varsity crew regular season streak that would last until 1969 and would establish Harry Parker's reputation as a great crew coach.

Paradoxically, the streak would be ended in 1969 by the Penn crew coached by Joe Burk, who had first recommended him to Harvard.

The rowing world is small, indeed.

After the Ratzeburg crew returned home to Germany, and on the same day as the Harvard-Yale race, all the other major rowing colleges reassembled for the annual IRA, then held at Lake Onondaga in Syracuse, New York. Cornell again won the three-mile varsity race, besting western runners-up California and Washington.[253] Cornell's varsity lights and heavies were rewarded with trips to the Henley Royal Regatta.

Pennsylvania's varsity was tenth in the IRA, the JV twelfth, and the Freshman twefth. Amidst the thrill of international visitors, and the strengthening of rowing in Europe, Penn's collegiate rowing fortunes appeared to have waned during the regular college season.

The 1963 Penn regular college season ended on a low note. But some of the graduate oarsmen from boats in 1961 through 1963 continued to row together out of the Penn boathouse, as if they had a further prupose.

They did. The prospect of the 1964 Olympics in Tokyo did keep near the Penn Boathouse in the summer of 1963 some of the members of the stronger Penn crews from 1961 and 1962 who kept rowing after graduation in the hopes that Olympic glory might come their way. These graduate stalwarts would be enlivened by the presence of graduates from other schools whose eyes were also focused on the next Olympic rowing contest in Tokyo.

Whatever disappointment Joe Burk might have felt at the 1963 collegiate season was buoyed by the presence in the boathouse of this Old Guard. With no special announcement, Penn rowing graduates like Woody Fischer, Penn '62 and stroke of the '62 Henley Varsity, Al Wachlin '61, Fargo Thompson '62, Jim Fitzgerald '62, simply kept rowing out of the Penn Boathouse. The veterans occasionally rowed with the Penn undergraduates and sometimes rowed by themselves when the undergrad racing season approached.

Whether they envisioned it as such, Burk and the graduate oarsmen were fashioning—on the fly—a sort of American Ratzeburg—a rowing club out of the same boathouse as the Penn undergraduate effort but clearly focused on making the U.S. Olympic rowing team in 1964. Burk did not explain his motivations or publicize his efforts, but he seemed to be harkening back to the Penn effort in 1936 under Rusty Callow. Readers will remember that Rusty Callow had strengthened his Penn undergraduate crew for the Olympic Trials by putting Burk and two other Penn graduates into what Callow then called "the graduate boat." That formidable "graduate boat" had led Washington's *Boys in the Boat* until the final 500 meters of the 1936 Olympic Trials.

There was also another model for post college rowing besides Ratzeburg, the Pocock-influenced Lake Washington Rowing Club, which had won the 1960 U.S. berths in the Rome Olympics in both coxed and coxless fours and coxed and coxless pairs, and brought home gold and bronze medals in the coxless four and the coxed pair respectively. These recent historical examples tempted those who felt they had more rowing to do. Those so tempted became a sort of *coalition of the willing*—to employ a more modern usage.

Burk began to enter crews in local races under the name of College Boat Club, or CBC—with substantial organizational help from Woody Fischer (Penn '62), who, because of his intensity and drive, operated as the *de facto* captain of the group.

College Boat Club has a storied history, interwoven with undergraduate rowing at Penn. It was first established in 1872 by Effingham B. Morris as a club for Penn undergraduates to race other Philadelphia club crews. The Club entered into its first intercollegiate rowing in 1879 when it battled undergraduate teams from Princeton and Columbia for the Childs Cup, named for the cup's donor George Childs, then the publisher of the *Philadelphia Public Ledger*. The oldest of "cup races" in American collegiate rowing,[254] the Childs Cup, remains on the Penn crew schedule to this day.

Because the CBC was a legal entity separate from the University of Pennsylvania, Burk used it to join oarsmen within and outside of the Penn rowing community. How much formal permission he got from the University for this combination is not recorded. By the spring of 1963, the combination had attracted the attention of Lyman Perry Jr., Navy stroke for the 1960 crew that had been disappointed at the past Olympics.

In 1963, Lyman was contemplating his future while serving out his Naval Academy obligation of service aboard a submarine. Perry was a squared-away, second-generation product of the United States Naval Academy[255] whose father Lyman Sr. had been an all-American football player on the 1918 Navy team and later director of athletics at Annapolis. Lyman Perry Jr., as an undergraduate at Navy, had rowed three years for Rusty Callow, and in his senior year—the 1960 Olympic year—for Coach Lou Lindsey when he succeeded Callow, who had retired due to ill health.

The younger Perry had experienced the heady atmosphere of the 1960 Olympic Regatta, and after considering the stinging defeat he and his teammates had suffered there, he decided in 1963 that he was not yet finished with rowing.

"Having won the IRA once—and stroked [Navy] to two second places, I thought I was going to be a pretty good sculler," said Perry. "I watched Harry [Parker] train in the single, and I thought 'I can do that.' So I wrote a letter to Joe, and he of course remembered me and said, 'I'll be happy to coach you in the single, and I'll bet you'll do pretty well.'"

The Navy still had a program encouraging its best athletes to train for the Olympics, and Perry, with his 1960 Olympic pedigree, was soon assigned to Philadelphia to train for the 1964 Tokyo Games. He remembered arriving at the Penn Boathouse in the summer of 1963:

So I came down to Penn with my single on top of an MG. On the day I arrived at the Penn Boathouse, it was hot as the hinges of Hades, and as I was unpacking my single from the top of my MG—out comes Frank Shields [Penn heavyweight captain '63]. Because I had rowed against him, I introduced him to my wife Kate—and she thought he was the most handsome thing she had ever seen.

Kate Perry's judgment was good. Frank's daughter, the model and actress Brooke Shields, was born two years later. She would inherit her father's good looks and his lean, athletic build.

Shields was not the only former rival Perry met that day.

"Out walked Al Doering [Penn '61] . . . a Penn oarsman I had rowed against. He was older than I was, but I rowed against him at least two or three times. And he was going to law school and got serious about life—and [later] said 'I can't row anymore.'"[256]

That summer, Perry moved his boat into the boathouse, and settled into a routine of two a day practices. "Joe would send me out ahead in the single and another guy in the single named Dave Robinson. So the College Boat Club [eight] and two guys in a single would row as a group once in the morning and once in the evening."

Perry respected the guys in the eight and quickly characterized some of them 60 years later: "Woody Fischer, who was pretty much the organizer of it all, the captain of the '62 crew . . . gone to Henley . . . Al Wachlin, who was as strong as a bull, and Fargo Thompson."[257]

The greater rowing community quickly came to understand that Joe Burk was gathering a mixed graduate and undergrad team—and the goal was the 1964 Olympics. The Baltimore *Evening Sun* even included in its sports chat section the following:

> **Looking Ahead**—Six Penn undergraduate varsity oarsmen joining four grads to row this summer as College Boat Club under Quaker coach Joe Burk. They have a full schedule planned, intend to be active throughout the year, then enter next spring's Olympic trials.[258]

Joe Burk was making no secret of his Olympic aspirations for College Boat Club. Today, few oarsmen remember that the Club was in that quest for Olympic gold in Tokyo. The plans of another Philadelphia based Club, Vesper, and their success would come to dominate, completely, later historical memory.

Burk's use of College Boat Club for his graduate crew caused some confusion in the press for 1963 summer regatta results. The AP Wire story for the results of the Schuylkill Navy Regatta of June 22, 1963, erroneously compared the earlier intercollegiate results of the Penn undergraduate results at the IRA—where the undergrads finished 10th —with the sparkling performance of the graduate crew which won against strong opposition of a Vesper Boat Club eight, but they were totally different crews.[259]

The CBC eight that summer was:

Bow	Charles Eddy
2	Tom Meeks
3	Dave Robinson
4	Mark Thompson
5	Steve Sawyer
6	Frank Shields
7	Fargo Thompson
Stroke	Woody Fischer
Coxswain	John Hartigan

That same crew also won the July Fourth Regatta in Philadelphia, beating a Potomac Boat Club crew that led for over half the race, as well as a Vesper eight.

At that same regatta, Burk also boated Frank Shields and Steven Sawyer in the coxed pair with James Fuhrman steering, that also won gold.[260]

The overwhelming majority of members of the 1963 CBC felt positive about their chances at Tokyo, and following the summer racing season, continued to show up for fall practice with Burk.

Exactly how Burk decided how best to train his returning undergraduates—the job for which he was paid—while at the same time coaching his potential Olympic oarsmen, is lost to history. Burk did not preserve his training logs from the era. Memories of those differ on details. Somehow, all crews—both graduate and undergraduate—rowed the practices they had planned to row.

It is interesting to consider for a moment whether Burk had even asked the powers in the Penn Athletic Department whether he could use the Penn owned boathouse and equipment for graduate oarsman—or in Perry's case not even a Penn grad. In the modern world of litigation and the mandatory liability waivers for entering U.S. regattas, far more scrutiny is paid to such details. The narrow focus in 1964 was victory—if you said "yes" to that challenge—no further questions asked.

Sometime during Lyman Perry's time at CBC—probably during the early 1964 season—Burk asked Perry if he might be interested in coaching the Penn freshman heavyweight crew. Burk made clear the question was only preliminary, Perry said later. "I have to tell you, with me, it was just a passing comment. It wasn't a formal thing—no salary was discussed. He just said, 'Hey, would you come coach . . . you'd be good at it.'

"I said I was trying to get into the Penn architecture school at the time." I said to Joe, and I said to Joe, "I think I'll stick with that."[261] Since Burk's long-term plan had previously been to bring in Harry Parker as his replacement, he was obviously beginning anew his search for his own eventual replacement at Penn. He might also have felt that a new approach at the freshman coach position was needed.[262]

Several of the CBC oarsmen of that era remember oarsmen other than those mentioned just above gathering along Philadelphia's Boathouse Row in attempts to get to the Olympics in Tokyo. Among them were a pair of Yale graduates, Emory Clark and Boyce Budd, who were wanting to row in a pair.

One CBC member recalled that Clark and Budd had inquired of Burk in the fall of 1963 whether they could possibly join the CBC. According to that version of events, Clark and Budd had emphasized that they were intending to row as a pair. Burk explained the CBC effort was focused on the eight oared Olympic race, then referred them down to the Vesper Boat Club. Another source thought that Burk believed their Yale styles (both had rowed at Yale for Rathschmidt) incompatible with CBC's style.[263]

Neither Emory Clark's book about that time—*Olympic Odyssey*[264]—nor his Vesper teammate Bill Stowe's book, *All Together*,[265] mention Clark and Budd approaching Burk. But what Clark's book does reveal is the generosity Burk showed both men by occasionally following them and offering comments on their performance—initially to Clark alone as he rowed a single out of Vesper awaiting Budd's arrival. "Joe would take a look at me two or three times a week and kindly offer some tips,"[266] Clark explained.

Later after Budd had arrived and the two were daily rowing the pair, Burk would simply watch them and comment, or comment after joint practices or races with the CBC pairs.[267]

There were many such examples of Burk offering encouragement to oarsmen who would later go on to win Olympic medals in 1964. And Burk, then an acknowledged master of the sport, freely offered his guidance without obligation. *The sensei.*

As Joe Burk as coach managed the tides of rowing as the Penn coach, Joe Burk as father also had another responsibility, since in the spring of 1964, his son Roger would graduate from high school and go to college. Roger had been an excellent athlete at Harriton High School, playing football and baseball as well as wrestling. Roger laughingly confessed that of the three sports, he was best at wrestling, "But I didn't like it that much," he said with a wry smile. Today he still has the stature of a lightweight oarsman, short but tightly muscled, with a wrestler's walk.

His father had urged him not to row during high school, a surprising admonition for a man who himself was so involved in rowing. While he didn't say so, Joe Burk likely thought his own broad sports background had been both a pleasure and an advantage to him when he reached college, and he likely wanted Roger to have the same advantage if he chose a sport in college. Burk might also have felt the quality of high school coaching in the area did not lend itself to creating future college oarsmen.

The older Burk relented in Roger's senior year when Dick Burgee, whom Joe knew and trusted, became the Harriton High School rowing coach. Roger rowed his senior year with his high school friend Rick Stehlik on the Harriton Varsity. Before that, Roger had sculled occasionally from the Penn Boathouse and spent time around Boathouse Row.

The Harriton eight under Burgee was quite successful. Roger stroked, and Stehlik rowed at two. Philadelphia provided many opportunities for races or practices with other high school crews, and the boat developed good speed. Stehlik remembers with pleasure the Harriton team rowing against traditional prep power Kent School, founded in Connecticut by a former Columbia coxswain, which in 1927 had been the first American schoolboy crew ever to compete in Henley Royal Regatta. The Harriton team with Burk and Stehlik aboard defeated the Kent School Varsity in 1964.

Roger discussed with his parents the colleges to which he might apply. Interestingly, his father suggested his son *not* go to an Eastern college but instead consider Midwestern or Western colleges. Despite his devotion to Penn, Joe Burk thought the atmosphere at colleges in the East had an elitist tinge, and he felt Roger would get a more realistic view of the whole of society if he went west.

"The idea was that if you are going to lead people, you need to know what their lives are like," Roger explained. Was this advice the residue of Rusty Callow's influence on Joe Burk? Or George Pocock's influence? We cannot now know.

Roger applied to three leading rowing schools: the University of Washington, the University of California at Berkley, and Wisconsin. Roger favored Wisconsin, but planned to row at whichever school admitted him.

He attended the University of Washington starting in the fall of 1964. Roger found that while he enjoyed a warm relationship with George Pocock who was like "a third grandfather to me," he was viewed with some suspicion by a few Washington oarsmen and some of the coaching staff.

"When Ratzeburg started to have success [in 1960 and forward], several things happened . . . that started out the rivalry, sort of, between the Catholics and the Protestants. Back at the University of Washington, everything was traditional. All of a sudden, Pocock saw that Eastern crews were beginning to buy shovel blades and go to Donoraticos [the Italian shell used by Vesper in their 1964 gold medal eight in the Tokyo Olympics in Fall, 1964], whereas before Pocock had been top dog. So I found myself in a really tough position at Washington coming from the East Coast—almost as a spy."[268]

The dissonance grated on young Burk. But in some respects,

Seattle felt like home. George Pocock and his family welcomed him into his shop and often told him stories about Joe's working with George to adjust specifications on the singles George built for Joe. George also provided a certain measure of confirmation to Roger in much the same way that he had been a sounding board and guide for his father Joe.

There were other residues of his father's path through the world of rowing: Roger's coxswain at Washington was the son of Washington Olympic 1936 coxswain Bobby Moch of *The Boys in the Boat* fame.

But Roger's rowing progress at "UW" was modest. He did not make the freshman first boat, nor the second. Pictures from the era reflect what might be viewed as a certain Washington "bias in somatotype" in favor of tall, muscled blonde men—lumberjacks. Roger Burk did not fit that mold. He was shorter—lean and powerful. And he was from the East.

In his last two years at UW, Roger would only scull in his single, storing it in the Pocock Boathouse and rowing from there. He spent much time in the Pocock shop, absorbing lessons by just observing and from time to time discussing rowing matters, and life matters, with George.

As Roger Burk was finding his way as a freshman at UW, Howard Greenberg, a Penn freshman, was trying to find his own footing. Greenberg had been a middling football player in high school, but did not see himself competing in college. He decided to go out for rowing, having never rowed a stroke in his life. While as freshman, he was coached by Jim Beggs in the fall of 1963 in the bare rudiments of rowing, in the winter of 1963–64, he had the chance to be personally coached by Joe Burk. Greenburg remembered the event over fifty years later:

> Freshman year, we had very short workouts. There was no reason for Joe to think I could develop into anything—literally no reason—and in those days, there were tanks under the gym at Penn, and they were really prehistoric. I think there was one tank on side for port or starboard, and if you couldn't make practice, you had to go the tanks, and I remember

numerous times, as many as ten times, I would report to the tanks, and I would be the only guy there. And Joe would coach me—alone—and tell me do this, do that.

He was a master, in or out of the boat [meaning in the tanks, saying] "take your hands up a quarter of an inch," minor things, one thing at a time, because he knew we [the freshmen] were not smart enough to do two things at a time.

And *the guy really taught me how to do it—a little bit at a time.* He was an incredibly patient man, and you know, I felt like he was just concerned about me. He was worrying about me even though there were twenty-five guys on the squad . . . but when he was in the tanks, or out on the river, and looking at you, he was concentrating on you and trying to help you do what you were trying to do better.[269]

Burk's coaching gift—and his patient willingness to teach a freshman in the tanks at the same time he was attempting to assemble an Olympic crew—would earn the loyalty of all his oarsmen, as well as pay dividends later in the form of the ascending fortunes of the Penn crew in future years.

Also in the fall of 1963, a graduate of Middlesex School, the prestigious boarding school located on the edge of Concord, Massachusetts, showed up at the Penn athletic facilities for a standard test given to all freshmen. His name was Nicholas Biddle Paumgarten. Born into a prominent Philadelphia family, his father was Harald Paumgarten, who himself had twice been named an Olympic skier for Austria, in cross country and in ski jumping.

Nick had rowed for five years at Middlesex in prep school, though, in his words, he was "sort of a dorky guy." Tall and slender, he had started as an end on the Middlesex varsity football team. He had originally had plans to follow in his father's footsteps and to focus solely on skiing, and had first considered applying to Middlebury College, which boasted a strong skiing program. But an experience while on winter vacation from prep school, skiing with Olympic-level candidates in Europe made it clear to him that Olympic grade performance in that sport was beyond him. "I was a good precise skier," he said, "but in seconds these other guys were halfway down the hill in front of me."

Was rowing the reason he chose Penn?

No.

"I had a girl friend who was a year older, who was a freshman at Penn when I was a senior at Middlesex . . . I was so unhappy . . . I went to Penn because all the year before, I knew all the guys at St. A's (a prominent Penn preppy fraternity) were hitting on her."

(Nick and his Penn girlfriend, Carol Marshall, would marry in 1966 and remain inseparable until her death following a long illness in 2020.)

As a freshman at Penn, Paumgarten had to take a standard battery of physical tests, or as he described it, ". . . that little athletic thing you have to do where you have to run around squares, and things, to show whether you had agility. And then you had to do pull ups, and I could never do a chin up, and there was Joe Burk, sitting underneath the bar, and I thought to myself, 'Well, I'm screwed now.'

"But I ran a little obstacle course, and the fencing coach came up to me, and said, 'Well, Nick, I hear you're an oarsman, but you should become a fencer because you are very quick.' And I said, 'I don't think that's for me.'

"So that's the first time I laid eyes on Joe Burk, and that was a really embarrassing moment. Just like when I came back from my honeymoon, in the beginning of my senior year, when Joe looked at me and said 'Nick, you have some work to do.'"

Nick Paumgarten would go on to great success in life, receiving an undergraduate degree in history from Penn and an advanced business degree from Columbia, followed by a successful career in investment banking and private equity. Yet even now, the memory of Joe Burk, sitting silently beneath the pull-up bar that day in the fall of 1963, while Paumgarten struggled, leaves the younger man humbled.

Such was the power of Burk's reputation, his quiet example, and its role in the molding of a man who would become first, captain of the Penn Crew in 1967, and later the chairman of the Friends of Pennsylvania Rowing.

As the traditional rowing colleges restarted their training programs in the fall of 1963, with at least two teams, the impact of Ratzeburg's 1963 spring performances in America had induced coaches to reconsider their training techniques and their equipment. It is well known that Harry Parker adopted the European boats and larger bladed oars for his Harvard crews in the fall of 1963, he was not the only one. Although not now well remembered, Parker's mentor Joe Burk also tried to employ the larger blades for his crews that year. While Burk did not purchase any European made boats, he did employ the larger bladed oars but diplomatically ordered oars from both American manufacturer Pocock and the German manufacturer Karlisch.

Allison Danzig highlighted the shift for Penn in an article appearing in *The New York Times* on May 1, 1964, entitled "Penn Crew Tries Radical Changes." The article outlined that Penn was "rebuilding from predominantly green material from the freshman, junior varsity and third varsity eights of 1963," but emphasized that "Pennsylvania offers something altogether different this season in its rowing establishment."

At Penn's first spring race in 1964, the Childs Cup against Princeton and Columbia, Burk's Varsity and Junior Varsity raced with what reporter Allison Danzig called "tulip-shaped" blades. In his report of the Childs Cup regatta printed May 1, 1964, Danzig noted:

> The varsity is pulling German oars made by Karlisch, exactly the same as used by Ratzeburg. The junior varsity is equipped with a set of blades of German design manufactured in this country by Pocock. "We switched to these oars in October [1963]," said Burk. "We found that we were definitely aided by them. We go faster. The men like the feel of them and find them more comfortable to row with."[270]

Danzig did note that the Penn varsity and JV that day did not row at the high cadence that both the German crew and Penn crews in past years had used:

The reason for the big drop in the rate was explained today by Burk. The change, he said, is only temporary. It was necessitated by the inexperience of the oarsmen.

"The crew is so green," he said, "and had to work on so many things it had to keep the stroke low. As we develop and gain coordination and smoothness, we will gradually go higher. I expect that by the time of the sprint championships, we will be up to handling our normal rate."[271]

Penn 1966 coxswain Joel Kantor remembered that college race distances before 1964 varied from 1.25 miles up to the three-mile race for the IRA.[272] But the 1964 college season would contain a huge change that while reported, has not been adequately appreciated in considering the effect it had on equipment choices considered by America college coaches in 1964. The Intercollegiate Rowing Association decided that for 1964, the three-mile distance would be replaced with the Olympic distance of 2,000 meters, or 1.24 miles.[273]

Burk would have planned his 1964 equipment choices with that revised IRA championship distance in mind. All Eastern college coaches had watched Ratzeburg struggle with the headwind (and the consequent longer race duration) at the morning heats of the 1963 Eastern Sprints, and then win in the afternoon when there was no headwind.

Burk might have judged that the larger blades were suitable for the shorter 2,000-meter distance, and maybe less than ideal for a three-mile distance.

This is the general theme that Kantor remembers now from 1964. "For the 2,000-meter Olympic race, which was the standard European race distance, crews would use the shovel blade but it was impractical for the 3-mile distance."[274]

Kantor could not recall with certainty whether all races that season were rowed with the shovel blades, but the evidence of the picture and the Danzig article make clear that for at least part of 1964, Burk as well as others would try out the larger European-styled oars. Lyman Perry remembered that in 1964, the CBC Olympic hopefuls Burk was coaching rowed the wider shovel blades, since both the Olympic Trials and the Olympic race were both 2,000-meters.[275]

To an extent now hard to comprehend, Harry Parker's Harvard 1964 crews dominated the college rowing season. Even before the first race of the spring season, *The New York Times* sports section bore the headline "Crew at Harvard Healthy, Hopeful: Varsity Rated as Potential Olympic Trial Contender."

Some observers agreed the Harvard Varsity might have Olympic potential. But most of the rowing world thought the publicity given Harvard at that early stage was unearned and overblown. *One victory over Yale and now the favorite for the Olympics?*

Parker was quoted by Allison Danzig as saying, "We are physically stronger than a year ago. Our replacement strength though makes for a better varsity . . . The question is whether we can come up with the kind of speed required for the Olympic 2,000-meter distance. We have been a better distance crew in recent years . . ." (Meaning better at distances longer than 2,000 meters.)[276] When he said this, Parker may have been thinking of the 1963 varsity rowing like Ratzeburg and not making the Eastern Sprints finals, and rowing their prior style and upsetting Yale at the longer four-mile distance.

Parker knew well the danger of speed at one distance not necessarily assuring victory at another. Parker had been the two-man on the 1955 Penn crew that had been undefeated in shorter races until the IRA with its longer three-mile length—and there Parker and his crewmates had been upset by Cornell and finishing fifth overall. Parker was alive to the possibility that a crew could have strengths at distance and not at another.

But in 1964, Harvard won all its cup races before the Eastern Sprints, and then dominated the varsity race, beating Cornell by a length with Yale third. Burk's Penn Varsity did not make the finals and did not place boats high enough to win points for the Rowe Cup, the heavyweight team championship at the Sprints.

Parker after the Eastern Sprints was identified as an innovator because he had adopted virtually all the Ratzeburg characteristics—wider oars, a European boat, non-sequential rigging: "Using the

German-style tulip-shaped blades with which it had been experiment-
ing, Harry Parker's undefeated, marvelously synchronized eight won
the Eastern Association of Rowing Colleges championship on Lake
Quinsigamond," reported Allison Danzig of *The New York Times.* [277]

Some of the coaches whose crews lost to Harvard at the Sprints
were quick to praise the Harvard crew and its coach. 'A heckuva crew,"
said Stork Sanford whose Big Red were clocked in 6:36 behind Harvard's 6:32 for the Olympic distance.[278]

Harvard's early identification as a possible Olympic boat went against
the fears that both Jack Kelly and Burk had made in 1962 about college eights falling behind European standards. Parker's sudden success as a head coach at Harvard—and his being characterized as an
innovator—did not sit well with Kelly or the other Vesper members,
who had made clear in 1962 that Vesper was attentive to the European
lessons and had brought in a Hungarian coach to Philadelphia to help
the Club absorb the European approach. Since the 1962 article, Kelly
had also brought over a former Ratzeburg oarsman, Dietrich Rose,
and was now attempting to fast-track Rose's application for American
citizenship so he could join Vesper as an oarsman as well as a rigger,
coach, and adviser for the 1964 Olympic Trials.

Even though Parker himself had rowed for Vesper when he had
been the U.S. sculler in 1959 and 1960 when Burk coached him, his
early success as Harvard's Head Coach—and the almost immediate
adulation of the established sporting press—seemed to isolate him
from the world of Philadelphia rowing. *"Too much too early,"* the whis-
pers suggested. *"Parker hasn't quite paid his dues . . ."*

It did not help that Parker was naturally reticent with those he did
not know, which made some take him as arrogant. Once his coaching
record was more established, this same manner was celebrated. One
book on Parker was entitled *The Sphinx of the Charles*, and by 2016
when it was published,[279] the image of the Sphinx carried the conna-
tion of mystery, quiet, and a certain permanence over time.

But Joe Burk in 1964 after the Sprints was quick to praise his student, now turned competitor: "This kind of crew comes along every
ten years or so," he told the press.[280] It was Burk's way of smoothing

Parker's acceptance with older coaches—focusing on the quality of the rowing team Parker had brought to fruition so quickly.

Advocating for due respect for Parker and his crews would prove, for Burk, a difficult task. The younger man's success seemed so precipitous that envy was bound to come, regardless of what Burk might say. The disgruntlement, particularly on Philadelphia's Boathouse Row, would later deepen, and Joe Burk would find himself with two simultaneous roles: that of Parker's mentor and his opponent.

In June 1964 after the end of the year's collegiate season, Burk's College Boat Club eight displayed good early speed. The boating of the eight had been modified by the loss of Frank Shields and Al Doering, who turned to other paths:

Bow	Charles Eddy
2	Woody Fischer
3	Tim String
4	Al Wachlin
5	James Fitzgerald
6	Richard Schwartz
7	Fargo Thompson
Stroke	Lyman Perry
Coxswain	John Hartigan

This College Boat Club crew, rowing the same type of equipment used by the 1964 Penn undergrad varsity—shovel oars and a Pocock boat—won the first major eights race of the season, the American Henley in Philadelphia in early June. *The Philadelphia Inquirer* reporter Frank Bates was impressed with the boat's showing:

A smooth-rowing College Boat Club eight-oared crew made a real bid for the 1964 U.S. Olympic Team when it rowed away from some of the country's best to win the American Henley Regatta on the Schuylkill River Saturday.

Stroked by Lyman Perry, a former Navy oar, and with seven Penn grads and one from Cornell aboard, the Philadelphia crew, considered the dark horse of the field, came from behind shortly after the start and led nearly the entire distance of one mile and five-sixteenths.

The crew trained from the University of Pennsylvania Boathouse all winter and spring under the tutelage of Penn coach Joe Burk, but there was an air of mystery about the boat, even though Burk confided the crew was "pretty good" and aimed to be at its peak for the Olympic trials in New York a month hence.

The CBC boat "under-stroked its rivals at nearly all stages," Bates remarked, and beat a Syracuse alumni boat, and Vesper Boat Club's "big senior crew, steered by coach Al Rosenberg," as well as a Schuylkill Navy eight, and crews from both the Detroit and Potomac boat clubs.

Bates added that a Penn eight had never rowed at the American Henley, but this boat appeared "about to go places . . ."[281]

All Olympic hopefuls moved on to the Schuylkill Navy Regatta held in Philadelphia on June 27, 1964, just two weeks before the Olympic Trials held in New York's Orchard Beach Lagoon. In the interim, the Vesper team had sought to demonstrate what they thought was the true strength of their club's eight.

Vesper's progress in forming an effective eight had until then been impeded by the reluctance of two of its potential members to give up their hopes of becoming Olympians in smaller boats. Brothers Joe and Tom Amlong—longtime members of the club, and each ferociously strong men—had been focusing their hopes on rowing the coxless pair. They had always rowed together, and most frequently it was just the two of them.

When asked to consider joining the eight for the American Henley race, they voiced a preference for the pair in characteristic fashion. As Vesper's Bill Stowe remembered it, "The Amlongs were calling everyone 'pussies,' and were determined to row in their pair where they felt they had the best chance of making the Olympic team." This confidence had been shaken at the American Henley by their loss in the coxless pair race to Jim Edmonds and Tony Johnson of Potomac Boat Club.

Stowe later said that while the Vesper eight had been beaten by Burk's CBC boat, "[t]he best news of the day was that the big-headed Amlong brothers, who chose not to row in the 'pussy' eight in favor of their pair without," lost to the Potomac Boat Club pair of Tony Johnson and Jim Edmonds.[282] That loss—together with a second loss to Budd and Clark in a practice pairs race Rosenberg engineered in order to impress the Amlongs with their vulnerability—set the stage for the Vesper eight as it would row in the future.[283]

The Vesper eight would finally include the Amlongs but would lose stroke Dietrich Rose. Despite Jack Kelly's dogged effort, the former Ratzeburg oarsman had been unable to obtain American citizenship in time to meet the eligibility requirements for the Olympic Trials. As a result, Bill Stowe moved to stroke, and the Amlongs—at their insistence—took the six and five seats.[284]

All of this maneuvering at Vesper was done in full view of Burk and the oarsmen at CBC. It is the nature of life on Philadelphia's Boathouse Row that you row amongst your potential adversaries every day—on good days and bad days. Stowe remembered a Vesper time trial against an opposing eight—not CBC—which was witnessed by Joe Burk. Stowe wrote:

> Somewhere during three-week period before the Schuylkill Navy Regatta we had a practice race against some other eight and Joe Burk—rowing's paragon as Penn's coach—followed in his launch, witnessing the new Vesper combination. At the end of the 2,000-meter row, Rosenberg called over to Burk and said, "My stopwatch failed. I didn't get the time, Joe. Did you?"
>
> Burk responded with his usual shy smile, not revealing the time he may or may not have clocked, and replied, "No. But your guys are very fast."[285]

240

Joe Burk was forever a clear-eyed judge of rowing ability. And he was always the gentleman and would compliment good rowing, whether it came from his crew or an opposing crew. The Vesper crew in its new form dominated the Schuylkill Navy Regatta on June 24, beating Burk's College Boat Club eight by two lengths.[286] Lyman Perry remembered the race over fifty years later:

> And then, right before the Trials, they beat us. And that took the wind out of Joe's ambitions. And I think he said to us, "Well, you're going to have to do more to beat Vesper. Do you want to go to the Trials?"
>
> And I think we all voted to go to the Trials.[287]

The Olympic Trials were held at the Hunter Island Lagoon outside New York City.

On July 8, the eight trials began with sixteen boats contesting in four separate heats of four. *The New York Times'* Allison Danzig identified Harvard and California as the "Top Choices" for the event.[288]

Burk's College Boat Club was in the heat with the University of California at Berkley, idenitifed in rowing circles simply as "Cal." California beat CBC by one and one-quarter lengths, and the Laconia Rowing Association—an impressive mix of MIT and Wisconsin oarsmen—was only half a second behind CBC.

Harvard won their heat by two and one-quarter lengths, and Vesper won theirs by three lengths, both crews rowing with the newer-style shovel oars.

These trials also included the single scullers, and Dave Robinson, who had sculled with Lyman Perry, was in his heat a distant second to Sy Cromwell, the 1964 Henley Diamond Sculls champion. In another heat, former Cornell oar Don Spero won, followed by Jim Storm from San Diego Rowing Club.

The College Boat Club eight had to go to the *repechage* in an attempt to advance to the semifinals, where they surprisingly failed. Burk's chance for a winning eight for this Olympic Team was gone.

Only Dave Robinson, the sculler who had trained with Lyman Perry, was still in contention in the single.

Harvard met Vesper in the semifinals, with two other crews, Laconia and the University of Washington JVs. Burk warned Parker that he had personally timed Vesper rowing 500 meters as fast as 1 minute, 21 seconds, a time that suggested Vesper would be formidable.[289] Burk's warning was prescient: Vesper won, beating Harvard by two lengths, but since the first two boats in each of the two Semis would advance, it was not clear to outsiders whether Harvard had rowed especially hard in the race once Vesper took a lead.

Parker was quoted before the finals as saying he thought the main competition would come from California, whom Harvard had not yet faced. The July 11 final would be between Harvard, Vesper, Yale and California. At the start, Harvard and California got away quickly, and Vesper, whose stroke Stowe said they never started well, trailed in the early going. But Vesper was soon even with California, and about a half-length behind Harvard after 500 meters. Harvard tried to surge at 1,000 meters but made no progress on Vesper, who then surged in reply. "We were able to gain a seat with each stroke," Stowe later wrote.[290]

By 1,200 meters, Vesper had a length, and rowed conservatively thereafter, winning by a few feet of open water.

In the single sculls trials, Don Spero of the New York Athletic Club defeated his former doubles partner Sy Cromwell. Cromwell had just made it back into the country from England after winning the Diamond Sculls at Henley. Third in the single was a tall sculler from San Diego Boat Club, Jim Storm. Burk's own College Boat Club sculler, Dave Robinson, was fifth.

After the finals, Jim Storm approached Joe Burk, and introduced himself. "Because Burk was my hero," Storm said with no embarrassment over fifty years later.

Burk was my hero.

The old champion was most gracious. "Why don't you come down to Philadelphia and stay at my house. We'll get you a single and I'll go out with you on the water and tell you what I see."

Storm was surprised, and delighted to accept.

Burk would host Storm as offered and watch him closely as he sculled up and down the Schuylkill. After the practice, Burk gave the young man encouraging and characteristic advice, "Don't let anybody change what you're doing—you're doing pretty well."

Interesting advice from a champion sculler who carved his own unique path to victory almost thirty years before.

The incident has stuck in Storm's memory, and Storm followed Burk's advice of not allowing anyone to change his stroke too much. Storm would go on to combine with Sy Cromwell to win the double sculls in the next round of the U.S. Olympic Trials weeks later. They would go on to win the silver medal in Tokyo.

Most importantly, Storm remembered fifty years later the warmth and welcome the old champion had given him when he was just attempting to reach the heights that the older man had known for decades. It was Burk's generosity of spirit that impressed Storm.

College Boat Club regrouped and split itself into small boats for the second trials a few weeks later in August. Dave Robinson and Lyman Perry teamed up to row the double. Lyman Perry remembers his parents watching his double in the lead at 500 meters, but his boat was soon passed by the eventual winners Cromwell and Storm.[291]

The coxed four consisted of Charles Eddy, Mark Thompson, Woody Fischer, and Fargo Thompson, with coxswain Jay Furhman.[292] They would reach the finals before ultimately losing to Harvard.

Dick Schwartz, who had rowed six in the CBC eight, partnered with Air Force Captain Wayne Frye to enter the coxed pair, and were coxed by Bob Wisner. They would lose to Conn Findlay, Ed Ferry, and Kent Mitchell—the eventual gold medalists in Tokyo.[293]

All of Burk's CBC efforts had fallen short. But Burk was a realist, a measurer. His numbers early in the summer had given him some reason to hope for victory by the CBC eight, but no assurances. He had watched Vesper Boat Club's eight grow faster and could see the chances for CBC recede. When asked, he had, in his paternal manner, encouraged Jim Storm on a path that would lead to a Tokyo silver medal in the double with Sy Cromwell.

But Burk remained undismayed and looked to the future. Burk seemed to be following the same advice he had given Jim Storm: "Don't let anybody change what you're doing—you're doing pretty well."

During the time period after the Olympic eights trials, Burk also began sharing with the Vesper Olympic eight an invention Burk had been working on to measure the pressure exerted by oarsmen during the rowing stroke, nicknamed "The Wizard." The invention had been developed by John McGinn, a Penn-trained engineer who worked for General Electric, whom Burk convinced to help develop the prototype.

The device itself consisted of a black metal box, with lights and wires hooked to each oarlock, which was equipped with a strain gauge. The box itself was located between the stroke and the coxswain and measured the pressure which each of Burk's eight oarsmen exerted on their oar handles by measuring the pressure in the oarlock pins. The device measured force at four levels, and signaled the level achieved with four lights, triggered at ascending force: 215 pounds gets one light, 240 pounds gets two lights, 265 pounds gets three lights, and 285 pounds gets four lights. [294]

The system also transmitted the lights to a duplicate box in the coaching launch. Each oarsman had a bank of lights at his own station that indicated the pressure on his own oarlock.

Vesper three man Stan Cwiklinski remembered the experience of trying out The Wizard:

Vesper was right next door to Penn . . . so we had a lot of interface with Joe and his gang . . . Joe was always dabbling with inventions, one of which was a strain gauge he put on the oarlocks. So somehow or other, he invited the Vesper eight to row in [the boat with The Wizard] to see who was pulling. Allen Rosenberg seemed to be for it. So we got into the boat and we rowed it around. And Joe and Al were in the launch, where he could observe the goings on in the eight with the strain gauges . . . I think the way it turned out, it didn't mean beans to me, but the Amlongs were concerned about which one of them was pulling more than the other, and Tom Amlong

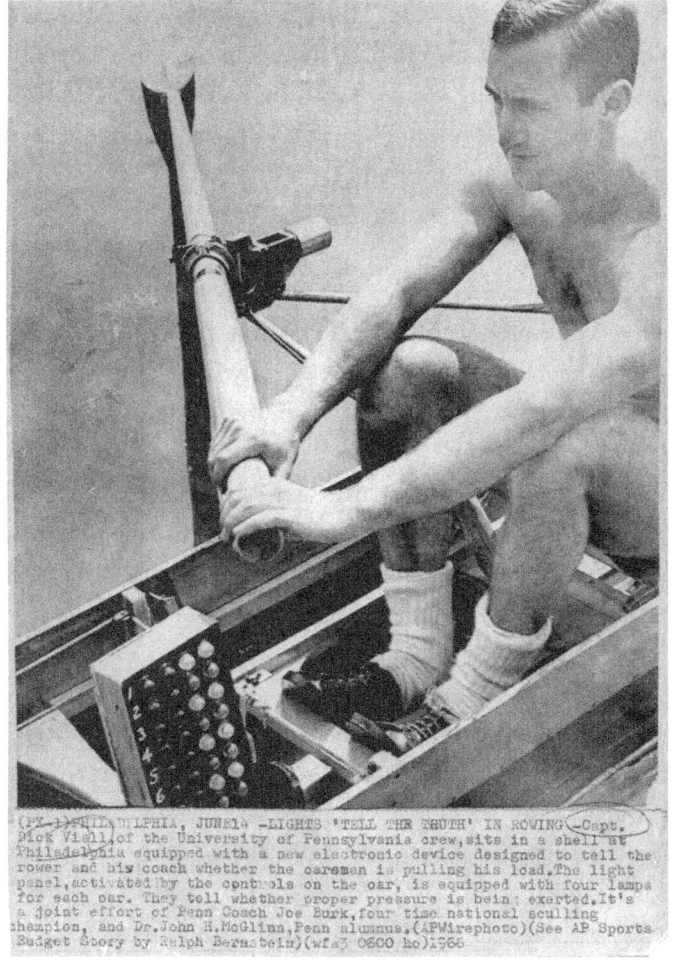

Dick Viall and the Black Box, AP Wire Photo, from Ed Woodhouse collection

finally broke the strain gauge. He was so concerned about a machine that could tell how hard he was pulling, that he pulled it so hard he actually broke the oarlock . . .

Tom was at four, and I was at three..... [295]

Vesper did not ask to use The Wizard again. When asked over sixty years later what he remembered about the Vesper eight's reaction, Vesper adviser Dietrich Rose remembered some of the oarsmen saying: "We don't need that shit . . ." [296]

Harry Parker was named the U.S. small boats coach for the 1964 Olympics by reason of his Harvard coxed four's win at the Trials. After so quick a rise in the world of rowing, Parker found himself leading more seasoned oarsmen like Conn Findlay who had already won medal in two Olympics. It would be a challenge to prove himself in such company.

On Olympic rowing finals day in Tokyo, weeks later, the early races were marred by rough water and at times unfair conditions based on which lanes the crews were assigned. The wind was generally a cross wind blowing from lane 6 across the course to lane 1. The result was the water would be best at 6, and a choppy mess at 1, where the water had collected in waves against the side of the course. The first two races, the coxed fours and the coxless pairs, finished more or less according to the lane assignments—lane 6 winning and lane 1 being dead last.

Parker protested the unfairness of the conditions, and maintained that the unfairness was proved out by the early results. Race officials at first simply said racing would continue. Parker—to his credit—stood his ground and repeated his protest. He even kept Conn Findley's coxed pair in the boathouse for a period while he renewed his protest.

The racing *was* finally delayed for twenty minutes.[297]

When racing finally resumed, the conditions were better, but not good.

U.S. singles sculler Don Spero, hampered by the conditions that day finished sixth in the singles final.[298] He would win the Diamond Sculls at Henley the next year. In good water two years later at the 1966 World Championships, he would win the Gold.

Conn Findlay and Ed Ferry with co Kent Mitchell would win the gold medal in the coxed pair. Kent Mitchel years later would tell Peter Mallory, "We would *not* have won the gold medal without Harry Parker . . . [T]hanks to Harry, we had our chance."[299]

The Stan Pocock-coached the coxless four, with 1960 gold medalist Ted Nash at stroke, would win the bronze medal.

Cromwell and Storm would win the silver in the doubles.

The Vesper eight, racing in the darkness because of the weather delay, would beat the Ratzeburg eight by a length and a quarter to win the gold medal.

CHAPTER TWELVE

1965–1969 Burk Adjusts His Approach

F ollowing the 1964 Olympics, Penn changed freshmen heavy-weight rowing coaches. Jim Beggs, who had coxed at Yale and for the Stanford Olympic coxed pair in 1952, and then coached the Penn frosh for Burk for many years, stepped down. Ted Nash, who had rowed on the 1960 and 1964 four without coxswain, winning the Olympic gold and bronze medals respectively, was named as coach of the Penn freshman crew.[300]

Beggs himself was quoted in Peter Mallory's *The Sport of Rowing* as saying that he had lost confidence, and did not understand the type of freshmen he was seeing coming to college. Those who lived through that era would probably agree that the tenor of college life was changing.[301]

Jim Fitzgerald (Penn '62) maintains today that Beggs was the reason Fitzgerald made it through his own freshman year. Fitzgerald was not lacking in talent—he would later become a distinguished jurist and member of the Pennsylvania Supreme Court. But he struggled with certain classes as a freshman, and Beggs pulled him through with personal tutoring before exams. Other freshman Fitzgerald knew told the same tale.

Newspaper reports of Beggs' retirement were factual and neutral: Beggs had stepped down and Nash had come aboard. Because Nash had stroked the U.S. Olympic coxless four in Tokyo, and the Olympics had not ended until October 24, 1964, Nash did not arrive at Penn until late in the fall.

The fact that Burk had, just a year or two before, inquired of Lyman Perry in 1963-4 whether he might try coaching suggests that succession had been on Burk's mind.

Burk would continue as head coach for the next five seasons at the University of Pennsylvania. Throughout that time, Ted Nash would work with frenetic diligence to recruit, develop and pass on to Burk well-trained, fit, and motivated young athletes with which to form great varsity and junior varsity boats. It was the beginning of a golden age of Penn heavyweight rowing.

Those in the rowing community familiar with both Nash and Burk might emphasize their differences in manner, which contrasted most obviously between Nash's outward bravado, and Burk's quiet mentoring. These differences were clear for all to see.

But there was also a common rowing heritage. Both Burk and Nash were products of George Pocock and the greater University of Washington diaspora. Burk was coached by Rusty Callow (who himself was coached by UW's first rowing coach Hiram Conibear) and later advised by George Pocock. Nash was coached by both Pococks at the Lake Washington Rowing Club.

To a man like Burk, so deeply influenced by George Pocock in the 1930s, and still brainstorming with him about a possible sculling comeback in the late 1940s, Ted Nash fit with Burk's philosophy of rowing as a life-long passion. Neither man had allowed himself to slip into an easy lifestyle. Both remained determined oarsmen themselves.

Nash was a tall, heavily-muscled man, who used his physical presence to influence those he coached. He could be disarmingly persuasive, and when he wished to be, intimidating. He had served six years active duty in the Army as an officer following his graduation from Boston University, where he had rowed. Nash often had stories about combat training, and others, like Stan Pocock, had seen him execute alarmingly daring flying in military aircraft.[302]

The two coaches would in the next four years make an astonishing team: elevating Penn rowing to a dominant position in collegiate rowing. Nash's burly assertiveness would inspire the freshmen oarsman, who in the following year would be passed on Burk, the quieter figure, for further refinement and employment in the varsity, junior varsity, or third varsity boats. While Burk's rowing record could only be found in the history books covering the period before the Second World War, Nash purposefully put his athletic awards and numerous rowing shirts in displays Nash inserted in the Penn Boathouse to keep his charges focused on the ultimate in rowing honors that might lie ahead for them if they lived up to the standards both men espoused.

Nash always demonstrated professional deference to Burk while he served as the senior man's freshmen coach. Nash referred to Burk as *Coach Burk*. The military knew hierarchy, and Nash's behavior was always military.

One of Nash's first acts when he got into the Penn Boathouse signaled to all what would become his approach. Lyman Perry, who was still around the boathouse in late 1964, seeking to enter the Penn School of Architecture, remembered:

> The first thing [Ted] did when he got into the Penn Boathouse—because I was there—he told the freshmen "Line up . . . we're going to shave your heads." And then he stirred them all up with this almost impossible physical routine, because he had been an Army Ranger, and he thought these guys were a bunch of wimps.[303]

Nash would be the first change in the late fall of 1964. But there would be another change. Burk began to rethink his own theoretical framework of training for rowing.

The approach Burk began to study was a training routine that had been developed by Arthur Lydiard, the renowned distance running coach from New Zealand. Burk's son Roger remembers his father

251

beginning the work in late 1964. At the Tokyo Olympics in the late fall of 1964, Lydiard's runners had repeated their exceptional results from the 1960 Rome Olympics, and Burk took notice.

What had looked like a fluke in 1960, two Olympic golds (800 meters and 5,000) meters and one bronze (Marathon), in 1964 looked like a growing trend. Using a framework of constant high mileage running at moderate pace and peaking late in the season with a careful addition of hill running and speedwork, Lydiard's runners again took two golds (1500 meters) and one bronze (800 meters). All this from a coach who had left school at age 16 to train as a shoemaker, who coached only those runners drawn almost entirely from the villages surrounding his own in the Auckland area.

The New Zealand Amateur Athletic Association was at that time largely staffed with socially prominent people, who in their middle and late years enjoyed attending meetings and events and largely left the athletic training and coaching to athletes and coaches who would, as in Lydiard's case, work for free. Lydiard's obituary in 2004 stated that "his running revolution was not embraced by the establishment."[304] Those were measured words. Lydiard thought most of running's administrative hierarchy and all orthodox distance running training was foolish, and he would tell anyone who would listen.

Joe Burk was one of those who listened.

Lydiard developed his training theories in the early 1950s, using himself as a guinea pig. His earlier background had been in rugby, but his self-developed running training—in which he ran up to 250 miles a week—allowed him to run for New Zealand in the marathon at age of thirty-three in the 1950 British Empire Games,[305] where he finished twelfth.

Roger Burk remembered the form and color of some of the Lydiard material his father obtained in late 1964:

> Lydiard wrote a little pink pamphlet that Dad got—and thought this is the way we should be going. With the University of Washington sort of long-distance training—but he would take it to another level and then use the interval

training method [advocated by Karl Adam] as merely polishing tools at the end.

So all of a sudden in . . . the last four years of his coaching career . . . he started having the twenty-mile non-stop workouts . . . the East Germans had come to the same conclusion . . . I can guarantee you that people were saying Dad was copying the East Germans. No. He was copying Arthur Lydiard . . .

In the early sixties, he was beginning to try to copy Karl Adam . . . but from '65 on, he was copying Arthur Lydiard.[306]

Roger confirmed that earlier in the 1960s, his father had learned to read German so that he could follow the success and philosophy of Karl Adam and the German approach to rowing that had garnered such success in the 1960 Olympics. But Burk's emphasis on Karl Adam's interval training now changed. The long-distance training that Lydiard prescribed would constitute a far greater proportion of the training Burk prescribed. Timed 500 meter pieces would be the focus only for "polishing" as racing approached. Even then, the intervals were mixed with long recovery rows.

Burk must have sensed that his 1964 approach to College Boat Club's 1964 training had contained some errors. The center of the Adam approach had emphasized carefully measuring a crew's progress in racing over 2,000 meters by testing speed over 500-meter pieces in a repeated fashion—up to eight to ten repeats of 500 meters—a quarter of the race—with limited rest while the boat turned around to cover the same water in the opposite direction.

This was Burk's approach in the summer of 1964 with CBC. Lyman Perry remembered:

When we were training . . . and [Burk] was trying to figure out if we would go to the Trials, we would row ten 500 [meter pieces] back-to-back. And they ended up being 800 [meter pieces] because we started 300 yards before the [starting line] . . . and [Burk] would be on the mark . . . [so] we would be up to speed when we hit the [start of] the 500-meter mark.

If we could hold the speed, we could qualify in his mind to be a good boat. That was one of the methodical ways he used.[307]

But how had the 1964 Olympic season played out for College Boat Club? Burk likely focused on the fact that the CBC eight was fast in its earliest race—which it won—but seemed to slow down relative to the Vesper boat over the summer. Likewise, Lyman Perry's double in the Olympic Trials final had been first at 500 meters, but had faded to fifth at the finish, suggesting that the season's peak of the double had been reached and passed with perhaps too much interval work speeding the decline.

Burk must have suspected that he had over-tested the team in his quest to obtain a true sense of the speed of his crews.

As Roger Burk had described it, Arthur Lydiard's approach was similar to the University of Washington's rowing approach of building up long, steady mileage throughout the whole year in gradually ascending distances and speeds. But compared to a race pace at 2,000 meters, the speeds of these long, aerobic, practices pieces were between 70 and 90 percent of the final race speed.

The benefit of this approach was to gradually allow the athlete's body to adapt over many months to the ascending training load, building what is now generally accepted as the precursor of all good rowing—a massive aerobic base. Only in the few months before the racing was the Adam interval training method needed—and then only sparingly.

Lydiard in a recorded talk in 1963 said that many runners "would come to hand pretty quickly"—meaning the speed of the intervals done would increase without much effort.[308]

In Lydiard's mind, until the season was underway, a wise coach deferred bringing on the peak that hard interval training and testing led to.

Barry Magee, Lydiard's 1960 Olympic marathon bronze medalist, remembered receiving dire warnings when he starting working with Lydiard. One fellow runner told Magee Lydiard's methods were dangerous: "He'll kill you Barry! He'll kill you. Don't do it!" Those warning Magee were assuming all work was done at a killing pace. They were wrong. Magee himself found Lydiard's method, with its gradual and measured lifting of athletes slowly over time to their peak, brought the grocery store owner an Olympic bronze medal in the Marathon.

Burk, whose own training methods in the single in the 1930s had at the time been deemed extreme, likely viewed the independence of Lydiard's thoughts in a favorable light. Lydiard, like Burk, had thought through his training on his own. In the hills around his home in Auckland, New Zealand, Lydiard had been as alone as Burk had been on Rancocas Creek in New Jersey. Left to their own wits, both men had found their way forward.

Burk in 1965 would not be alone. Lydiard, a garrulous, opinionated man with big heart, had not been shy with speeches all over the world advocating his approach. He influenced the training regime which Oregon track coach Bill Bowerman used to develop scores of long-distance runners, such as Olympic talents like Kenny Moore (4th Munich Olympic Marathon), and Steve Prefontaine (4th 5,000 meters Munich).

Burk began to shift Penn's training in the fall of 1964. Interestingly, two *New York Times* articles in 1964 reported that individual runners from Yale and Harvard had both improved their distance running after each of their parents had separately arranged for their sons to train with Arthur Lydiard for three months in New Zealand.[309]

After 1964, Lydiard began to train distance running coaches in other countries, including East Germany, Finland, Japan, and Mexico. In East Germany, with its state controlled and standardized development of sports coaches, the rowing coaches soon learned to apply the Lydiard techniques used successfully by the running team.[310]

Burk's new approach followed Lydiard's key suggestion: practice rows were longer and generally in stretches without stops. Burk would have races every Friday, and Nick Paumgarten, then a sophomore, remembers you got a number assigned for how your boat did in the Friday races, which were usually between three boats:

> You started at the top of the Schuylkill and you rowed three miles down, and the first boat got ten points, the second boat got seven, and the third got five. Don't get fives! And at the end of the year, Joe would give—would actually carve—three oars [for the three highest point getters] . . . Nobody but me ever won three oars [during my three seasons of rowing for Burk].
>
> . . . My first year [rowing for Burk, 1964–65], I was in first place in the last race of the season. We rowed in the morning in those days—it was *dark*—and I finished [in the] third boat. And [the competition for points] was so tight that year that I went from first to third in that one race. But I got an oar.[311]

But Paumgarten was clear—the boatings for the spring 1965 races were not strictly done by points on the races. The prize for being one of the top three point getters that year was to get one of three-foot model Penn oars Burk had built in his shop. It was Burk's own judgment that determined who would sit in the Varsity or JV. Paumgarten spent time in both.

Paumgarten also remembers rowing in the seven-seat as a tall and slender sophomore in an early spring line up that did some practice pieces against the then re-forming Vesper eight, which contained five of the eight oarsmen[312] who had won the 1964 Olympic gold medal the year before.

Paumgarten remembered the day: "In my sophomore year, I was rowing briefly at number seven, if you can believe that . . . I was six foot two, and hundred and sixty-eight [pounds]. We lined up against the Vesper crew—about half of them were the same guys who won the Olympics. The seven-guy in the Vesper boat was Fargo Thompson, who went to Penn.[313] He and I have been friends forever, his wife Nina, who was in my class, she was an Olympic swimmer. And so Fargo says, "Nick, what are you weighing in at these days?"

And I looked over and whispered, "Oh, f**k . . ." Then to Fargo: "Well, I'm one sixty-eight, Fargo, what are you?"

"Two fifteen."

Paumgarten added, "That's the last time I saw them in that practice."[314]

Penn's varsity got off to a promising start in 1965, leading Yale until the final moments of the Blackwell Cup, when the Elis pulled ahead. At that point, the Penn Varsity boating was:

Bow	Rusty MacMulllan
2	Jack Barclay
3	Steve Sawyer
4	Bob Dubbs
5	Steve Dexter
6	Henry Saltonstall
7	Phil Seaton
Stroke	Mark Thompson
Coxswain	Jay Furhman

The Penn JV won its race by a slender about half a length.

The Penn freshmen, trained but not recruited by Ted Nash, finished second to Yale.[315]

In the Adams Cup, Harvard won all races by wide margins, and the Penn Varsity was not able to match second place Navy in the three-way race, finishing third.[316]

The 1965 Eastern Sprints were a disappointment for Penn. Neither the Varsity nor the JV qualified for their six-boat finals. But Ted Nash's freshmen crew were beginning to surge, finishing 4th in their finals. Harry Parker's Harvard crews swept all three heavyweight races.[317]

In the Madeira Cup contest against Cornell on May 23, 1965, the Penn Varsity—an average of eleven pounds per man lighter than their Cornell opponents—lost by two and one-half lengths. The JV lost by almost four lengths, and the freshman by a length. The race in Philadelphia was also the site of the tenth reunion of the Penn 1955 Henley crew, celebrating the tenth anniversary of their win.[318]

Before the 1965 IRA, Burk's continued use of the black box strain gauge device in practices and some races generated publicity. The *Philadelphia Daily News* published a brief article entitled "Penn Crew Really Wired For IRA Test:"

> Penn's varsity is on the hot seat, even though the Quaker crew isn't picked to win the Intercollegiate Rowing Association Regatta here today.
>
> They're on the hot seat, because the shell has been wired electrically, with the wires hooked to a string of bulbs that tip off the coxswain as to how much effort each rower is making in applying himself to his sweep.
>
> "It's been a big help," Burk says. He has juggled his crew on the basis of the readings on the gauge, which was installed a month ago.
>
> John Barkley is Penn's new stroke, presumably because his wattage is high. While Penn's crew is improved, it is still ranked a longshot in the tough unwired field.
>
> Cornell, Washington and California are rated among the favorites with Brown and Navy in the darkhorse category.[319]

At the finals of the IRA, the Naval Academy boats swept all the races that year. In the fourteen boat Varsity final, Penn finished eighth out of fourteen entries. The newspaper articles about the race results took no notice of "The Wizard" or Penn's use of it.[320] Burk was nowhere quoted what he thought of the device's first racing test. As sometimes happens when innovations are being tested, the rowing world's attention was elsewhere.

The attention of the U.S. rowing community was at that time largely focused on a brewing controversy between Harvard and Vesper Boat Club. On Wednesday, June 16, 1965, before the IRA, the tabloid *Philadelphia Daily News*, published an article concerning the increasingly bitter rivalry between Vesper leader Jack Kelly and Vesper coach Al Rosenberg on the one side, and Harvard coach Harry Parker on the other.

The feud between Vesper and Harvard was driven in large measure by the positive press the 1965 Harvard Varsity was receiving for its undefeated streak in collegiate rowing. The reigning 1964 Olympic champions at Vesper took umbrage over what they viewed as Harvard's attitude of superiority and what Kelly and Rosenberg viewed as the Harvard coach's reluctance to test whatever claims of greatness Harvard had in a race against Vesper before the two met at the Henley Regatta. The article, entitled "Vesper Crew Is Up in Oars Over Harvard's Runaround" . . . began:

> When the Vesper crew finally gets to row against Harvard at England's Henley next month, they may need barbed wire for the lane markers.
>
> Not since the Monitor and the Merrimac collided have two American crews exchanged the kind of sniping that's been going on between the Olympic champs and the college folks.
>
> "The Boston papers have been calling Harvard the wonder crew," Jack Kelly says, "so when we got to the American Henley last week we looked around and said, 'Yep, they're the wonder crew . . . we wonder where they are today.'"

Daily News reporter Stan Hochman characterized the rivalry with journalistic precision: "All season long, America's top two crews have been avoiding each other, and nobody wants the blame."

Hochman deftly outlined the competing claims:

> "We could have met them in the Eastern Sprints," Vesper coach Allen Rosenberg says grumpily. "But our application was refused by the colleges. The year before they invited

Ratzeburg, the championship German crew. The fact that Vesper is this year's world champion somehow escaped them."

"When they didn't get into the Eastern Sprints," says Harvard coach Harry Parker, "we invited them to a race on May 22 [a week after]. They didn't even bother to reply."

Hochman noted that Parker had rowed at Penn but neglected to note that Parker had sculled as part of Vesper Boat Club in 1959 and 1960. Whatever club loyalty Parker had earned as a 1959 Pan Am gold medalist, and 1959 Diamond Sculls and 1960 Olympic finalist, all representing Vesper, was apparently inconsistent with the journalist slant developing.

It would get more extreme.

In its June 28 issue that year, *Sports Illustrated*'s cover featured a picture of the Harvard 1965 varsity in midswing forward. In the foreground, as if standing on a platform above his crew, was Harry Parker in a red polo shirt, arms folded. The caption read: "Harvard Coach Harry Parker and the World's Best Crew."

In fairness to Harry Parker, it is unlikely that the editors at *Sports Illustrated* asked for Parker's input on the subtitles to be used if the magazine chose to put the Harvard crew on the cover. Parker was taciturn in public—one book written about him years later was titled *The Sphinx of the Charles*—and guarded in what he said to the press in terms of predictions or assessments. This was the style he had seen with Burk and with Tom Bolles.

And caught in the middle of this controversy—ever maintaining warm relations with each side—was Joe Burk, a man who praised all good rowing, wherever it occurred.

It was the same generosity of spirit that Burk had learned firsthand from his own coach, Rusty Callow, when Penn broke Navy's multi-year winning streak in 1955. The old lumberjack's call, shouted heartily from his launch to Burk's right after the race, "Congratulations."

No qualifications. No side comments. No bitterness.

"Congratulations."

Harvard and Vesper finally met overseas—in the semifinal of the Grand Challenge Cup at Henley in July, 1965. Awaiting the winner of that heat, on the other side of "the draw" that determined how the winning crews would advance, was the 1965 Ratzeburg crew, the same crew, down to the man, that the Vesper Olympic champions had beaten in the darkness of the Tokyo final the year before. The Vesper crew had three substitutions on its crew, Fargo Thompson, Penn '62, rowed at the seven-seat. Bill Stowe's Cornell teammate John Abele rowed at five, and Tony Johnson—formerly of Potomac Boat Club, and the bow of the U.S. Olympic coxless pair in Tokyo, was at four.

ABC's *Wide World of Sports* covered the Vesper-Harvard race live, and early in the race itself, the broadcast announcer noted the rivalry between Harvard and Vesper, and quoted Vesper coach Al Rosenberg as emphasizing the size and the athletic maturity of the Vesper crew by saying of Harvard, "They are boys, and we are men."

It made for good copy.

Vesper beat Harvard by a full length, setting a Henley course record in the process, and blowing the claim of the *SI* cover out of the water. Jack Kelly must have felt vindicated.

Harvard's loss to Vesper in 1965 after appearing on *Sports Illustrated* is still discussed today among oarsmen old enough to remember the event, and students of the sport devoted enough to study the controversy. Among sports enthusiasts, often over beer, there have been discussions about a phenomenon called the "*Sports Illustrated* Curse." Fans would often bemoan that the fortunes of their team seemed to drop suddenly after the team had been placed on the cover of *Sports Illustrated*. The Parker cover and the words used by the magazine, "the world's best crew" seemed to fall into that category. Such a designation asks the question: How does the "world's best crew" get beaten by another within weeks of the *SI* publication, and then that winning crew is itself beaten by a third?

Articles have been written in several popular magazines that seek to explain the phenomena. Those who like the "curse" theory will remain unpersuaded. The scientific explanation is a statistical concept called *reversion to the mean*.[321] The greater the deviation of any one event from the mean of such events, the greater the probability that the next event will deviate less far. Wolfram MathWorld summarizes for the number-impaired: an extreme event is likely to be followed by a less extreme event.[322]

This *SI* cover is still remembered with derision today in parts of the rowing world. This picture and its caption have erected a wall of bitterness between the Boston and Philadelphia rowing worlds that has yet to be entirely torn down.

Vesper met Ratzeburg in the Grand Challenge Cup final. The Germans started at over 50 strokes a minute and grabbed an early lead from Vesper. Vesper clung to Ratzeburg, with each rowing at or near 40 strokes a minute down the course. Closer races have rarely been run. But Ratzeburg won the Grand Challenge Cup at Henley by "a canvas,"—about 8 feet.[323]

Vesper—their attention now fixed upon their old West German rivals Ratzeburg—accepted the Germans' invitation to race again in Ratzeburg the week later. The results were the same: Ratzeburg by a bigger margin because one of the Vesper oarsmen caught a crab near the race's end.

Bill Stowe remembered years later that the two crews went out and drank far too much after the race in Ratzeburg. "We all got drunk, and the Vesper guys sang to their Ratzeburg opponents, 'You won the race, but we won the war.'" Alcohol had apparently allowed both crews to think it was funny.[324]

Almost sixty years later, Fargo Thompson would remember the Vesper '65 eight—"I look at that boat as the strongest I have ever rowed in."[325] While Vesper crews in later years would assemble able eights, that 1965 boat was the last effort for the majority of the Tokyo gold medalists.

In later years Harvard would continue to post impressive records in both the collegiate season and in international competition, but their major collegiate opponents would be different. Joe Burk's Pennsylvania crews would gradually work their way back to the top to row against Parker's Harvard crews on roughly equal terms.

Part of the reason for Penn's ascent *vis a vis* Harvard during this time period had to do with the torrid efforts Ted Nash as the freshman coach was making in recruiting young athletes to come to Penn. The Olympian undertook this task with the same uncompromising approach he had used in winning two Olympic medals: he did everything he knew to do get likely freshman to come to Penn, and if at Penn, to row.

Sean Colgan's father Charlie had rowed for Penn in the 1947 Seattle Invitational. By the late 1960s, both Colgan's were fixtures on Boathouse Row. Sean remembers the extent of Joe Burk's recruitment before Nash's arrival. "Joe Burk's recruiting would be to send my father season tickets to the Penn football games, figuring my father might put in a good word for Penn to some the local high school graduates he knew might row in college. That was all."[326]

Nash began a letter writing campaign to any young athletes he knew—whether they had rowed or not—urging them to consider applying to Penn. Those that showed interest would be invited to visit the campus, perhaps on a football weekend. Tickets would be provided for those who expressed interest.

Such energetic work by Nash was paying off.

At least by the time Nick Paumgarten had advanced from the freshman crew in the fall of 1964 to the varsity squad, Burk had added a small additional incentive for the Friday intra-squad races. Each week, the oarsmen and coxswains were awarded five points for a third-place finish, seven points for a second-place finish, and ten points for a first-place finish. The three people with the highest scores in the practice races would be awarded at the end of the year a three-foot long miniature Penn oar, which Burk had made in his workshop.

Paumgarten won the first of three such oars in his first year on the Varsity, in the season ending in spring 1965. Until the start of the 1967–8 season, the model oar was the only certain reward for a Penn Varsity squad member could be assured of for one of the top three point winners. Before that season, Burk's judgment of the overall performance of oarsmen and coxswains, on the water, with The Wizard or without, determined who made the varsity, the jayvee, or the third boats.

As the 1965–6 season began, Joe Burk kept using The Wizard in practice but made a change—he discontinued use of the wider German-style blades used in 1964 and 1965 and returned to the traditional narrower oars made by George Pocock. Thereafter, as long as Burk was head coach, Penn oarsmen would row with the narrower blade.

At the start of the 1966 collegiate season, in the April 14, 1966, edition of *The New York Times,* reporter Allison Danzig noted Burk's return to the American traditional narrower oar in an article entitled "Penn Rejects German Influence in Favor of U.S. Oars and Shells". The Ratzeburg visit in 1963 was recited as the start of the trend of American crews adopting European equipment and training techniques, led by Harvard and Vesper. But Danzig pointed out that Joe Burk was returning to the traditional American equipment:

> ... strangely Joe Burk has refrained from jumping on the bandwagon. Rather, he has dropped off. He is one of the few coaches who is not employing some feature of the "new wave of the future" in rowing. He is standing by the standard Pocock oars and shell.
>
> "We will stick to the conventional old-fashioned oars and equipment," said the Penn coach, a great oarsman in his college days and twice a winner of the Diamond Sculls.
>
> "Perhaps you could say this is typical of Pennsylvania. But we have used foreign oars and we have rowed high and rowed low and we have come to the conclusion that you win if you have the horses and you don't win if you don't have them."

The article ended with Burk's measured comments about the upcoming year. The strong 1965 freshmen were now entering Burk's squad, which Danzig said would strengthen the team. Burk made special mention of Dick Viall, whom Danzig said was "the first Pennsylvania captain who [had] never rowed in the varsity."

"Viall is the best captain we've ever had. He weighs only 160 pounds. Pound for pound he is the best oarsman I ever had," Burk told Danzig.[327] Leadership in the Penn Crew was not size related. One of Viall's boatmates remembers him today as "lightweight in size, but very inspirational as a Captain."[328] Captain in 1967 Nick Paumgarten says today "I was voluble as a Captain—Dick did it better, he was a steadying influence."[329]

In 1966 Steve Gladstone was in his first year as coach of the heavyweight freshmen at Princeton. He is today convinced that Burk's success as a coach was based on his being open to innovation, but only when tested against long established training principles in rowing. And while Burk was not afraid to try innovation, he was equally unafraid to discard it when the evidence so indicated. To Gladstone, Burk's returning to the narrower oar blades in 1966 was a sign that in Burk's judgment, a better blade had not then been introduced.

"There was never any evidence," Gladstone said, "that the Macon [another term then used for the symmetrical wider blades used by Ratzeburg in 1963 and thereafter] were faster than the pencil blades. The real, the profound point, and obvious change [in oar blades] was when people went to the 'hatchets.' [meaning oars with asymmetrical shapes where the blade edge nearest the water is far wider (and thus deeper in the water) than the upper edge of the blade.]

"Interestingly enough," Gladstone said "the pencil blades had greater wetted surface area [when compared to the Macons]. And the Macon shape, the Macon shape is just pretty. It has nothing to do with [efficiency], if you think about it, why would you have the same amount of material on the leading edge and the top edge. It was just very pretty."

"Like so many things in life, it was monkey see, monkey do," said Gladstone. "And Ratzeburg was having success, and they happened to row the Macon shape."

Gladstone relayed the history of the turnaround in American collegiate coaches at the time of the Ratzeburg visit in the 1960s: "The

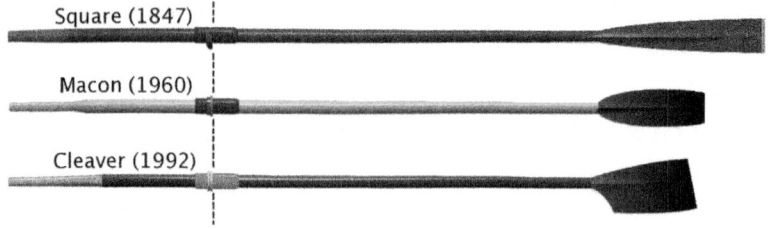

Evolution of the oar according to Wikipedia.

history, [in 1966] . . . all the masters [of U.S. coaching] were gone, or on the way out. And the new groups that came in, they were not that schooled, they did not come out of a tradition of . . . *very simply they did not have the guidance of George Pocock that all the older guys had had* . . . they were all newbies.

"So they were very susceptible to this new thing of interval training . . . that Ratzeburg introduced. And I can remember when Karl Adam came over to the United States, he was a very very generous guy with his knowledge, and he was giving a lecture down at Vesper Boat Club, and I was standing next to Stan Pocock, and just taking notes and sucking all this up, and Stan sort of leaned over to me and said, 'Well, that set American rowing back ten years' [Pocock meant the focus on intense intervals rather than long steady distance work]."

Gladstone continued: "And of course it did. It set it back, and of course when the East Germans developed [their international rowing program after 1965[330]], they went back to the same thing all our old coaches were doing, a lot of miles, and at low cadence. So Stan was spot on. The Ratzeburg thing was very much in vogue, none of it understood, it was all imitation."

"As I said, the only person who did an analysis of training from a physiological standpoint, interestingly enough, was Joe. And he did it [originally] tooling around in his single."[331]

Burk's habit of innovation while rowing had simply carried over to his coaching.

Burk was fascinated throughout his rowing career by the quantification of effort. How hard an oarsman was rowing was not a matter only of judgment, but of measurement. Burk's focus on measurement had driven his own progress as a sculler on the Rancocas Creek, and now drove his fascination with The Wizard, first used in Penn practices starting at the end of the 1964 season and thereafter. The Wizard was as data driven as the work Karl Adam was doing advancing the fortunes of the Ratzeburg crew.

The Penn oarsmen over time developed a certain ambivalence about *this* innovation. Some feared that the device meant there was nowhere to hide if you were having a bad day. That much was undeniable.

They began to joke among themselves in crude terms that their coach had a love affair with the machine. Others simply saw that it was another measurement point and simply tried to light the lights. Others began to theorize that there was some way to "rig the system." Speculation arose that by hitting the catch hard, an oarsman could light all the lights up but not pay the price of full effort thereafter.

What Burk noticed a boat with the box turned off (Penn had only one), if given it was turned on the next day, would perform better than the day before. The major question in his mind was whether the fifty pounds of extra weight offset any benefit from the enhanced effort the machine induced in the oarsmen aboard.

The Penn Varsity, using The Wizard in the first two Cup Races in 1966, won both. In fact, the whole team did well, although only the Varsity had The Wizard. In the Childs Cup against Princeton and Columbia, all three Penn boats, the Varsity, JV, and Freshmen won—the frosh by a huge five length margin.[332]

At the 1966 Adams Cup in Philadelphia, a Harvard Varsity with only one returning oarsman rowed the first part of the Henley distance about a length ahead of both Penn and Navy. Nick Paumgarten up in his bow seat remembered that his boat went well in the early going—Harvard was leading but not gaining. Paumgarten could see the lights of one of the Penn oarsman drop off—slowly at first, then suddenly. The Harvard Varsity began to pull away. Harvard's margin would be three lengths at the finish. Penn barely managed to pass the Navy Varsity near the race's end.

The Penn JV did better against the Harvard JV, lowering the Harvard JV victory margin by one and half lengths. The Penn freshmen—the first class both recruited and coached by Ted Nash—beat the undefeated Harvard frosh boat. Coxing the Penn frosh boat was Ken Dreyfuss, who would later become Captain of the 1969 crew, and a member of multiple U.S. National Teams, and later a coach at numerous schools including the Naval Academy. [333]

At the Penn Boathouse, as the coaches and crews gathered after the race, Burk shook hands with Parker, and said, "Congratulations, Harry!"

Penn captain Dick Viall, stroke of the Penn JV boat, overheard Parker's response to Burk's congratulations: "That settles some old scores."

Viall was surprised by the younger coach's tone. *What scores needed settling? Why not just say 'Thank you'?*

In later years, Viall recalled the stories around Boathouse Row about Joe's being able to beat Parker when they sculled together during Parker's 1959 and 1960 competitive seasons. Viall said later "it's conceivable that Harry still had a chip on his shoulder." But he had no doubt of the words. "As Joe and Harry walked into the Penn Boathouse right in front of me, I was stunned by Harry's comment."[334]

Burk had determined by May 1966, that while the Wizard's weight would not be a disadvantage at longer distances, at the 2,000-meter distance of the Eastern Sprints, it might be. Penn thus did not thereafter use it at that race.[335] The Penn Varsity qualified for the Finals, but finished sixth at the back of the pack, 13 seconds behind winner Harvard. The Penn JV finished fifth, thirteen seconds behind the winner Cornell. Ted Nash's freshmen won over Harvard by a bare tenth of a second.

At the very end of the 1966 college season, the Penn heavyweights were not expected to do especially well at the IRA, an event that would gather all the crews save Harvard and Yale for a final three-mile race on Lake Onondaga.

Burk decided to have his varsity use The Wizard, and for the first time, some rival coaches expressed concern. According to *Sports Illustrated*:

. . . there were immediate cries of unethical by some officials, but Burk points out that the wizard does not make the boat go faster. The rowers do that. All it does us tell them how. Like a stopwatch, only better. Confronted with such logic, the race committee gave the wizard its tentative blessing, and Penn went out and finished eighth in a field of 15. No celebratory bell began to peal at this result, but when you consider that Penn was picked to finish dead last, it was something to ponder.[336]

At the time of the article—June 6, 1966, before the IRA—Burk explained to the *SI* reporter the effect the lights had on the oarsmen who were given that feedback. Burk had two boats racing one another. The boat with The Wizard in it had the device turned off. After one test piece, Burk instructed the coxswain of The Wizard boat to turn the wizard on, and that boat surged ahead on the next piece. "It was amazing . . ." Burk said.

Burk also pointed to the bow and two-man of the 1966 varsity, Nick Paumgarten, 6'3" and 175 pounds, and John Henderson, 5'11", 175 pounds, and said, "they would never have rowed for the varsity except they kept the lights winking. They were simply much stronger than they looked."[337]

The *SI* staff were quick to note in the article that Burk used the box to quantify and predict how Penn would do with a consistent light achievement versus its opponents, and that Burk had done the same thing himself when he sculled in 1936 to 1940. He would predict a pace that would lead to victory and then stay with it. According to the *SI* writers, the Penn boat, like Burk in his single in the thirties, would maintain an even pace and a high cadence. In the years to come, they would frequently be victorious.

The magazine writers' assessment that The Wizard was part of Burk's plan to estimate a winning pace overlooks that Burk was estimating winning paces years before The Wizard was built. Fred Lane remembered Burk looking for even splits with the Penn Henley-winning crew back in 1955.

The magazine writers were quite correct in pointing out that Burk was respectful of tradition, yet fully able to discard it if he thought of a better idea:

> Besides snapping his oars in and out of the water at a rate that approached pure frenzy, Burk [in the 1930s] also ignored the advice of experts who urged him to race the other fellow, not himself. Burk was very respectful of the old ideas, because he is that kind of person, but he simply did not believe them. So he began sculling with a cheap pocket watch stuck between his toes. "I had a definite stroke I knew would be good enough to win," was Burk's theory. "If the other fellow went off ahead of me, I let him go. He'd come back to me if I stuck to my stroke."[338]

While the *Sport Illustrated* article about The Wizard acted as "the teaser" to pique interest in the race, the more important story was the overall Penn performance on race day at the IRA, which showed a squad with gathering strength. Ted Nash's freshman crew won for the first time since 1924. Steve Gladstone's first Princeton frosh crew led the Quakers for over a mile and a half of the two-mile race before the Penn frosh passed them and gradually opened a one and one-half length lead, rowing at 40 strokes a minute at the finish.

The Penn JV, stroked by Captain Dick Viall had great race, taking second behind a Dartmouth crew that had in prior races *been designated as the Dartmouth Varsity*. Under the odd circumstances, the men of the Penn JV could reasonably conclude—as some did—they had really won in the JV category.

The Penn varsity, rowing with The Wizard aboard, finished fifth in the three-mile final, which was won by Wisconsin. The *Times*' Allison Danzig called the victories by Wisconsin, Dartmouth and Penn "unaccustomed glory."

Penn's overall glory was arguably the greatest, because the University won the Jim Ten Eyck Trophy, awarded to the heavyweight team with the best overall performance, for the first time in the school's history.[339] Progress had been made in the whole Penn heavyweight program, and those team members not graduating naturally looked to the 1967 season with high hopes.

Burk's re-focusing of the varsity training to emphasize the long, continuous workouts was slowly reshaping the Penn rowing program.

There is no evidence that Burk used The Wizard after the end of the 1966 season. No Penn oarsman interviewed for the book remembers why the device slipped out of use at Penn. Little is remembered of The Wizard's history today. No records have been found about whether the machine was ever disallowed, and a question recently posed to the U.S. Rowing website about whether the current rules would allow the machinery went unanswered. The current rules do not appear to prohibit such a device.

Burk's black box was the harbinger of the modern-day rowing ergometer as well as the EmPower oarlock, both of which today measure power applied by the oarsman in much the same fashion as The Wizard did in the 1960s.

During this same time period, Roger Burk stopped rowing in sweep boats (one oar per rower) for the University of Washington, and instead sculled (two oars per rower) in his single exclusively, often with fellow sculler Al McKenzie. He stored his single at George Pocock's workshop and spent much time with old master. Roger remembered an instance where Pocock had received a package from Ted Nash, which contained a Pocock seat with a proposed refinement to the design, and a note from Nash advocating its adoption by the Pocock works.

Stan Pocock had much praise for the Nash's toughness and had coached him to Olympic Gold and Bronze medals in 1960 and 1964 respectively. But Pocock *pere* looked askance at the burly rower's design suggestion. "He told me who had sent the seat," Roger remembered, "he examined it briefly, and then ran it through a band saw right in front of me."[340]

By the fall of 1966, the entire Penn heavyweight rowing organization was primed for the intense effort that would be needed to beat

Harvard. Nick Paumgarten, having rowed hard enough to get into the varsity for two years as a sophomore and junior, was electcd captain of the 1967 Penn crew at the start of the 1966 summer.[341]

Paumgarten was known for his loquacious encouragement of his teammates from the bow seat of the varsity—"I was known as *the Voice* at Penn . . ." he said with a laugh.

Many of the Penn oarsmen rowed throughout the summer to stay in shape for the coming collegiate season. Paumgarten had done so the preceding summer of 1965, boating from the University Barge Club. But *this* summer, 1966, he was getting married on June 24, and honeymooning with his bride in Europe.[342] The couple did not return until college started again in the fall.

When Paumgarten first bumped into Burk in the boathouse that fall, Burk looked at the rower's frame—grown thinner during his summer without workouts—then said very quietly, "Nick you've got some work do."

The remark brought back the sense of trepidation Paumgarten had first felt while dangling from the pull-up bar, nose-to-nose with Joe Burk on his first day at college, three years before.

Burk, perhaps again studying his Lydiard literature, had decided over the 1966 summer that still higher mileage was the key to Penn's further improvement. The date of the first day of the varsity squad's practice, Burk brought the team together in the second-floor varsity locker room and announced the new regimen just before the fall's first practice. He had not discussed the details with anyone beforehand—not even Nick Paumgarten, that year's captain, who heard the details for the first time that day with everyone else.

"Burk brought us all into the locker room and said, 'We'll row 18 miles a day and 24 miles on Saturday. We are going to draw all the boats out of a hat, use the point system [prior years' races were limited to Fridays only], but this year every day is a race day.'"

Paumgarten remembered the squad being silent as Burk announced the far more demanding schedule. The coach gave no reasons for the changes, they were simply outlined.

"When Joe was finished, he walked down the stairs, out to the dock, and stood next to his launch with his hands in his rear pockets, waiting. There was then a protest upstairs."

Sophomore coxswain Ken Dreyfuss, then in the varsity locker room for the first time as a member of the squad, said, "*I remember that day.* Some oarsmen said 'We're quitting. We're not going to do that. We didn't sign up to do eighteen miles on a Tuesday, that's crazy.'"

Nick Paumgarten then took his first action of the year as Captain. "Are we rowing for Joe," he asked, "or not. *I'm* rowing for Joe." Nick resisted the temptation to go right down, because he wanted to see how the squad would react. The room was silent for a few moments, and then one oarsman started down the stairs toward practice. Then another. One of those who had protested then cried out, "Shit! . . ." and himself started down the stairs. "God dammit," said another protestor, and started down. Soon the whole squad was in the boat bay, and the shells were being carried out.

In addition to the longer practices, and constant racing, Burk extracted an extra measure of effort from those he deemed as carrying too much weight. "The fat boy squad," as Paumgarten called them, were required to run after practice from the boathouse upstream and back for a distance most remember as three miles.

The Penn oarsmen followed the regime, but the upward adjustment of the miles rowed extracted a price. Nick Paumgarten remembered, "I'd just gotten married and I don't know how much I saw of my wife in the evenings . . ."

In retrospect, Paumgarten thought that however much the long mileage helped with the endurance, the team could still have benefitted from more emphasis on rowing technique. "I never thought we looked that good—shooting your tail, where your arms are at the catch, there's little bit of individual taste, but there is a little bit of professionalism about it, too. Anyway, I think Harry [Parker] spent a lot of time it . . . but we didn't."[343]

Gardner Cadwalader was part of the freshman crew in the spring of 1967. He had cause to visit the small office both Burk and Nash shared at Weightman Hall and remembered years later the difference in office style between the two men. Cadwalader was struck by the difference in how the two men operated in that confined space—working side by side and apparently without rancor.

Nash, whose wide-ranging and energetic recruiting efforts are remembered today by oarsmen who received them, got a lot of mail in response to his wide solicitation of potential young oarsmen. The surge of responses would leave Nash's desk overflowing with letters and lists, and the file drawers assigned to him would hang open as if he were forever in mid-search.

Burk, by comparison, would have no papers on his desk whatsoever. He would routinely receive, read, and respond to correspondence immediately, and seemingly without effort. Papers were not on his desk—they were filed.[344]

Skimmer Day at Penn was scheduled for April 23, 1967, as Penn hosted Princeton and Columbia in its first season race. Penn swept the other crews, with the varsity winning by just under two lengths, and the JV and frosh boats winning decisively.

In the 1967 Adams Cup, the Penn oarsmen had reason to feel they might have a chance against the Harvard crew. Earlier in the season, the Harvard varsity had been run hard to defeat a Northeastern crew in the first race of the season. It was Northeastern's only third season of crew. English coach Ernie Arlett, whom readers will remember had hidden behind Burk in the bicycle line after provoking Stuart MacKenzie at the start of a heat of the Diamond Sculls at Henley in 1962, had become the sculling instructor at Harvard's Weld Boathouse before starting the program at Northeastern. Then in his third season at Northeastern, Arlett had the pleasure of seeing his varsity lead Harvard until the final moments when one of his oarsmen caught a crab, allowing Harvard to slip by for a narrow win.

Doubters wondered if cracks in the Harvard façade were beginning to show. The Penn frosh lost by one length, but the Penn JV won by over fifteen seconds, or more than three lengths.[345] Burk's squad, now gradually bolstered by the steady stream of Nash-trained freshmen, might prove deeper than Parker's.

But the hopes were premature. The Harvard varsity beat Penn by almost three lengths.

At the Eastern Sprints, Harvard again won the varsity race, and Penn was second. But the margin was smaller—two lengths, not three. Penn was second overall, with Northeastern sprinting fast to finish third.[346] Harvard also won the frosh race, and Penn the JV race.

After the Sprints, Howard Greenberg was moved up from the Penn JV, which at that point had lost no races that season. Burk had first begun to see the young man's tremendous potential in the tanks in Weightman Hall when he coached Greenberg early in his time on the team.

"Howard Greenberg came in and made a difference," said Nick Paumgarten, recalling the change. "He helped with the boat's swing, he was a great personality, and you know, these things matter."

Greenberg, like all Penn oarsmen worked to make his way through the point system Burk was then using for Friday races. What had impressed Greenberg as he had worked under Burk was his coach's abiding fairness.

"Joe had a thing to choose boats—I remember it was the Friday races—and you got rated on those Friday races. And one year, one of those Friday races fell on a Jewish holiday—Yom Kippur, I think—so I said, 'Joe, I can't do it, I can't make it.'

"So I assumed I would get a zero, because I didn't show up. What you did performance wise he had always averaged out with your most current score. But in this case he took my average for all the other races, and he gave me the average for [the missed race] race. Because he thought it would be fair. I was just touched by that."

Greenberg would graduate from Penn and go on to law school. He has just recently retired from law practice as this book is being published. He never forget his old coach's example. A picture of Joe Burk, given to him by his 1966 JV boatmate Roland Steiner, hung on the wall of Greenberg's law office until the day of his retirement, it was then brought to his home to hang in the study.

Penn's last race before the IRA was the Maderia Cup against Cornell. Often the latest Eastern college getting on the water in the spring, Cornell could be especially dangerous at this point in the season, as they rowed themselves into shape for their peak race, the IRA.

The revised Penn boatings more than met the Cornell challenge that weekend. The Penn Varsity, with Greenberg aboard won by 16 seconds, the JV by 23 seconds, and the Frosh by 35 as astonishing seconds. Penn returned to Philadelphia to make their final preparations for the IRA weeks away.

Soon after their return, the relatively calm of collegiate athletics was roiled by a dangerous turn in world affairs—the Six Day War between the Arabs and Israelis from June 5 to 10 of 1967. Howard Greenberg remembered:

> I remember distinctly, Joe would sit at this little, tiny table in the varsity locker room, and he would read *The New York Times* in the morning as we were changing. And Joe—who had been a heavily decorated World War Two hero, which he never talked about, he didn't tell you that—he was reading it, and I could tell, he was clearly rooting for the Israelis, because they were against incredible odds, and they won the war.
>
> Burk was impressed. He was clearly impressed.
>
> Those were the two things [his attitude towards the Israeli armed force and not penalizing Greenberg for his absence from practice during Yom Kippur] that made an impression on me. He was a one hundred percent fair man . . . nobody fairer . . . and it didn't matter if you were a rich guy, a middle-class guy . . . there weren't too many poor guys at Penn.
>
> If you went to prep school, if you had a background in rowing . . . I never saw a boat until I got to college. Nothing mattered but how you performed. What greater encouragement could you give to an athlete—particularly one new to a sport[347]

Nothing mattered but how you performed.

Nick Paumgarten in his senior year, Captain of the boat, had a habit of speaking to the crew, and the coach, as practice went along.

> On a morning practice in June the week before the IRA, Paumgarten remembers the scene: We were above the island, going up the course, it's seven in the morning, it was about ninety degrees out, no humidity, a great morning to row, no wind out, the sky was absolutely desert-like red, sun was coming up, and I'm looking around, and I'm talking to people, and I see this frickin' dead body to my right . . . and I said, "Joe, Joe . . ." The boat kind of comes over, he's got his megaphone, and I say, "Joe, there's a dead body here."
>
> And Joe says, "We'll get him on the way back."
>
> It's a true story, and it did happen. But rather than do that, Joe took his boat over to where the park guards were [and informed them].[348]

When asked about the same general story having been told about Ted Nash, and published in *The Book of Ted*, Paumgarten, at the time of the interview the Head of the Friends of Pennsylvania Rowing, said, "Well, that's such bulls**t. It was Joe."[349]

By this time, the college rowing season had settled most internal disputes by race results—Penn the day before the IRA was considered the favorite in all three boat classes—varsity, JV and frosh eights. "Joe Burk says—and the competing coaches agree—that his Pennsylvania crews can win all three races Saturday in the Intercollegiate Rowing Association championships," said *The New York Times* in a teaser article before the race.[350]

Ted Nash's freshmen won by almost eight seconds, or two lengths, over the two-mile freshman course. Penn's JV eight was second to Navy in a race where an incredible storm created unequal conditions that penalized the superior Penn JV. The varsity crew won the three-mile race—the last IRA that would be rowed at that distance—beating Wisconsin by two lengths and with Cornell third. "Penn, rowing at a steady, distance-eating 33 strokes a minute,

Joe Burk left, 1967 Captain Nick Paumgarten with Trophy, and IRA official. (From Nick Paumgarten collection.)

moved into the lead a mile from the start and steadily pulled ahead the rest of the way."

The aerobic base formed by Penn's long-distance practices had shown over the three-mile race. The Photo here shows Joe Burk with Captain Nick Paumgarten holding the IRA Cup awarded minutes before the picture was taken.

Penn's entire heavyweight performance ensured they captured the Jim Ten Eyck Trophy for the second year running for best overall heavyweight performance. Immediately after the race, Penn, beaten only by Harvard, announced it would compete against the Crimson in the trials for the [U.S. eight berth in] PanAmerican Games next month in New York."[351]

The tenor of the IRA was captured by *The Philadelphia Inquirer* columnist Frank Dolson, who published a long piece on the details of the hours leading up to and after the race, entitled "Long Hours of 67-Year Wait". The article described how various teams were busy with enthusiasm displays—painting on bridges near the racecourse—while the

Penn men arrived without such materials or ritual routines. "All they carried was the weight of the collegiate rowing world on their shoulders," Dolson wrote.

"'Why so glum?' Coach Joe Burk asked Nick Paumgarten, his varsity bowman, as the group of all well-muscled athletes strode silently past.

'We're not glum,' Paumgarten replied. 'We're ready.'"

Ted Nash told Dolson that Burk was "as keyed up as I ever saw him," but then claimed the head coach was good at hiding it. Ted was wearing his "lucky shirt."

Dolson asked Burk whether he had a lucky item.

"I gave up charms when I was sculling . . . if you depend on a charm and you lose it, you're finished."

Dolson noted that Burk was dressed in his usual style for the IRA—a buttoned-up blue blazer. All IRA victory photos from this year and two future years would show Burk in a blazer, dark trousers, and business shoes.

Burk could have been silent—but he mentioned how long the wait until the finish seemed to be, and then observed, ". . . the longer you coach, the longer you live, the more you realize something can happen."[352]

Burk's words were prophetic—but applied in this instance to the race after the IRA. Four days after the Penn victory at the IRA, the *Philadelphia Daily News* published a small news note in the sports section that read simply:

> Pennsylvania University's IRA championship eight is preparing to compete in the Pan-American crew trial July in New York City.
>
> The Penn crew will be missing senior Howard Greenberg and coxswain Art Sculley from its varsity boat, but coach Joe Burk will fill in with Pieter Fosberg and junior Dave Carroll. Also entered in the trial is Harvard, [the only] crew to defeat Penn this year.[353]

The *Daily News* also published a long sports profile of Burk the day before the Pan Am Trials for the eight at Orchard Beach Lagoon in New York City. Entitled "Penn Out to Make Big Splash in Final Test", reporter Ed Conrad sought to give color to a local hero now embarking on a large mission.

> Penn's crackerjack crew goes after a big fish tomorrow—a victory in the Pan-American Trials—and coach Joe Burk thinks they can make the catch. "It won't be easy because one of our opponents, Harvard, is undefeated in 28 consecutive intercollegiate races," confessed Burk. "In fact, they beat us twice this year."
>
> "But we know we have improved since those two losses to Harvard, and the question is if Harvard has improved a great deal since then."

Characteristically, Burk offered a note of realism: "One of our jobs preparing for this years' Pan Am trials is getting our heads out of the clouds. The longer time you haven't won something, the higher the clouds."

Burk also mentioned the difference in distance between the three-mile IRA and the 2,000-meter Pan-Am (and Olympic) distance. Burk also mentioned Harvard's larger size, and the quality of the two Vesper entries.

Conrad's piece concluded with what he understood at the time was the case—but turned out to be incorrect: "If Penn wins, the season will be extended indefinitely but if victory escapes the Quakers, the season will more or less grind to a halt."[354]

The trials for America's Pan American Team took place at the Orchard Beach Lagoon in New York City. There were four crews—Harvard, Penn, and Vesper Boat Club's "A" and "B" crews. The Vesper "A" crews still contained three of the 1964 Olympians from Vesper's Tokyo boat. That crew took off from the start at 50 strokes a minute—reminiscent of Ratzeburg's Henley start against Vesper in the Grand Challenge Cup final at Henley in 1965.

Vesper's lead dwindled as Harvard came back in the second 500, and Harvard led at the 1,000-meter mark. Burk's Penn boat then made its way past Vesper into second but could not gain on Harvard. Vesper's stroke Bill Stowe sprinted furiously at the end, and Vesper slipped by Penn to finish second, but with Harvard still ahead by a length.[355]

Nick Paumgarten told Peter Mallory years later that the Penn boat sorely missed Howard Greenberg, and "we just fell apart." Paumgarten said the chemistry was different. No one person's fault—Penn's chances had just been impaired by the loss of Greenberg. [356]

Nick Paumgarten would attribute Penn's improvement in the 1967 season to the long distance put in at Burk's insistence. Paumgarten noted that the distance work the Penn crew did mirrored the mileage done by an international champion sculler who had been successful that same year: "After two Olympic silver medals, the East German sculler Achim Hill, won the European Single Title that year of 1967. His training was based on mega-miles, and that's what we had done, too."[357]

Some of the Penn eight stopped rowing after the Pan Am trials in the eights. But since the spring, Ted Nash had been eyeing the possibility of one of his freshman oarsmen, Gardner Cadwalader, rowing in a coxed pair with a big senior rowing as the seven man of the JV boat, Robbie Meek, with coxswain Jay Fuhrman aboard. He proposed the possible combination to Gardner sometime in the spring. Cadwalader had spent a year in the freshman boat—which in all boathouses of the period meant being largely ignored by the upperclassmen. He was surprised when Nash asked him to join a senior in the coxed pair. He readily agreed.

Nash was broadening his role at Penn, and Burk seemed willing to let him do it. Having established himself as a reliable recruiter and supplier of well-trained athletes to Burk, Nash had begun to think of possible opportunities beyond the strict role of freshman coach. He was looking well beyond the college schedule—and imagining boatings beyond the eights.

Nash felt if Penn won in the eights, fine. But if not, Nash's own Lake Washington experience showed there was championship rowing to be done in the small boats. Cadwalader was convinced Nash had shared his thoughts with Burk.

The return to small boats had been a strategy Burk had used as a coach with the College Boat Club in 1964, and Nash had been part of the same strategy at Lake Washington in 1960 and 1964. As the 1968 Olympiad approached, why not try whatever was possible?

Nash's plan for Cadwalader and Meek was the first of many promising small boat combinations Nash would envision over his coaching career. Burk's main goal at that point was to get ever closer to Harvard in the eights. And the results showed that he was succeeding.

The margins of Harvard victories over Penn were gradually diminishing. Perhaps the next year Penn could win in the eights at the Olympic Trials.

In the denouement of the 1967 international season, Harvard won the gold medal in the Pan American Games, and the silver medal in the European Championships in Vichy, finishing less than two seconds behind the winning Ratzeburg crew. While no one then realized it, the Harvard race in Europe would represent the final high-water mark for U.S. college eights in international competition.

Gardner Cadwalader, Robbie Meek, and Jay Fuhrman would win the gold medal at the Pan Am Games, and then finish eleventh the European Championships. East Germany's Achim Hill—employing the same long mileage routine Burk had employed that season—would win his last international medal, winning the gold medal in the single at Vichy.

All eyes were now turned toward the '68 Olympic Games.

CHAPTER THIRTEEN

The Student at Harvard vs. The Master at Penn

Penn's long-distance practices, which had provided the massive aerobic base for the strong 1967 performances, continued in the fall. Sophomore Gardner Cadwalader, after a brief respite away from practice due to his late racing at the Pan Am Games and the European Championships, rejoined the varsity practices in the mid-fall.

The goal for this year's work: Win. Beat Harvard. Go to the Olympics.

Coach Burk was conducting races each Friday and awarding ten points for first, seven for second, and five for third. The point totals would determine who sat in the Varsity, JV and Third boats.

Races would occur each Friday the teams rowed, and the result would continue to be counted during the racing season, so the varsity boatings of one week might change in the next week.

Most followers of Penn rowing had been aware of intra-squad racing for points, but very few focused on whether there was a one-to-one correlation between race point totals and boatings. Many

The King of Clubs card Cadwalader carries
to this day

did not understand that at the start of 1967–68 season, Burk made the announcement that the race results would be binding—even on Burk.

Through the vagaries of Friday race results, Gardner Cadwalader, identified in the 1967–1968 Penn playing card system by having his name written on the King of Clubs, suffered a long series of defeats in Friday practice races. The reason for such defeats is not clear. Cadwalader as a freshman had had a full international season—as good a run as anyone in the boathouse—and had taken time off, at Burk's recommendation, at the start of the fall. Still the losses came.

It was as if the card itself was weirdly unlucky. Gardner Cadwalader to this day still carries a King of Clubs in his wallet. He produces it as a talisman against the bizarre string of luck he had during his sophomore season. *Slam!* "This was the card of death," he now recalls. "I lost thirteen straight races in Joe Burk's point system which gave me numerically impossible average to ever get in the varsity boat."

With the help of a few Penn faculty, some oarsmen who were

critics of the point system—and Roger Burk and his sister Kathy remember those critics certainly existed—had earlier tested the statistical validity of the point system and reported to the coach that it was found wanting.

Gardner Cadwalader seemed to be the 1967–68 season's poster child for such a statistical challenge. He already had by that time an impressive athletic career. He had played football and rowed in the first boat St. Andrews for three years—taking only his senior spring racing season off. He had played freshman football in the fall of his first year at Penn, but then returned to the water and rowed so well on Ted Nash's freshman IRA winning squad that Nash had managed his inclusion in a post-season coxed pair that had brought home a Pan Am gold medal.

But the anomaly of the King of Clubs remained. Cadwalader would start the season in a Third Varsity four. But he would receive an extraordinary opportunity at the end of the regular season—one he would seize, to the benefit of Penn rowing.

The collegiate eight-oared season in 1968 was, to a large extent, a fight between Harvard and Penn for supremacy—which all expected would lead to the winner constituting the U.S. Olympic eight.

As tradition dictated, Penn and Harvard met for the first time at the Adams Cup, held that year at Annapolis on the Severn River. Both Harvard and Penn varsities were undefeated. Navy was struggling.

Penn won all the preliminary races: Second freshmen, First freshman, Third Varsity four race—where Pan Am gold medalist Gardner Cadwalader was then mired—and JV.

Each of the races had been rowed on flat water. But as the varsity crews reached the stake boats, the wind on the Severn River shifted and the water began to get choppy.

Penn's varsity went off the start at 42 strokes a minute and took an early lead over Harvard, which was rowing at 40. By the 1,000-meter mark—the race had been shortened to the Olympic distance of 2,000 meters—Penn held a lead of about seven seats, meaning the stroke of Penn boat was about level with Dave Higgins, the bowman of the Harvard eight.

If that big a lead could then be increased, Penn might slip away and not be caught. Burk must have thought the tide was turning for all Penn's boats. But the Harvard eight took a surge at 1,000 meters, and by the 1,250-meter mark—the Route 50 bridge over the Severn—only 750 meters to go, the crews were even.

Penn was spent. Harvard's boat drew further and further away as the finish line approached. At the end, it was a two-length victory.[358]

Harvard and Penn were scheduled to meet again in one week's time at the Eastern Sprints on Lake Quinsigamond in Worcester, Massachusetts. Since at least the mid-1960s, the University of Pennsylvania had operated on a spring semester schedule that gave Penn a significant sports disadvantage at the Eastern Sprints, since in the week before that race, Penn had exams. Most other schools, such as Harvard, who had exams after the Sprints.

For Adams Cup races, Penn and Harvard oarsmen were on an equal footing each could race the other without having faced the disruption in schedules that exams would have posed. But at the Eastern Sprints, Penn's exam schedule would be a disadvantage.

Characteristically, Burk never complained publicly.

At the Sprints, Nash's Penn freshman heavyweights won the frosh final by two lengths, an unusually large margin. The Penn Junior Varsity won by a length. Harvard crews were second in both races.

In the varsity race final, Harvard met its goal of not losing ground to Penn at the start. Harvard coxswain Paul Hoffman was quoted as saying he thought the start had been crucial. "We jumped out a full seat on the first stroke," he said. "We had to, after last week."

The Penn Varsity clung to Harvard all the way down the course. There was no Penn fading at the end of the race like the week before. It was a far closer race, but Penn lost by just less than a boat length.

Notwithstanding the pressure of exams, Penn had cut the Harvard margin of victory in half in one week. Harvard's time of 5:54.5 was recognized as showing both teams rowing near Olympic levels.[359]

The two American collegiate eights viewed as the principal opponents at the Olympic Trials each took a different path. The Harvard crew's next race was the four-mile classic in New London, Connecticut, against Yale. Penn's next race would be a dual meet with Cornell—and then the IRA where it would oppose all the best collegiate crews except Harvard and Yale.

For Harvard, the Yale race was a formality, a tradition to be kept up, but no challenge. The Yale crews were not up to the task, and the races would be a formality. All of the Harvard crews won decisively.

Penn's Madeira Cup race with Cornell was less than a formality. Cornell had a history of picking up speed late in the racing season and surprising the unsuspecting at the end of the season. But this year, Penn's crews were dominant—Penn won all three races decisively.[360]

During the week before the IRA, the *Philadelphia Daily News* ran an article about Burk and the Penn crew. It was a warm endorsement of a coach who had seen good and less than good results—and maintained his resolve through it all.

Stan Hochman had penned the article—entitled "A Tough Crew":

. . . You cannot knock what the Penn crew symbolizes. These are young men doing tough work because it is what they want to do. Not for money, because there is no such thing as professional rowing and besides coaches are skimpily paid.

And the way Joe Burk runs crew at Penn! Race after race after race during the week. Shuffling the crews by flipping cards. And letting the results of those midweek races determine who rows in the varsity boat.

What it does is snatch away the crutch of alibi. No one can claim that the coach does not like his posture. Or his haircut. Or his attitude. Or the way he sticks his oars in the water.

"What it does it does is make men out of them," Burk said earlier in the afternoon. "They come face-to-face with life in the raw. They have to stand on their own two feet.

"I don't believe in the omnipotence of coaches anyway. So many of them make it sound like putting the pieces of a jigsaw puzzle together. As though this man can only row number five and not number three or number seven. Me, I just want to put the best eight men in that boat.

"The test of a racer is going head and head against someone. The point system makes every practice race a real race.
By the time we get to the IRA (Thursday) they will have
rowed 125 races.

"You're more anonymous in rowing than in any other
sport. They don't do it to get their names in the papers, because half the time the names are misspelled. They do it for
inner satisfaction. Like mountain climbing."[361]

Burk's words quoted above have in them the ring of Rusty Callow.
Both coaches, when describing what was their real goal in coaching,
do not describe victory but the formation of character through seeking and bearing the challenges inherent in sports. To the modern ear,
the words seem old-fashioned, even quaint.

Perhaps they should be studied afresh.

In 1968, the distance to be rowed at the Intercollegiate Rowing Association Regatta in Syracuse was changed to 2,000 meters, the Olympic
distance. Burk had supported the change, which had been mentioned
by Jack Kelly as far back as the 1962 *The Philadelphia Inquirer* article as
being needed for American crews to match up better with their European counterparts in international competition. If an Olympic berth
was the goal of college eights, then race the Olympic distance.

This change in college rowing has endured down to this day. Many
young oarsmen think the four-mile race of the Harvard-Yale is an
anachronism. It is, and as of 1968 and the change of the IRA distance,
it was the last such spring race in America.

On race day, Nash's freshman won by a length and a half—their
third consecutive victory at the IRA—and sent an enduring message
that the Penn heavyweight pipeline would be full for years. The junior varsity, remembering that they had been denied victory by a freak
storm the year before, surged to a two-length victory.

The varsity had a slow start, but rowed through the field, beating second place Washington, the Western favorite, by one and
one-quarter lengths. It was the first three boat sweep by Penn of the
heavyweight races in the seventy-four year history [including war

years] of the regatta. Since Penn had been one of three founding members of the IRA, it was hard to imagine a more complete victory for Joe Burk and his coaching methods.

Within a few days, *Sports Illustrated* would come out with a story on Burk's team's sweep, which would trumpet the victories as the triumph of Burk's card system: "A Straight Flush for Joe Burk" would headline a two-page article with a picture of Penn overtaking and then pulling away from the University of Washington eight.

Within the article, Burk would be quoted: "I like the card method, because it keeps everyone working with the hope that he'll make it up to the varsity boat. Day after day we row, until the consistently good ones come to the top like cream."[362]

But before the *Sports Illustrated* Article could be printed, Joe Burk would set aside the card system and use a different system for the selection of the Pennsylvania entry into the Olympic Trials. And two oarsmen, the first, Luther Jones, a member of the freshman boat who had not been eligible to row in the varsity, and the second, Gardner Cadwalader, already a Pan Am gold medalist who had not earned a seat through the card system for the varsity, would get their chance to join the Penn Varsity and line up against Harvard and the other crews vying for the U.S. Olympic eight oared berth.

There is an irony that as the *Sports Illustrated* IRA article was going to press, Burk was changing the selection system that the article would tout in print.

Freshman Luther Jones, a tall, muscular high school athlete who had grown up in Blackfoot, Idaho, had greeted his father and two brothers when they reached Syracuse days before the start of the IRA. The three men had driven the 2,100 miles from Blackfoot to Syracuse, east through the Great Plains, through Omaha and Chicago, and then up to Syracuse.

The three westerners were there to watch the races and then to drive back to Philadelphia with Jones, pack him up, and drive with him back home to Idaho. Jones had already packed up his things in Philadelphia. But with Penn's victory in the varsity race, new plans were afoot, and Jones was to find himself pulled into the coming change.

Ted Nash approached him just after the varsity had won their last race. "Luther, Coach Burk wants to talk to you."

Nash always said, "*Coach Burk*."

"I thought, 'Oh crap,'" said Jones. "'What's that going to be because I was ready to go home.'"

"So I went back to the boat trailer, or somewhere, and the coach said basically he's like me to stick around and see if I could make a seat in the trials boat—for the Olympic Trials. He said, 'I won't guarantee anything, but we'd like to give you a chance.'"

Burk was repeating the move Ted had suggested for Cadwalader the year before in 1967: bring the strongest freshmen up early to strengthen the team. In that year, it had been for filling the coxed pair. In 1968, it was to strengthen the Penn Varsity eight.

Jones did not agonize over the decision.

"I went and told my father and told him to turn around and head back home. But what they did, they followed me back to Philadelphia, and we chatted in Philadelphia for a day, and then they took off. That's when my career with Joe got started."

Gardner Cadwalader, then in his sophomore year at Penn, had only been able to work his way up to the jayvee boat by the time of the IRA. He was gratified by the jayvee win—but then surprised with another sort of victory following close on its heels. After the race, Joe Burk asked him to come back to the Penn Boathouse and also try out for the trials boat. Cadwalader readily agreed.

But Cadwalader must have wondered—*Why was Burk not using the card system as the method of selecting the crew for the Olympic Trials?*

Only two men had full knowledge of the making of the decision to consider adjusting the Penn first boat after the IRA: Joe Burk and Ted Nash. Neither are here to give us their stories, and there is no record of either ever having given a detailed explanation of their thinking. But we can infer from what both had said and done in the past to construct a fair picture of what they likely considered.

Without doubt, Joe Burk would make the final decision, but the inclusion of Nash's freshman Luther Jones in the possible mix makes clear that Nash had been consulted. All oarsmen who ever rowed for

Nash know he would have given his views to Joe without reservation, but with the deference Nash felt "Coach Burk" deserved.

The training between the IRA and trials would involve comparing the speeds of the crews with various combinations—including some "seat races"—where rowers are switched between two completing boats, or between sets of speed trials in one boat. These techniques were used because there was neither sufficient time nor enough people available to race two eights for a continuation of the card system computation.

The card system that had developed to be a maker or breaker of all who rowed for Burk was to be set aside. This was change enough, but there were further modifications in the selection process—less well known—which involved an oarsman never associated with Penn rowing.

That oarsman was former 1964 Vesper eight Gold Medalist Joe Amlong. Amlong in the summer of 1968 was still rowing at Vesper, next door to Penn. When the Penn team came back to Philadelphia, at some point Amlong suggested to Burk that he would like to be considered for inclusion in the eight to further strengthen the boat. When this request was made is not known—as Burk, Amlong, and Nash have all passed.

Few now living remember the details of how Amlong was evaluated—but this much is certain: Cadwalader recalls that while Amlong was tried out for a few practices, Burk finally decided to keep the boat an all-Penn crew, and Amlong was not included, although it is Cadwalader's recollection that he had won the seat races in which he had participated.[363]

In the end, two of the three seniors in the boat, 1968 captain Phil McKinley and Nick LaMotte, were replaced by Gardner Cadwalader and freshman Luther Jones. The boat would be rearranged so that both Jones and Cadwalader sat in the "engine room," the four seats in the middle of the boat where the biggest and strongest oarsmen were traditionally placed. McKinley and LaMotte would go to Long Beach as spares, in case either a port or starboard oarsman might get sick.

It is a testament to the high regard all the Penn oarsmen had for Joe Burk that the change from the earlier card-driven system was met with acceptance and deference to Burk's judgment. The Penn oarsmen's past experience with Burk had convinced them that he would be fair in his selections.

The ultimate quality of the Penn effort at the Olympic Trials and the oarsmen's view of their coach would wear well over the years.

The 1968 Olympic Trials represents a watershed moment in collegiate rowing. The intensifying Harvard and Pennsylvania rivalry, which existed between both crews and coaches, one the former teacher of the now-ascendent younger coach—would engage the attention of *The New Yorker* magazine and its most prominent writer on sports, Roger Angell.

Those who have read Angell know his delightful style—his piece remains one of the best examples of a beautifully-paced, elegant prose not often found on the sports pages. He had the advantage of having rowed at Harvard in the 1950s. Angell focused on the appearance of the Harvard crew when he visited them before the race in their dorm rooms at Long Beach, the site of the Trials:

> No matter how many of [the Harvard Varsity] were there, the room seemed crowded, for they were large, thickly muscled young men, averaging two hundred pounds. The room also seemed stuffed with hair. None of them, apparently, had wasted any time at the barber's in the previous months. They resembled athletes from another age—a band of Ralph Henry Barbour heroes.[364] I counted three separate mustache styles.[365]

While Angell did not note explicitly the difference between the "Harvard hair" and the crew cut, military style of the Penn crew, he did mention that the Harvard men had engaged in some "lighthearted disparagement of the Penn crew's intensity and generally gung-ho attitude toward the sport."

The Harvard guys in the room described how at the Eastern Sprints "they had heard the Penns roaring like Storm Troopers as their carried out their shell."[366]

The Penn oarsmen still had a hair length standard under Burk and Nash. Angell was noting what anyone who visited a college campus the year of 1968 could see. There was a growing divide over Civil Rights and the Vietnam War. Martin Luther King Jr. had been assassinated in April, and Robert Kennedy had just been assassinated after winning the California Democratic primary in June.

In *The New Yorker* article, Angell portrayed Burk enjoy[ing] "a Poseidon-like eminence at the Trials, for in addition to the Penn eight he had at one time or another coached five of the single-scullers vying of the singles berth at the Trials, as well as the Vesper stroke, and Harry Parker who is a Penn graduate. Burk is a lanky, remarkable affable man, with the weathered look of a Maine lobsterman. He twice won the Diamond Sculls at Henley, and he was a much-decorated PT-boat skipper in the Pacific."[367]

Before the race, oarsmen from both Harvard and Penn had, like trial lawyers, elaborated the advantages each side enjoyed. The Harvard men emphasized their experience, the Penn men their gradually improving performance against the Harvard boat over the three races already rowed.

Angell concluded "I instantly discarded any long theories I had developed about the two crews. If their positions had been reversed— if Penn had been on top for five years and Harvard had been on the rise—they would have spoken each other's words."[368]

The race itself was perhaps the most exciting eights race in American rowing. Penn led Vesper after 500 meters by less than a second, and Harvard by a second and one-half. Vesper fell off the pace of Harvard and Penn at 1,000 meters, and Penn continued to lead Harvard, rowing a beat or two higher. Penn still led by one and a half seconds at 1,500 meters.

Roger Angell was standing near the finish line:

The shells surged toward us up the bright water, quicker and larger, bending and reaching together, and we were all on our feet and shouting. Harvard's stroke of thirty-nine was holding Penn's of forty-one, and now the Harvard sprint began. The beat rose and then, incredibly, rose again, with Penn roughening and splashing a bit now and Harvard, the nearer shell eating up the margin . . . Harvard was gaining visible inches at each exchange. They went across the finish line together to the sustained, incredulous roar from the banks, and there was no way—absolutely no way—to tell which had won."[369]

Jim Dietz, who had competed in the singles trials, remembered being near Burk as the two crews swept by. "He had his blazer and tie on and looked very distinguished."[370]

It took the judges seven minutes to review the finish photo. Ultimately, they determined that Harvard had won by four inches. Bill Tytus, who was also at the Trials as a contestant in the singles trials, was standing right next to Joe and Kay Burk when the results were announced.

Joe Burk was silent at the news, a slight smile remaining on his face. Kay Burk spoke out, "Well, that's the way the mop flops."

No one nearby had a response to Mrs. Burk's remark.

As Gardner Cadwalader would say later, "Penn led Harvard all the way except for the last four inches."[371]

To the press, Burk was as analytical as ever in the moment of a tough loss. But he had analyzed the odds and knew the risks. He told *The Inquirer*'s Frank Dolson after the race, "Remember what I told you about Harvard having the better sprint."[372]

The two coaches had been at the boathouse "where they shared a bad view of the race. Burk, showing no trace of his undoubted despair, examined the finish photo and exclaimed, 'Isn't that great!' Parker looked at it and said, 'Isn't that beautiful.'"

The hand-held watches had the time difference as 0.2 seconds. The Longines timing system at the finish line measured the difference at one five hundredths of a second—which became the subtitle of *The New Yorker* article—"0:00.05."

The Inquirer's Frank Dolson was with Burk when he spoke to his crew. "You have nothing to be ashamed of. Disappointed, yes, but not ashamed. You rowed a great race. Harvard did, too. We know they'll do a great job in the Olympics Games. You would have done a great job, too."[373]

Years later, Harvard four-man Fritz Hobbs would mention to his friend Nick Paumgarten over lunch that Joe Burk had come up to him soon after the race and extended his hand. "Congratulations. Great race," Burk told the exhausted Hobbs. Hobbs still remembered the moment of the old coach's unvarying sportsmanship fifty-five years later.[374]

Ted Nash recalled that when he and Burk had their first private moments together after the race, Burk said to him, "Ted, you are the small-boats specialist here. Why not take this crew and make boats for the next set of trials?"[375] Nash at first resisted. Later that day the two coaches agreed to offer later in the day the opportunity to the oarsmen to come back to Philadelphia and try to form boats that could win the small boats trial weeks later.

Luther remembered to Peter Mallory: "The team met in Joe's hotel room. He commended us on the race and congratulated Harvard. He said that although the [Penn] eight was not going to the Olympics, there would be an additional chance to go in one of the small boats. It was an individual decision for each of us. All but two decided to return to Philadelphia to train."[376]

After the talk in the hotel room, when the two coaches were alone, Joe Burk simply shook Nash's hand, and said, "I'll see you in the fall."[377]

No fanfare, just a change of command.

And Burk was gone.

Burk and his wife returned to Philadelphia where they began their usual trek to Montana, with one difference. Now they were looking for property upon which to build the retirement cabin about which they had so long dreamed. When they reached Troy, Montana, they discovered there was a magnificent piece of property for sale next to the Kootenai National Forest near the Canadian border.

The current owner, who had bought a large parcel from one of the state's original homesteaders, had been injured and was having difficulty keeping up his land. The Burks learned of this man when they inquired at a gas station in Troy. The injured owner met the Burks and decided to sell them a portion of his holdings.

As Roger later explained, "They were lucky in one way—had Penn won, Mom and Dad would not have come up then, and by the time they could have gotten there after the Olympics, the land would have been gone."[378]

By contrast, the Olympic dreams of the Harvard crew would after the Trials seem to recede from their grasp as the Olympic date approached. The Mexico Olympics were to be held at an altitude of 7,500 feet, which meant all competing crews had to face the task of adjusting to the more challenging environment. At that point in the history of rowing, no one had any experience in making such an adjustment.

The U.S. Olympic rowing team decided to attempt an adjustment to altitude by practicing at the Blue Mesa Reservoir at Gunnison, Colorado, where the altitude was 7,700 feet. All found the change difficult. The Harvard stroke Art Evans suffered especially, both in Colorado and Mexico City. Team physiologists warned Parker and the other coaches that races could trigger bad reactions. In the preliminary heats in Mexico City, Art Evans struggled so badly in the last quarter of the race, that Harvard failed to advance to the next stage of the contest and had to go to the repechage. Evans, later a doctor, assessed that he was near to requiring intubation at the finish.

Evans could not safely compete again, and Harvard had to shuffle its lineup for the remainder of the regatta.[379] Former Harvard '67 captain Jacques Fiechter, who after graduation had rowed at Vesper and become a spare for the Olympic team, rejoined his former Harvard teammates at the three-seat. The three-man Steve Brooks, a sophomore, moved from the three-seat to the stroke-seat.

While Harvard made the Final through the *repechage*, they finished last in the six boat finals.

A Penn coxed four, with the middle four oarsmen from the Trials eight—Jones, Purdy Martin and Cadwalader, with John Hartigan (Penn '62) as coxswain—won the Olympic Trials, and were fifth in the finals. Ted Nash, who had phoned in training plans to the Penn men while they struggled at Gunnison, became dissatisfied with what he felt was inadequate coaching the four received from Harry Parker and the small boats coach Parker had appointed, decided to travel to Mexico City at his own expense to coach the team during the regatta.

The Penn four made the finals and finished fifth.

In 2018, for the fiftieth anniversary of the Class of 1968, Captain Phil McKinley penned an elegant remembrance of the 1968 Varsity in all its forms, entitled "'68 Penn Heavyweight Crew." It started with the most compelling of truths: "There are few superstars in a University eight-oared shell."

As a poignant example, Captain McKinley wrote of LaMotte's and his removal from the boat after the IRA: "The lineup in the Penn boat was changed hopefully to increase its speed by displacing myself and another senior oarsman, Nick LaMotte, who had been drafted the day of the National Championship IRAs, but thanks to the efforts of Joe Burk, was able to return under the Army sports program. We were replaced with two underclassmen, Luther Jones and Gardner Cadwalader."

The tragic four-inch loss to Harvard was revisited, and the Penn coxed four making the final was proudly recounted. McKinley ended the piece with the elegantly simple declaration; "Indeed 1968 had been an extremely good year for Penn Heavyweight Rowing."[380]

McKinley's gracious recounting of the Penn '68 crew history, and the absence of complaint by either LaMotte or McKinley makes it clear that Joe Burk's goal in the race system had been fulfilled—rowing for Burk had, in their coach's own words, *made men of them.*

As this book was being prepared for printing, Nick LaMotte passed away in late January of 2025. After graduating from Penn, he had been drafted into the Army in 1968, where he served in Vietnam in the Fifth Infantry Division (Mechanized). He was twice wounded in battle and was awarded the Bronze Star for valor in combat, and two Purple Hearts.

CHAPTER FOURTEEN

The Final Contest

The college rowing season began as normal in 1969. What was not normal was the increasing number of students now being drafted for service in the Vietnam War. Burk's son, Roger, who had graduated from the University of Washington, was attending graduate school at Florida State University in Tallahassee when he received his draft notice. He was inducted into the Army at Jacksonville, Florida.

Roger would have his Basic Training and Advanced Infantry Training from April to August 1969, at Fort Dix, New Jersey. "Ironically the Army at the time tried to send the trainees far away from home. It made no difference. We were confined to base, with no visitors. But Mom and Dad did come to graduation."[381]

Despite their own deeply etched patriotism, it was a difficult time for Joe and Kay as they worried about Roger's future deployment, likely to the jungles of Vietnam.

Joe Burk kept his conscious thoughts on coaching rowing and tried to focus on the upcoming season. He again employed the point system, and the crews worked the river with long rows starting in the fall.

But Burk instituted one change in the point system. Roger Burk remembered the issue and the change. "One thing Dad found, the smaller guys tended to get into shape faster than the big guys, and so if a smaller guy was building up a big point total lead in the fall, it did not necessarily mean that he was going to be the best boat mover in June. So Dad had to start weighting [the race results]. The question then was: how far back do we give full credit for all this?"[382]

We can now recognize that this adjustment was obviously triggered, at least in part, by the anomaly of Gardner Cadwalader's slow start in the 1968 point totals, which as a matter of mathematics excluded him from the Penn Varsity.

In the fall of 1968, Burk decided that for the upcoming season, he would count only the last fifty races, so that the earliest results were dropped off the average to more closely reflect the improvement in any oarsman's boat moving ability as their rounded into form.[383] This adjustment would tend to focus the point system on performance as measured in the latter part of the season when the racing occurred. This adjustment was consistent with Burk's approach since his days of sculling. Measure carefully, consider carefully, and adjust. True measurements would be fair measurements and were apt to lead to victory.

The day before 1969's first spring race for the Penn crew, the *Philadelphia Daily News* ran a piece by Ed Conrad entitled "Burk Shuffling Another Top Hand?" in which Conrad quoted Burk as optimistic—but as usual, cautious:

> "I don't like to be evasive, said . . . [Penn's] likeable skipper, "But I have to admit one thing – we could be *very* good this year.
>
> "Of course, you don't know for certain until you see the team in competition. You can keep looking good in practice, but, until the boat is in competition, you never really know for sure."

The article confirmed that the Penn crews had again been picked by Burk using the card system after "many grueling practice sessions and quite a few shuffling of the cards."[384]

The Philadelphia Inquirer columnist Frank Dolson the next week wrote a column entitled "No Job Security for Penn Oarsmen." The article focused on the seemingly anomalous result of Burk's 1969 point system. Joe Burk was conducting a race three days a week, which had resulted in three of the men from the Penn Varsity that had raced in the 1968 Olympic Trials, and two who rowed in the Olympics, not being in the varsity for the starting race of the 1969 season. Gardner Cadwalader and Tony Martin's points had landed them in the JV, and Luther Jones, the freshman who had made the varsity for the Olympic Trials and rowed in the four with in the Olympics, was not even in the JV, but in the third boat.

Frank Dolson applauded the result. "There is no room for sentiment, no preferential treatment for Olympians on a Joe Burk crew . . . Last year's star can be this week's spectator."

Burk was quoted as saying he recognized that a great Olympic year effort might leave an oarsman depleted, and he used as an example the 1956 Yale Olympic champions. "It's hard to set up new goals . . . I know when the Yale Olympic team of 1956 came back they were *never nearly as good as before. They'd lost their incentive.*"

To Frank Dolson, that was the brilliance of the Burk system: "At Penn," he wrote, "the system [weekly racing and points] supplied the incentive."

Dolson thought Burk had the answer: "It's a matter of pride. They're trained not to give up in a race, to keep coming back . . . pushing . . . pushing . . . Look at Gardner last year. He was hopelessly behind [in the points] but he didn't quit."[385]

For Burk's 1969 Varsity, the two beginning "Cup races"—the Blackwell and Childs Cups—had all been victories. But the most important race lay just ahead. Penn would face undefeated Harvard—then holding a thirty-four-race regular season varsity winning streak – dating back to the last race of the Harvard 1963 season.

The Harvard streak had been truly historic. There have been years of dominance by a few college programs—Washington, California, Cornell, Yale, Navy, Harvard under Tom Bolles, and others—but the Harvard streak of the 1960s was as long and as complete as any. But such success could cut two ways. The story of Harvard's dominance also acted as a catalyst for the revival of the fortunes of Penn heavyweight rowing in the last years of Burk's coaching tenure.

In the spring of 1969, Penn Varsity was now starboard stroked by the Penn junior Somerset Waters, who had rowed seven in the 1968 varsity that fell only four inches short of an Olympic berth. Behind Waters was a powerful group of veterans whose main goal that year was to end the Harvard Varsity's winning streak. The Penn Varsity's 1968 performance had allowed them to reduce the Harvard Varsity's margin of victory from two lengths at the Adams Cup to four inches at the Olympic Trials.

Both the Harvard and Penn varsities came to the 1969 Adams Cup undefeated. The site of the Adams Cup that year was the Schuylkill River—Penn's home water. The water on race day was rough. Harvard's Varsity, usually rowing a Swiss made Stampfli shell, made a conservative choice and planned to row instead in a more forgiving Pocock boat it had brought along just in case. The results of the races before the varsity showed strength in both squads: Ted Nash's freshmen had won by two lengths in a boat stroked by Gene Clapp,[386] but the Penn JV boat never found its rhythm and finished several lengths behind both the Harvard winner and Navy.

The Penn Varsity rowed a careful race, striking at a cadence lower than Harvard's during the body of the race, and coming from behind to win at the finish by one and half lengths and rowing 40 strokes a minute at the end. Here was the breaking of the Harvard streak, the decisive victory Penn and Burk had sought for years.

Race day was Penn stroke Somerset Waters' twenty-second birthday.

The Philadelphia Inquirer the next day proclaimed that "[t]he Penn boat is now favored for the Eastern Sprint Championships next week at Worcester, Mass."[387] An AP story that ran the morning of the Sprints final included a quote by Harry Parker saying that the seeding of Penn ahead of Harvard was "fair from my point of view. It's hard to tell what might happen, but I think it may take something special to beat Penn."[388]

Parker sounded like Joe Burk or Tom Bolles—measured and cautious.

At the Eastern Sprints, four things changed between Harvard and Penn. The rough water that had been on the Schuylkill the week before was replaced by the flat and calm water at Lake Quinsigamond. Harvard's varsity decided to return to the Stampfli shell it normally used. The Penn crew had to manage race preparation and exam week, while the Harvard crews were unburdened by the press of exams which were scheduled later in Cambridge. And lastly, Parker decided to make some major changes to his varsity lineup, changing the seating of the eight oarsmen to try and improve the boat's efficiency. *The Boston Globe* outlined the changes:

> Parker had to make changes to get more power and speed from his big boat. He moved Steve Brooks from bow to six, Charlie Hamlin from two to five, Fritz Hobbs from five to seven, Mike Livingston from six to bow, and Cleve Livingston from seven to two. [389]

The wording in the *Globe* report implied the change took place the day before the race,[390] but Fritz Hobbs and Cleve Livingston remember the change took place on the Monday practice after the Adams Cup defeat.[391]

In the final of the Sprints, the Harvard varsity took a slender lead over Penn at the start, and ever so gradually increased it throughout the race. Try as they might, the Penn crew could not stop the widening margin. The difference between the crews at the finish was 3.2 seconds, or just three-fourths of a length.[392]

Sports Illustrated covered the race with a two-page article entitled "Underdog Bites Back" which featured pictures of the assembled college crowd at Lake *Quinsigamond*.[393] Hidden among the pictures of the racing crews and their fans was a picture of a spectator, sitting with his date on the beach beside the lake, wearing a white tee shirt with a red clenched fist defiantly pointing upward centered on the back of his shirt. Positioned horizontally in the mid forearm of the fist, in black letters, was the word STRIKE.

The photograph of the "Strike" shirt at the regatta is a reminder of the context in which this event was being held. This was the 1969 championship of the Eastern Association of Rowing Colleges, and for at least three of its schools—Wisconsin, Penn, and Harvard—student strikes earlier that spring had roiled the quiet of campus life. At the University of Wisconsin, a group of black students had submitted a list of demands to the administration and threatened a boycott if those demands were not met.[394] The student protest at Penn, "started on February 18 as a greater Philadelphia area protest organized by the Students for a Democratic Society (SDS) against the University City Science Center (UCSC) over its displacement of residents as well as its Defense Department contract and secret research provisions."[395] SDS also threatened a boycott at Harvard.[396]

The ubiquity of protest had paved the way for the casual use of protest shirts at sporting events that spring. Such was the tenor of the times.

This changing tide of political sentiment on campuses was obvious to former Lieutenant Joseph W. Burk, and yet he had by that point made no particular statement about it. His worries about his son Roger notwithstanding, Joe was a rowing coach, and he had stayed in his lane.

But his restraint for a moment later that summer would slip.

After the Eastern Sprints of 1969, the race results between Penn and Harvard would stand without further resolution. Unlike 1968, there would be no rubber match between Penn and Harvard. The crews would not see each other again for the rest of the season. Each side would naturally view the race that they won as the true test of the contest. Penn had the argument that when neither team had exams, Penn was the best. Harvard had the argument that the last race was the real test, and there they were the best.

What could not be foreseen, however, was Penn's victory in the 1969 Adams Cup, would mark an apogee in the fortunes of Harvard heavyweight rowing. There would be Harvard victories and streaks to come, yes, but Penn had breached the citadel, and Harvard's winning streak would never again grow as long.

The weekly races and point system continued under Burk's eye. Parker was different. He would rarely change people out of winning crews, and as of the afternoon of the Eastern Sprints, the Harvard boat was set.

But Burk had his cards and point system, and he continued it. Practice race results after the Sprints altered the balance of points, and the varsity stroke, Somerset Waters, was dropped from the varsity to the six-seat of the junior varsity without any public explanation from Burk. In Waters' place, varsity six-man Rick Crooker would stroke the varsity for the Madeira Cup, and other varsity members switched seats within the boat—the positions themselves within the boat being a result of Burk's judgment, not necessarily point totals.

Thus, as of May 24, the day before Penn's race against Cornell, the Penn Junior Varsity was to contain two 1968 Olympians, Luther Jones and Gardner Cadwalader. Not only that, but Somerset Waters—the only stroke oar to have defeated a Harvard Varsity in collegiate racing since 1963—was not stroking but listed in pre-race line ups made public two days before the contest as the six-man of Penn's jayvee boat.[397]

Many Cornell jayvee oarsmen thought Penn had somehow stacked their junior varsity.

Was this what the points system had wrought?

On race day, at least one of these odd outcomes was changed. Burk made a further shift in the JV. Burk's JV boatings had been published in the Ithaca Journal on May 24 as Luther Jones at stroke, and Somerset Waters at six. But in the report of the Saturday, May 25, race, *The Ithaca Journal* mentioned that Waters (at six) had switched place with Jones (at stroke) in the JV. The May 24 boatings had been adjusted after being released publicly. When and why the change was made was never publicized.

One anomaly was removed but one remained—the point system had still placed two 1968 Olympians in the 1969 JV.

On race day, the result was decisive. Penn swept the Madeira Cup races.

Waters admitted years later that some Cornell men had been suspicious. Every bit as much the gentleman as his coach, Waters said that the boatings had been the result of the weekly racing—and said nothing more.

Waters was ever the loyal Burk oarsman.

But another even more sublime example of loyalty to Burk was soon to appear.

In 1969, the Penn rowing alumni had again been moved by the courageous display of determination by the heavyweight team. The varsity had defeated Harvard—the first to do so in college rowing in five years. Did not such a crew deserve to go to Henley? Among themselves, the alumni began an informal discussion about raising the funds necessary to send the 1969 varsity to Henley.

The alumni reached out to the elected 1969 captain, then varsity coxswain Ken Dreyfuss about the discussions. Dreyfuss was asked to approach Burk. Would the coach consent to go to Henley if the funds could be raised outside the University?

Burk privately agreed, but on the condition that the varsity would have to win the IRA first. All involved agreed. All likely thought that imposing such a condition was a way of avoiding the repeat of the 1955 situation, where Penn decided to go to Henley after winning the Eastern Sprints, only to lose the IRA.

The Ithaca Journal published a brief report on June 9, 1969, under the title "Penn Crew's Pace Slower:"

Dateline Philadelphia—For several years now when Pennsylvania varsity crew shows up at Syracuse for the IRA regatta, crew buffs were on hand to find out which new factor Coach Joe Burk had added into the program. One season it was the "Wizard," a system of lights on the shell, and then came Burk's famed card game. This year, "We really don't have anything new, only a change in our approach to the regatta," explains Burk.

To be more specific, the Penn crews have not rowed as many miles as they have in the past. There are several reasons for this and two factors stand out. Due to the many oarsmen participating in the Olympic trials, and the Olympics themselves, many of the Penn oarsmen did not row in the fall.

Secondly, Burk decided on a slower pace for this year, particularly for the IRA. It was the feeling that last year the Quakers were not as sharp as they might have been and were even a bit too tired. Thus, Burk set a different pace. "I don't know if it helped, but we'll find out."[398]

The Henley plan was now in motion. Only the challenge of the IRA lay ahead. On the day *The Ithaca Journal*'s article about the Penn workout schedule was published, the last of the point system races was yet to be run and seat positioning for one seat was still in flux. Captain Ken Dreyfuss had coxed the varsity all year. But since the Madeira Cup victory against Cornell, JV coxswain Bob Tanzik had nosed ahead of Dreyfuss in Burk's point standings in the weekly races.

At stake was who would be the coxswain of the varsity for the IRA and—if the team won—for Henley.

The Inquirer columnist Frank Dolson devoted his Tuesday column to the outcome. The column headline: "To the Henley or the Jayvees."[399]

The coxswain whose boat won the race on Monday, June 9, on the Schuylkill would cox the Penn Varsity at the IRA the following weekend, June 14, at Lake Onondaga. Tansik had been the varsity coxswain for all of 1968, and Dreyfuss for all of 1969—so far.

Columnist Dolson emphasized the finality and the basis for the Burk system:

The points were final. Mathematics would decide the boatings, not a coach's opinion. Burk would add up a man's score for the last fifty races—three points for a victory, two for a defeat, one for a bad defeat—and let the totals speak for him. High man would be in, low man out, even if the difference was practically microscopic.[400]

A year ago, Tony Martin made the varsity in the final point race. This year, Gardner Cadwalader made it in the final week.

Now the boatings were set—except for the coxswain. Tansik and Dreyfuss were still that close.

"Right now it's pretty much a matter of luck," Tansik said Monday morning as Burk shuffled the cards and one of his oarsmen spread them out on a table, face down. One by one, Somerset Waters turned them over. Silently the two coxswains watched the ritual. The lineups for the last points race were set. Tansik's boat looked stronger.

On that Monday, in the season's last race, Dreyfuss's boat took an early lead because of a poor start in Tansik's boat. But Tansik's boat came back finally winning by a mere seven tenths of a second.

Dolson's column noted the irony. Dreyfuss's approach to Burk had convinced Burk to make the Henley trip, and now Dreyfuss would stay home. A jayvee oar who had no chance to go to Henley had contributed to the travel fund, as had Dreyfuss himself. But Dolson described Dreyfuss after the race:

> ... dressed now, sitting on a bench behind the boathouse, overlooking the river. He was disappointed, of course, but there was no sign of bitterness. No anger.
>
> "I figured it would be close," he said. "When you have a point system like we have; when you have coxswains starting out about even in ability—well, it was exciting just to have been in the varsity boat as long as I was."
>
> The last point race of the season was over. Henley was out of reach. Monday's loser, the commodore[401] of the Penn crew, gazed out across the water and talked enthusiastically about how great it would be to end his career with a victory in Saturday's jayvee race in Syracuse.[402]

Burk was undoubtedly moved by the sportsmanship and generosity of spirit that Dreyfuss—like all the Penn oarsmen—had displayed in the face of all disappointments, whether at the hands of fate as dealt by the cards, or by the grind of defeats at the hands of Harvard, or

1969 Penn Varsity at the morning heats of the IRA.

simply by the chill of a long cold wind on the Schuylkill. The loyalty and steadfast support Burk had inspired throughout his twenty years at the helm now stood in stark contrast to what he saw on college campuses that summer.

In a moment of rare candor, Burk gave a quote to Dolson that was placed in dark lettering in the column of *The Inquirer*:

> "It's fellas like [my oarsmen] who are, to me, the antithesis of the revolutionaries and the reactionaries and the hippies who are in college," Burk said. "I think if the public knew about the young men of this type, they'd feel more kindly disposed towards people of university age."[403]

Ken Dreyfuss would enjoy a storied rowing career after graduating from the University of Pennsylvania. He steered the U.S. coxed pair in the 1974 and 1975 World Championships and won the gold medal in the coxed pair at the 1975 Pan America Games. He would go on to coach crew at the U.S. Naval Academy, Stanford University (where he won Pac-10 Coach-of-the-Year), and Potomac Boat Club. He coached the senior women's team at the 2003 World Championships.

As politics and protest continued to roil college campuses across the nation, Joe Burk's final Penn Varsity kept their heads down and prepared to row at the IRA. It is a testament to Burk's confidence in his card system that the final varsity did not include Luther Jones, one oarsman who had already rowed in one Olympics, and would eventually go on to represent the U.S. in a second Olympics and several world championships.

The final boat is shown at the start of the heats of the IRA on Thursday, July 12, 1969.

The history of IRA Regatta shows that victory in the varsity contest would swing between the many fine crews that came to contest each year's final race. The accomplishment of three wins a row was rare. Rusty Callow's great Navy crews had done it in the 1950s, and Stork Sanford's Cornell crews did in the late '50s and early '60s—but such dominance was not the rule.

And for Penn, such a three-win streak had last occurred in 1900, when it won for the third time in a row against a far smaller contingent of opponents. Since 1900, Penn had not won even a single varsity IRA until the breakthrough in 1967.

Burk's 1969 varsity, like a knife sharpened against the whetstone of competition with Parker's Harvard, now faced the challenge of repeating a three in a row win for the first time in sixty nine years of Penn history.

In the Penn Varsity boat, each of the eight footboards for the oarsmen was covered with white athletic tape with blue lettering "HENLEY?"

Such overt motivational tools were not Burk's style. The likely source was Ted Nash. But no one, Burk included, removed the tape.

In the race, motivation seemed to have supercharged the Penn Varsity. They surged off the start and soon reached open water over Cornell, who traditionally had a strong IRA performance. The Dartmouth Varsity then surged, cutting the Penn lead and pushing past Cornell. The Penn crew held steady and kept their lead, and as the Dartmouth surge subsided, Penn regained its full-length lead.

The varsity's victory at the finals of the IRA was enough to garner an AP story that focused on the fact that Penn would only go to Henley if it repeated its two prior victories at the IRA. *The Baltimore Sun* headlined the story as "TRIP INCENTIVE TO PENN'S CREW: Henley Visit Hinges on Victory In IRA Row." The paper featured Burk's assessment of his varsity after their IRA win:

> Joe Burk, Penn's coach, said, "I'm real proud of my boys. They did a great job. In many ways I feel this year's boat was better than last year's boat. I didn't expect them to start out that fast, though."[404]

The AP article announced that the Penn freshman boat would also go to Henley to compete in the Thames Challenge Cup. Nash's freshman crew had tied with a strong University of Washington boat in the freshman IRA race. Penn's jayvee was third behind Cornell and Wisconsin.

In late June 1969, Joe Burk made what would be his last trip to Henley as the Penn coach. He was now fifty-five years old, and the times were changing. The legions of young athletes he had trained and mentored had moved into young adulthood and beyond. Kathy and Roger, too, had made successful lives for themselves. Kay was dreaming of a quiet summer home in Montana. The Henley Regatta seemed a fitting end to a season for a legendary coach and a varsity that had ended the Harvard winning streak at the 1969 Adams Cup.

But as he undertook the return to Henley, Burk did not foresee that the races in England would be his last as the Head Coach at Penn.

The Penn trip in 1969 was Burk's sixth pilgrimage to Henley: he had won the Diamond Sculls in 1938 and 1939 and accompanied the 1951 Penn lightweights. He had coached the 1955 winning crew in the Grand Challenge Cup, and the valiant 1962 Penn Varsity effort in the Grand when Penn had been beaten by an able Italian crew.

This 1969 effort seemed destined for a great performance. Burk was recognized as one of the greatest oarsmen ever to row at Henley, and the coach of many great crews. To most observers, it seemed like an opportunity for yet another peak in a string of great performances. But in an interview with Ed Conrad of the *Philadelphia Daily News*, Burk framed the contest not as a hope for victory but for his crew's best effort. The statement, made well before the contest, perhaps best captures Joe Burk's wisdom in how to seek athletic excellence:

> "We've got tremendous competition in this year's Henley," he whispered before departing for England. "I'm just counting on our guys to do their best. That's all I ask of them."[405]

Doing your best was the point.

The early heats showed Penn's chances were good.

In the quarterfinals of the Thames Challenge Cup, Ted Nash's Penn freshman defeated a crew from Bedford Rowing Club with what *The New York Times* described as "a convincing victory."

Burk's varsity, too, began with great promise. Penn engaged in what the Henley official history called "a great struggle against London University," where the latter overcame Penn's lead to narrow the gap to a quarter of a boat length at the finish, with both crews rowing at 42 at the finish.

In the semifinals, the Penn Varsity defeated the leading English crew—the Tideway Scullers—by three quarters of a length. But it was their second close race in two days—the finals would make three races in three days.

Both the Penn varsity and Penn frosh had made the finals at Henley. A possible two boat sweep at Henley lay in front of the Quaker crews.

The freshman raced first against Leander Club in the final of the Thames Challenge Cup. Leander, rowing on its home waters,[406] took an early lead and never relinquished it, despite the Penn frosh continually raising their stroke in attempt to break through. The margin at the finish was one length.

The varsity faced the East German club Einheit Dresden in the Grand Final. All crews in East Germany were by this time benefitting from a government sponsored, nation-wide approach to standardizing rowing excellence, which included the long-distance training that Burk had instituted at Penn in 1965. The East Germans were racing not just for their club, but also in a sort of socialist intramural contest to show whether they could best their putative Russian masters. East German oarsmen, while operating under a system where their own country was subservient to the U.S.S.R., were in fact intent on proving to their Soviet overlords that, while their nation might be subject to functional Soviet control, the emerging East German sports efforts could beat all comers. Their effort in the Grand was a chance to make good on that claim.[407]

The battle between Penn and Einheit Dresden is recorded in the official Henley history of the race:

> Einheit Dresden were one of the fastest crews ever to race at Henley, and although the outcome was never in doubt it says much for the quality of the Grand entry this year that, in the five races, there was only one occasion when the boats were not overlapping . . .
>
> In the final Einheit Dresden, starting at 43 [strokes per minute] to Pennsylvania's 39, led by a quarter of a length at the quarter mile and gradually increased this to half a length at the Barrier, three-quarters of a length at Fawley and a length at the mile. Pennsylvania made repeated spurts but could not close up and Dresden without spurting won by three-quarters of a length.[408]
>
> Burk was philosophical about the results.
>
> "Well, it was tough, as expected," said Joe Burk, Penn's coach, after his varsity's defeat.
>
> "Maybe three hard races in three days were a bit too much for us. But we are not too disappointed. It was a fine race and *this crew is the fastest I ever brought here*" (emphasis supplied).
>
> "We knew the Germans would lead early, but we hoped to pull it back. Then, when the crunch came, we couldn't. We didn't have enough left."
>
> Asked whether he would be coming back again next year, Burk, who has been at Henley several times since 1938 answered, "I certainly would like to."[409]

CHAPTER FIFTEEN

Towards the West

"Smart lad to slip betimes away,
From fields where glory does not stay." [410]

The quotation above from English poet A.E. Houseman's "To an Athlete Dying Young" is an apt description of Burk's decision to leave coaching at age fifty-five. As the poem illustrates, it is always a danger to linger too long and strive unproductively in a portion of one's life where success was once abundant. Most people have known individuals who cling to an early achievement too long and too closely and thus fail to move from strength to strength toward life's next challenge.

Joe Burk and Kay had planned carefully for this next stage of their life together, and while their children were young, they had used their car trips west to Kay's family's compound as an opportunity to discover where that next step in life might lead them.

Roger Burk shares a telling story about how his father's impetus in leaving rowing was rooted in his experience of watching an old oarsman at the Eastern Sprints. The oarsman approached Burk and his crew while they were eating lunch, and Burk said the man started telling the Penn oarsmen Rusty Callow stories. Burk later told Columnist

Frank Dolson that the Rusty Callow stories had little effect on his Penn oarsmen. "They had barely heard of Rusty Callow. They were ten when he was coaching. They didn't think of rowing then."[411]

Roger Burk also noticed another change in the reaction of groups of people who would ask his father about his naval service in World War Two. The old warrior would rarely give details about the combat he had been involved in. Instead, Burk was excited about the Navy's recruiting into the PT boat service so many athletes Burk had admired in pre-war years.

Joe Burk would tell questioners he had been "in the Navy with Bernie Crimmins," but have to explain the context of his own excitement: that Crimmins had been an all-American football player for Notre Dame who had also been a PT Boat skipper with Burk in Squadron 21.

The need of explain had to have been a reminder to Joe Burk that it had been almost thirty years since Crimmins had taken the field for the Fighting Irish football team.

Burk must also have been thinking of the change in college campuses. The World War Two medal winner can be forgiven if he felt the ground shift under his feet seeing the "Strike!" shirts on the backs of the college student watching the Eastern Sprints.

After Henley was over, Burk learned that Ted Nash was being considered for the head coaching job at Yale.

Ted Nash had joined the Penn organization as the freshman heavyweight coach in the late fall of 1964, and he had admirably fulfilled his obligations to both Penn and Burk. Nash had gathered, trained, and retained impressive classes of freshman oarsmen for Burk to hone on the varsity squad. The undefeated frosh crews of Nash's early coaching had a huge impact on the speed of the heavyweight varsity and JV crews.

Now Burk learned that Yale was looking for a varsity coach and that Nash was among those high on Yale's list of candidates. Yale was on the verge of making an offer.

Burk had planned on coaching one more year after 1969. Since the start of 1965, he and Nash together had amassed an enviable record, and they had reached a peak with the defeat of the Harvard varsity.

In a final act of loyalty to Penn, Burk amended his own plans for the benefit of the Penn rowing program. He accelerated his retirement, announcing it on July 10, 1969. Ted Nash was named Penn's head coach of rowing soon thereafter.[412]

Within the Penn organization, several steps had already been taken on the assumption that Burk would remain through the 1970 season. The talented Somerset Waters, starboard stroke of the '69 crew that had beaten Harvard at the Adams Cup, had already been named crew captain for 1970.

Waters and Burk were especially close, both quiet men with exceptional athletic talent beneath gentlemanly demeanors. While Waters respected Ted Nash, the two men were deeply different in temperment. Burk knew that, so while on his way to Montana after his surprising retirement announcement, he wrote his first letter to Waters from the Holiday Inn where he and Kay stopped for the night in Eau Claire, Wisconsin:

July 11, 1969

Dear Somey,

This letter is prompted by an unexpected change that I hadn't anticipated. Up until yesterday, I had expected that I would be back on the job as usual in September. However, with the late start that we shall get on the house, it now seems that it is better that my retirement from coaching comes now. It will eliminate a lot of uncertainty in my mind, as well as the minds of others.

I hope that you and the other varsity oarsmen give Ted the same great co-operation that you have given me. You have the potential for another good crew and with hard work you can go all the way.

Please convey to the others, in the fall, my sincere appreciation for their valiant efforts. They were a pleasure to coach and I'll miss them all.

To you, in particular, I wish to extend my thanks for the way you handled yourself—especially at the time of the Cornell race. Most oarsmen who stroke a few races soon think that they know all the answers and that they are bigger and more important than the rest of the crew. Your reaction to the pressure and the prestige of stroking has been a real joy. I never coached a stroke that I had more confidence in.

Please excuse this makeshift way of announcing my retirement. However, since the decision came up on the eve of our departure for Montana, there was no alternative.

Good luck to you all. I'll be back late in November and see you in person.

Sincerely,
Joe

The *Philadelphia Daily News* on July 22, 1969, reported Nash's appointment to succeed Burk, lauding both men. The headline ran: "Making Burk Proud is Goal of Nash Era for Penn Crew." At the front of the story was a gracious quote by Nash:

"A guy like Joe Burk comes along once in a lifetime and casts an enormous shadow. I don't pretend to be able to take his place, but I'll do my best."

Nash was skillful in handling in deflecting what must have been a reporter's question of why he had never followed Burk's point system in coaching Penn's freshmen. Nash emphasized that Burk had given him a free hand in developing the freshman training program according to his own view.

"Joe had an awful lot to do with our success [with the freshman crew] . . . I'm thankful that Joe allowed me to experiment . . . that's one of the reasons I've been very happy to be working under Joe. Don't forget, Joe could have easily said, 'Look here, Nash, this is our system and this is how we do things.' However, he never said it, although he had every right to do so."

Since Nash had never used the card system, it is likely he was referring to that difference. The article ended with as graceful a tribute as a younger coach could give a mentor: "We all have learned a lot from him. We just hope we can conduct ourselves the way he had over the years."[413]

Meanwhile, having written to Somerset Waters and drafted his farewell to the Penn rowing community for Nash to release in September, Joe and Kay arrived at the Montana property they had purchased the summer before after the 1968 Olympic Trials loss to Harvard. Working together, Joe, Kay, and Roger began building the cabin they envisioned along the banks of the Seventeen Mile Creek in Lincoln County. It remains there today.

The emotional foundations for this change had been laid years before. Burk and Kay had so enjoyed the cabin at the Whitney Adirondack estate during the summer of 1947 when Burk had coached Harry Payne Whitney. They resolved that they wanted such a rural summer home in retirement.

While laboring in Montana, Burk received a heartfelt response from Somerset Waters, who wrote:

Dear Joe,

Many thanks for your letter; I appreciate it very much. Needless to say, the shock was severe for me, but I have shared it with most of the others.

Frank Dolson wrote eloquently [referring to The Philadelphia Inquirer article entitled A Great Coach—And Man—Retires, which read in part: "Sadly there are not many college coaches like Joe Burk. Not that many men who are that honest with themselves and with others. Not many men who act the same, win or lose; who do what they believe is right and do not expect—or even want—recognition for it. Not many men earned the respect that Joe Burk earned throughout the world.] . . .

Certainly your greatness will live on, not so much in stories but in the temper you have demanded Penn rowers to display. Penn is known for its disciplined sportsmanlike attitudes based on fairness and a certain integrity . . . You have been responsible for a faith in all of us that rowing successfully is not an end in itself, but a means by which we mature. This will continue. The stories will be muffled after a while in Philadelphia, but that temper and faith are in us . . . to stay.

Burk wrote back to Waters on August 1. His letter read in part:

I know that you fellows will have great success under Ted. Maybe you will hate the toil and the sweat, but the victories will be well worth it because you can live with them and reflect on the fun part of it for years and years. There will be change and procedures that will be different, since no two men think and coach alike. But remember there are many different routes to success. What is one man's road for getting there doesn't necessarily have to be that of someone else.

. . .

But Joe gave Waters one last summary caution:

Don't ever let the others convince themselves and you that one can win without paying a price.

Don't ever let the others convince themselves and you that one can win without paying a price. Such was the importance of the message that Burk—so often in the past the quiet, understated coach—wanted to underline in parting to his last captain, the great truth behind all rowing.

In the fall, the next edition of the *Pennsylvania Rowing News* began to arrive in the mailboxes of Penn Rowing alumni. On the last page of the newsletter was the goodbye that Burk had penned for Nash entitled a "Letter to His Friends from Joe Burk," which read in part:

Ted Nash has asked me to write a piece for the Rowing News. I am happy to, as it will give me an opportunity to say farewell and thank you to the many loyal alumni and friends who backed us to the hilt whether we won or lost. Many times during my coaching career I silently gave thanks for my good fortune in being associated with such patient, understanding, and generous alumni. To cite just one example—what other alumni group would have waited so patiently for a victory in the I.R.A.? Many waited from graduation to grave for a victory that didn't come until three years ago. So, to all of you that suffered in silence during those lean years and wrote such kind letters when the tide turned, my sincere and everlasting thanks.

Close friends have expressed surprise that I should retire at what seems to them a comparatively early age and at a time when Pennsylvania's rowing is riding the crest of a wave. My reply is that I always planned to leave at an age when Kay and I could still do all the things we had dreamed about over the years. It was impossible to attempt them while still in coaching and trying to give the time and thought that these hard-working, young oarsmen deserve. Rowing coaching has gradually become a very time-consuming occupation. There isn't time for much else. So, if we were ever to do the things we talked about, we had to start soon. The years have a way of silently clipping by.

That, in essence, is why I am writing this farewell to oars while sitting in a "camper" in northwest Montana. Kay and I are living in these cozy, cramped quarters as we enjoy the pleasures, thrills, and aching muscles of do-it-yourself home construction. We are building a summer home that seems to have the peculiar trait of entrapping us like a gambler at Las Vegas. It has been a summer full of hard work . . .

For quite some time we had planned to return to this rather isolated bit of Montana that had enchanted us some fifteen years earlier when we drove through on the way to the West Coast. We said then that someday we would return and build a place for summer vacationing. By a sheer coincidence that borders somewhat on a miracle, we are now building on a spot only one mile away from the very place where we camped for a night during our first trip out this way . . .

I leave Pennsylvania with one simple request that is, hopefully, superfluous. It is that all of you give our Pennsylvania crews the same inspirational, financial, and moral support that you have bestowed in the past. These present-day oarsmen are the same type of dedicated, hard-working, and deserving guys that they were in your day and my day.

Joseph W. Burk[414]

In that summer of 1969, Joe and Kay themselves started to lay the foundation of their cabin only a few miles from the border with Canada. As the cabin took shape, the Burks developed their lives around bird banding (Kay), panning for gold (Joe), flying fishing (Kay), and further development of the property. Over the years they hand dug a pond and built a sturdy outbuilding for storing Joe's sluice box, which he used for filtering the flecks of gold that flowed down from an abandoned mine upstream of Burk's claim site. All of this done without outside labor.

Each summer, they were visited by friends, family, Joe's oarsmen, and fellow coaches like Steve Gladstone and Andy Anderson. Especially frequent visitors were Reed Kinderman and Ken Dreyfuss, who would bring oarsmen they had coached or family to meet Joe and Kay to enjoy the rustic hospitality. The photo appearing at page 324 shows a picture (taken by Ken Dreyfuss) of Reed Kinderman (Penn '67) with his son Ian, and Jason Stinson, who had rowed for Ken Dreyfuss at Stanford before transferring to row at UW. The woman in the center is Ethna Cook, who lived with her then ailing husband further up the valley from the Burks.

Reed Kinderman remembered the errand for the Cooks that the group had managed the day of the picture:

On that particular occasion, we were delivering some cut up and chopped wood to [the Cooks] who lived further up the creek from Joe and Kay. I remember she had a hot water heater hooked up to no source of electricity or gas, but put the chopped wood under the hot water heater to heat the water by fire. She also had a separator that spun milk down

Joe's outbuilding, still guarding his last mechanical sluice for
gold mining. (from Woodhouse collection.)

into regular milk and cream. Her husband was ill and frail and
she'd serve him pure cream, as his only source of nutrition.
There was of course, no electricity. Life was hard up in that
area of Montana . . .

Burley oarsmen that day were converted to lumberjacks and haulers
in service of neighbors in need. Coach Burk—even in retirement—
still led the way.

Another Dreyfuss oarsmen remembered being introduced to the
old champion and his bride in the wilds of Montana. John MacEachern rowed for Dreyfuss at Philadelphia's Chestnut Hill Academy and
accompanied Dreyfuss to visit the Burks in Montana late in the summer of 1976. He remembered almost fifty years later the great warmth
the Burks had for each other, and the hospitality they showed to
their guests. "I can still remember the smell of Kay's zucchini bread.
And I still have a small bottle filled with bits of gold flakes that Joe
mined for me." The two oarsmen—46 years apart in age—struck up
a friendship and continued to write to each other after having been
introduced.

Photos of Reed Kinderman Visiting

"The thing about Joe, you could always count on him to write back to you," MacEachern remembered. "He would type his letters out on an old typewriter, but would always sign them 'Joe.'" They corresponded for years.

MacEachern went on the row for Harry Parker at Harvard and was elected Harvard's 1981 Captain. On one of his last visits to Montana, he gave Burk his own Harvard racing shirt as a token of their long friendship.

A visitor to the home site today finds him/herself dwarfed by evergreens on all sides, girding the valleys with an endless mass of green sentinels. The Montana cabin's difference from the Burk's earlier suburban world of Philadelphia is stark.

One story that circulated in the Eastern rowing world during the 1960s was that, after he retired, Joe went touring with Kay west without an itinerary. According to the story, Burk had stopped at a barber shop in Montana.

The barber asked Burk what he did for a living, and Burk had told him he had just finished coaching the Penn crew. "What's crew?" the barber asked—and according to legend, Burk then proclaimed to his wife that they had come far enough West. That event (so the story went) had led to the cabin in Montana.

The story reveals about more the myopia of the Eastern rowing world than the Burk's true motivations.

For most of their marriage, Joe and Kay had made sure their children knew the East where Joe was raised, and the West where Kay was raised. The children's summers had been spent with Kay's family at the family compound in northern California. Joe's explanation that he and Kay had seen the land before, and it brought to their minds the image of the Whitney compound in the Adirondacks fits this "two-coast" model.

It should be added for those Eastern readers, that for Joe Burk, his two most important mentors—Pocock and Callow—lived the bulk of their lives in the westernmost part of Washington state. Rusty Callow's gravesite in Lake Forest Park, Washington was less than 400 miles due west of the Burk' cabin, and George Pocock's workshop about an equal distance away.

And two of the three colleges Burk had recommended for his son Roger were west the Continental Divide, and the third, the University of Wisconsin, is only a hundred miles east of the Missisippi River.

Joe Burk had returned to a land he knew well—the land of his teachers.

Roger Burk says that his parents never intended to make the Montana property a year-round home. The winters were ferocious, and snow could maroon cabins in the valley for days or weeks. His parents' original intent, Roger explained, was to spend part of the winters in Mexico, and have a home somewhere near the Mexican border. Their first trip was intended to be to El Paso.

But the Burks happened upon a new housing development then being built in Tucson, Arizona, around a golf course. Mexico was quickly forgotten. Joe and Kay bought a home before it was finished—and moved in as soon as it was ready. Their house was on the twelfth hole, though neither played golf. Roger remembers tournaments held at the course in the 1970s being broadcast to his work site in Africa. From his distant location of another continent, Roger could see his parents' home and assure himself that all was well.

On Monday, May 16, 1988, nearly twenty years after his early retirement from coaching, the University of Pennsylvania conferred on Joseph William Burk the honorary degree of Doctorate of Laws (L.L.M.). Burk had traveled from his home in Montana to attend the event. The citation conferring the degree recited the collegiate and post-collegiate rowing honors Burk had won in eight-oared boats and the single, but called out the traits and manners in Burk which fit more fully the accomplishments and mien of a man of full maturity rather than of youth and promise:

> You accepted all accolades with a gentlemanly modesty that even the English [at the Henley Regatta] respected. You experienced disappointment when the Olympics, where you were assured of a gold medal, were cancelled during World War II. Transferring your quiet, courageous leadership to the South Pacific you proceeded to win the Navy Cross, the Silver Star, and the Bronze Star, "for extraordinary heroism and intrepidity in action." During the nineteen years you later dedicated to coaching Penn's varsity crew, you instructed your mostly successful teams in the manly art of dealing with unfulfilled expectations, the equal importance of winning and losing well.
>
> The many Penn graduates, several of them Trustees of the University, who credit you with the example and education for life you gave them on and off the Schuylkill, welcome you "home" from the wilds of Montana, and salute you, Joseph William Burk, outstanding scholar/sculler, dean of crew coaches the world over, all-time American great . . .[415]

For all the successes for which Joe Burk had been known and celebrated, this last public honor did not focus solely on Burk's successes but on how he negotiated the variable winds of chance that buffet all lives. Nick Paumgarten, longtime head of the Friends of Pennsylvania Rowing, sums up the modern view of Burk: "A total gentleman, a great loser, and a great winner."[416]

Power Ten Dinner, NYC—Penn Attendees
Back Row, Standing: (1) Mike Meehan (2) — (3) — (4) Sandy Bierce (5) John Dale (6) Frank Shields (7) Tim Thompson, (8) — (9) —
Second Row, Standing: (1) Woody Fisher (2) Tony Palm (3) Nat Reece (4) Gardner Cadwalader (5) Somerset Waters (6) Pieter Fosburgh (7) —
First Row, Kneeling: (1) — (2) Fargo Thompson (3) Joe Burk (4) Harry Parker (5) Nick Paumgarten (6) Steve Cook

Today the Penn Boathouse bears Joe Burk's name in acknowledgement of his contribution to the University's rowing program. The preservation of Burk's memory at Penn is enduring proof that his extraordinary character continues to resonate over time, and that, in Somerset Waters' words, the "temper instilled in us will remain."

That temper is captured by the poet's lines:

If you can dream—and not make dreams your master;
If you can think—and not make thoughts your aim;
If you can meet with Triumph and Disaster
And treat those two imposters just the same . . .[417]

An organization called *Power Ten New York*, made up initially of New York-based former oarsmen led by '63 Penn captain Frank Shields was formed in 1988 as a fraternal organization to promote rowing in America. They cast as their premier event *The Power Ten Dinner*, held annually at the New York Racquet Club on Park Avenue. This dinner has been used since that time to honor various rowers and coaches for past accomplishments and has been described by some as a testosterone fest where large competitive men—most still very competitive— gather to drink, smoke cigars, and discuss past races. One year, the founders, many of whom are Penn men, honored Joe Burk.

Much to everyone's surprise, Joe Burk chose to attend. As is the tradition, speaker after speaker rose to regale the former oarsmen with tales of past glory, peppered with gibes at other speakers. Old races and old stories were recounted.

At the end of the evening—which one wag described as "well past Joe's bedtime"—the master of ceremonies asked Burk to say a few words.

Obligingly, Burk rose and walked to the podium.

The crowd immediately quieted.

"Thank you very much," Burk said. "Good night."

A photo of some the Penn oarsmen attending that, with Burk and Harry Parker, kneeling, center of the first row is included on page 327 of this book.

Epilogue

Joe and Kay Burk were married for fifty-six years. Kay Burk told her daughter Kathy that she had always expected to outlive Joe, since he was almost eight years older. When Kay's final illness made it clear that would not happen, mother and daughter had a candid conversation about how Kathy could help her father when Kay was gone. Kathy was living in Scottsdale at the time, and since Joe and Kay lived in Tucson, she pondered what role she might play.

She asked her mother. Kay told Kathy that her father was so good, he could appear almost naïve sometimes. Kay said that was simply his way. In relating this conversation, Kathy recalled that her mother often had had to terminate conversations at the front door when her husband was too kind to send Jehovah's Witnesses away. When Kay intervened, the visitor would exclaim, "Your husband's been so nice, we'll come back next week."

Kay had learned to say "No." Now Kathy would sometimes have to do so.

Kay Burk died on September 22, 2001.

Roger Burk had taken a leave of absence from his job at Chevron from April to September 2001 when his mother's cancer was diagnosed. He took early retirement thereafter when it became clear that "any caregiver from outside the family would not be a good fit for Dad." Joe and Roger lived together in the Burk home in Tucson from

2001 to 2006. They would winter in Arizona and go up to the Montana cabin in the summer, maintaining the rhythm Joe and Kay had kept.

Five years later, in 2006, Joe moved in with Kathy in her home in Scottsdale when she retired from her position as a licensed adviser at Vanguard. Joe's physical condition had declined such that his last trip to Montana was 2005. Thereafter, Roger would travel to Montana in the summers to see to the cabin.

Joe Burk passed away on January 13, 2008, in Scottsdale.

Kathy still lives in the home she shared with her father. Her son Kevin and his wife Joan visit from their home in Singapore. Kathy's daughter Katherine and her husband Michael Jekeli live in Duncan, South Carolina. They and their children exchange visits with Kathy.

Roger now splits his wintertime between Germany and South Africa. He goes to the Montana cabin in the summer, where he acts as "caretaker" for the cabin, which remains on the western half of the property which Kathy now owns. Roger has plans to build a second cabin on his eastern half.

Harvard 1981 Captain John MacEachern retired from his position at Groton school as this book was being printed, and will this fall coach crew at Cambridge Rindge & Latin School in Massachusetts this fall.

Joe Burk's example lives on.

Author's
Acknowledgements

T his biography of Joseph William Burk has been shaped by many
still living who were themselves shaped by Burk. Burk's own
children, Roger and Kathy, have welcomed me to Kathy's home
in Arizona, and to the Burk cabin in Montana, and made available the
voluminous memorabilia still in the family's possession. Among those
memorabilia is a priceless collection of wartime letters Joe Burk wrote
to his former coxswain Sid Phelps (Penn Varsity '34), which Sid kept
and gave to Burk in scrapbook form in 1992. These letters, together
with the wartime naval records gathered by Jeff Fuglestad (mentioned
below), tell the full story of Joe Burk's valorous naval service in the
Pacific in World War Two. Phelps' generous contribution to the Burk
record reminds all oarsmen and oarswomen alike how much of their
success is due to a fine coxswain.

Rowing historian Peter Mallory, himself a fellow Kent School
student, former Penn lightweight oarsman, cox, rowing coach, and
author of the magisterial history *The Sport of Rowing*, was an early sup-
porter of the writing of this biography, introducing me to generations
of oarsmen who have contributed their insights on Joe Burk. Peter
read early drafts of this book and provided comments.

Kent School and Penn oarsman Jeff Fuglestad, Penn 1967, provided voluminous naval records on Burk's service in World War Two

as a PT boat skipper. These materials provide the backbone of Burk's combat story told here.

My University of Virginia 1978 law school classmate and 1970 Yale lightweight oarsman Tom Weil reawakened my love of rowing history by his own devotion to it. Just before his death, Tom simply sent to me all the Burk photos in his collection without comment. I learned of his passing weeks later. Tom served as a naval officer during the Vietnam era. Fair winds and following seas, you proud son of Eli.

Dr. W. Reed Kindermann, Penn oarsman from the Class of 1969, and still a practicing eye surgeon, graciously shared with me his presentation on Burk given to the Moorestown Historical Society and other audiences, and toured Rick Stehlik and me through the towns surrounding Rancocas Creek in Burlington County, New Jersey, where Burk grew up, where he rowed after college, and where he perfected what became his world-beating rowing style. Kindermann shared with us the insight that the Quaker faith to which Joe Burk was exposed in his early schooling at Westfield Friends School was a force in molding the man Burk became. All my research for this book confirms this deep insight.

Gardner Cadwalader, Penn oarsman from the Class of 1970, 1967 Pan Am gold medalist, 1968 Olympian, and Cambridge Blue, provided key insights into the latter part of Burk's coaching career, and read and commented upon drafts of this book. Gardner's father, John Cadwalader Jr., had rowed with Joe Burk at Penn in the 1930s, and as a career naval officer served in the United States Navy during the Second World War

Somerset Waters, Penn heavyweight captain in 1970, and Cambridge Blue, who refers to Joe Burk as "a second father," maintained an active correspondence with Burk from 1969 until 2006. Somerset kindly gave me access to those letters and provided crucial insights into Burk's philosophies, many of which guided Waters' own life choices.

Ken Dreyfuss, 1969 Penn heavyweight captain, and National Team coxswain in the 1970s was the first to pique my interest with his stories about Burk while we were both candidates for the 1974 National

Rowing Team. It was the memory of those stories that was the first impetus for this biography.

Jim Fitzgerald and Fargo Thompson, Penn '62 oarsmen and members of the 1964 College Boat Club eight that contested the 1964 Olympic Trials, gave invaluable background to Burk's attempt to fashion a "graduate rowing club" to try for Olympic berths in 1964.

1960 Naval Academy graduate Lyman S.A. Perry, stroke of the 1960 Naval Academy crew that represented the U.S. at the 1960 Olympic Games, and stroke of the 1964 College Boat Club eight at the Olympic Trials, provided an outside perspective on Burk, the Penn crew, and its graduates with whom he gathered to try for a berth on the 1964 Olympic team. Perry rowed for Rusty Callow in Callow's last years at the Naval Academy and provided information linking Callow and Burk.

Fred Lane, stroke of Burk's 1955 varsity which won the Eastern Sprints and the Grand Challenge Cup, gave details of how the 1955 boat made its way through its successful season, but he also added key details about the less successful varsity boats in 1956 and 1957.

Dick Viall, Penn captain 1966, and his longtime coxswain Joel Kantor together filled in gaps in the established record about Burk's coaching and equipment choices during some of the leaner times in the mid-1960s, and provided much needed support and clarity in the last days of this book being written. During the Vietnam conflict, Viall served as an officer in U.S. Navy during his first tour, and volunteered for a second tour as an advisor to South Vietnamese sailors on riverine boats patrolling in the Mekong Delta.

Steve Gladstone, most recently Head Heavyweight Coach of the Naval Academy, and former Head Heavyweight Coach at Yale University, the University of California at Berkeley (twice), and Brown University and Head Lightweight Coach at Harvard, and, like me, a former Kent School oarsman, helped me understand the context of college rowing coaching during the years Burk was both oarsman and coach. Alone among all this book's supporters, Steve had participated in in the periodic meetings of major Eastern rowing coaches and the national media at Mama Leoni's restaurant in New York City, and his memories of those meetings have allowed me to understand the relationship between major college rowing coaches and the media. Steve also shared stories of his three visits to Burk in Montana, where he sought Burk's counsel during Gladstone's own career.

Nick Paumgarten, Penn Captain in 1967 and longtime Head of the Friends of Pennsylvania Rowing, gave key details on the changes in Burk's training regime and card selection process during the 1965 through 1967 seasons, and also clarified stories about Burk's demeanor both in the coaching launch and later when Burk was honored at a celebratory dinner in New York City in the 2000s.

Roger Burk's Harriton High School boatmate Rick Stehlik, now a mainstay and archivist of Philadelphia's Malta Boat Club, and himself a bronze medalist in the lightweight double sculls at the 1977 World Championships, and coach of the U.S. 1978 bronze medalists in the same event, restored Joe Burk's 1930s era Pocock single for its place in the University of Pennsylvania's Burk-Bergman Boathouse where it can now be seen. Rick provided countless insights and introductions into the world of Philadelphia's Boathouse Row.

Roger Burk's sculling partner at the University of Washington in the mid-1960s Al McKenzie, remains a mainstay of the Seattle rowing scene and works with efforts to preserve both UW and Pocock history. Al provided prior publications on Burk in *OARSMAN* Magazine, links to the UW community, and access to the books written by both George and Stan Pocock, all of which allowed me to gain a fuller picture of Burk's rowing lineage on both the East and West Coasts.

Oarswoman Dotty Brown, former reporter and editor at *The Philadelphia Inquirer* and author of the classic *Boathouse Row: Waves of Change in the Birthplace of American Rowing*, helped frame the historical and the political development of Boathouse Row in Philadelphia, the wellspring of countless great crews and Olympic champions. Dotty also read the final draft of this book and provided wise counsel that improved the final product.

My Kent School classmate and boatmate (as a coxswain) and University of Virginia Law School classmate John Reichner, a product of two Philadelphia families and a Penn 1972–5 lightweight oarsman, steered me through a maze of Pennsylvania stories and sources.

Bill Tytus, current owner of the Pocock Boat Works in Seattle, 1969 finalist at the Diamond Sculls at Henley Royal Regatta, and a 1970 and 1971 National Team member, occupies the enviable position of having learned sculling under George Pocock, Joe Burk, *and* Harry Parker. Many of Pocock's previously unpublished comments about Burk and his rowing and training habits came from Bill, who had heard them directly from George Pocock.

Peter Raymond, Princeton oar of the Class of 1968, who rowed in the Parker-coached 1968 U.S. coxless four in the Mexico City Olympics in 1968, and in the 1972 silver medal U.S. Olympic eight in Munich, and coach of the Navy plebe heavyweights, Princeton women, Harvard lightweights, Radcliffe crew, and the 1980 U.S. Olympic quad, provided insights on the relationship between Joe Burk and Harry Parker, and read and commented on drafts.

My Harvard boatmate and roommate Gregg Stone, himself the U.S. single sculler from 1977 through 1979, and coach of his daughter Gevvie Stone, silver medalist in the women's singles in the 2016 Rio Olympics, provided key links between Burk's coaching era and its relation to the current state of the art of international rowing, as well as read and commented on drafts.

Joe Burk's nephews John and Robert, born to Burk's older brother Paul, provided key background on their uncle's family life at the Rancocas farm, and his relationship with his brothers.

Dietrich Rose, former Ratzeburg Ruderclub oarsman and longtime coach of Vesper Boat Club, provided a "neighbor's view" of Burk and Penn crews during the period 1963 to 1969.

Fellow Kent School varsity oarsman and captain Fred Schoch (1967–9), thereafter University of Washington varsity (1970–1974), 1971 Pan Am silver medalist, and just retired director of the Head of Charles Regatta, and son of Delos "Dutch" Schoch, longtime Princeton coach, provided his recollections of the friendship between his father and Joe Burk in an earlier, more gracious age.

Penn oarsmen Al Wachlin (1961), Howard Greenberg (1967), Phil McKinley (Captain, 1968), and Luther Jones (1971) were generous with their time in granting interviews about their rowing under Burk.

Fritz Hobbs and Cleve Livingston from the Harvard 1968 Olympic eight and the silver medal 1972 Munich Olympic eight gave details of the rearrangement of the Harvard eight that lost to Penn's eight at the 1969 Adams Cup and then reversed that loss a week later at the 1969 Eastern Sprints.

Nick Bancroft, who rowed in Harry Parker's earliest 1963 Harvard varsity, provided his colorful recollection of the details of that crew's reaction to the visit of the Ratzeburg crew to America in spring 1963.

Stan Cwiklinkski, the three man of the 1964 Olympic gold medal Vesper eight, kindly provided details of Burk's offering the Vesper eight the chance to try out the "The Wizard" oarlock strain gauge he was then developing at the Penn boathouse.

Andy Anderson, a/k/a/ Doctor Rowing, gave me early guidance about writing a biography of Burk in 2020, and shared the two pieces he had written in *American Rowing* magazine about his visit to the Burks in the summer of 1995, noted in the Bibliography. Andy convinced me that to understand the full arc of Joe Burk's life, I had to visit the Burk cabin in Montana. Wise counsel, Andy.

John B. "JB" Kelly, III, grandson of John B. Kelly Sr. ("Jack") and son of John B. Kelly Jr. ("Kell,") and himself a former Harvard oarsman, kindly provided the use of pictures for this book from his family's collection.

Sean Colgan, Penn '78 oarsman and founder of the Colgan Foundation, currently supporting *inter alia* Penn, Vesper, Leander Club and New Zealand rowing, read and commented on drafts, and provided access to numerous magazines, Regatta Programs, and pictures. Sean's comment; "My father (Charles Colgan, Penn '50) kept everything."

John Maceachern, stroke of the U.S. Junior silver medal four in 1976, Chestnut Hill '77 oar under Ken Dreyfuss, and 1981 Harvard Captain for Harry Parker, relayed to me the story of his friendship with Joe Burk beginning in the late summer of 1976 when he travelled to Montana with Dreyfuss to meet the Burks. His later gift of his Harvard racing shirt to the Penn coach as a sign of respect is a fitting end to an era of intense rivalry between the two storied rowing powers. John has just retired from working in Development for Groton

School, and, following Joe Burk's example, will be coaching rowing at Cambridge Rindge & Latin School next year.

Any errors in this book that remain are mine alone.

Finally, my special thanks to the team at Mayfly Design of Minneapolis, Minnesota, especially Julie Scheife and Molly Mortimer, who provided shrewd guidance and seamless execution of the steps necessary to bring this book to print.

Edward James Woodhouse Jr.
Dublin, Virginia

Selected Bibliography

BOOKS

Ayer, Toby. *The Sphinx of the Charles: A Year at Harvard with Harry Parker.* Lyons Press, 2016.

Beresford, John. *Jack Bereford: An Olympian At War.* Cloister House Press, UK, 2019.

Brown, Daniel James. *The Boys in the Boat.* Viking Penguin, 2013.

Brown, Dotty. *Boathouse Row: Waves of Change in the Birthplace of American Rowing.* Temple University Press, 2017.

Bulkey, Robert J. *At Close Quarters: PT Boats in the United States Navy.* Arcadia Press, 2017 (originally published in 1962).

Chu, Victor. *American PT Boats In World War II.* Schiffer Publishing, Altglen, Pennsylvania, 1997.

Clark, Emory. *Olympic Odyssey.* Taylor Butterfield, Lapeer, Michigan, 2014.

Colgan, Sean. *The Book of Ted: Olympian, Coach, Mentor Ted A. Nash.* Colgan Foundation, 2022.

Cunningham, Frank, with Leslie Stillwell Strom. *The Sculler At Ease.* Avery Press, 2nd ed., 1999.

Cwiklinski, Stan. *My Lifelong Jottings During Peace and War: An Autobiography of Record.* Privately Printed, 2024.

Doyle, William. *PT 109: An American Epic of War, Survival, and the Destiny of John F. Kennedy.* Harper Collins, 2015.

Fairbairn, Steve. *Steve Fairbairn on Rowing.* Nicols Kaye, London, 1951.

Frkovich, Jo. *Enemy in the Mirror: World War II Tragedy in the Pacific.* Privately Printed, 2009, updated 2013.

Halberstam, David. *The Amateurs: The Story of Four Young Men and Their Quest of an Olympic Gold Medal.* William Morrow and Company, Inc., New York, 1985.

Hamm, Thomas D. *The Quakers in America.* Columbia University Press, 2003.

Hartman, Neil, et al., eds. *Moorestown Friends School: A History.* The Development Office, Moorestown Friends School, Spring, 1986.

Herberger, Dr. Ernst, et al. *Rowing (Rudern): The GDR Text of Oarsmanship.* Sports Books Publisher, Toronto, 4th ed., 1990.

Johnson, Frank D. *United States PT-Boats of World War II in Action.* Blandford Press, Poole, Dorset, England, 1980.

Keating, Bern. *PT Boats In World War II: The Mosquito Fleet.* G.T. Putnam's Sons (Scholastic Book Edition), 1966.

Kemp, Hovey. *The Hammers: The Story of Harvard's Underdog and Undefeated 1976 Crew.* Privately printed, 2021.

Lanouette, William. *The Triumph of the Amateurs: The Rise, Ruin, and Banishment of Professional Rowing in the Gilded Age.* Lyons Press, 2021.

Larkin, Andrew. *My Life in Boats, Fast and Slow.* Off the Common Book, Amherst, Massachusetts, 2018.

Livingstone, Keith (D.C.). *Healthy Intelligent Training: The Proven Principles of Arthur Lydiard.* Meyer & Meyer Sport, Maidenhead, UK, 3rd ed., 2013.

Mallory, Peter. *The Sport of Rowing.* River and Rowing Museum, Henley-on-Thames, Great Britain, 2012.

Matheson, Hugh, and Christopher Dodd. *More Power: The Story of Jurgen Grobler.* HQ, An Imprint of Harper Collins, London, 2018.

Newell, George, and Dick Erickson. *READY ALL!: George Yeomans Pocock and Crew Racing.* University of Washington Press, Seattle and London, 1986.

Nolte, Volker, ed. *Rowing Faster: Serious Training for Serious Rowers.* Human Kinetics, Windsor, Ontario, 2nd ed., 2011.

Pinsent, Matthew. *A Lifetime in A Race.* Ebury Press, London, 2004.

Pocock, George Yeomans. *Memories.* Undated. Privately Printed. Contact the Pocock Foundation, info@pocockfoundation.org, 3320 Fuhrman Ave East, Seattle, Washington, 98102.

Pocock, Stanley Richard. *Way Enough!: Recollections of a Life in Rowing.* BLABLA Publishing, Seattle, Washington, 2000 (Privately printed, but copies are available from the Pocock Foundation in Seattle. Contact https://www.pocockfoundation.org/contact-us).

Redgrave, Steve, with Nick Townsend. *A Golden Age: Steve Redgrave The Autobiography.* BBC Books, London, 2000.

Riesman, David, in collaboration with Reuel Denney and Nathan Glazer. *The Lonely Crowd: A Study of the Changing American Character.* Yale University Press, New Haven and London, 1950.

Roberts, Andrew. *The Storm of War: A New History of the Second World War.* Harper Collins, New York, New York, 2011.

Stowe, William A. *All Together: The Formidable Journey to the Gold with the 1964 Olympic Crew.* iUniverse Inc., New York, London, Shanghai, 2005.

Symonds, Craig L. *Nimitz At War: Command Leadership from Pearl Harbor to Tokyo Bay.* Oxford University Press, 2022.

Taylor, Bradley F. *Wisconsin Where They Row: A History of Varsity Rowing at the University of Wisconsin.* University of Wisconsin Press, 2005.

Walker, Vern. *Peter Snell and the Kiwis Who Flew.* David Lyng Publishing, Auckland, New Zealand, 2014.

Wildenberg, Thomas, and Norman Polmar. *Ship Killers.* The Naval Institute Press, Annapolis, Maryland, 2010.

University of Pennsylvania Booklets

Recollections and Records: A Tribute to Joe Burk (*On the Occasion of the Tribute to Joe Burk, Bronze scripture unveiled and dedicated May 22, 2005, University of Pennsylvania Boathouse.*

ACADEMIC JOURNALS

Breeding, William Paul. "Henry Robert 'Bob' Pierce: A Biography." Master's thesis, Western University, 1982. Digitized Theses, Digitized Special Collections. https://ir.lib.uwo.ca/cgi /viewcontent.cgi?article=8282&context=digitizedtheses (accessed March 1, 2024).

MAGAZINE ARTICLES

Anderson, Andy. *American Rowing, Joe Burk: A Rowing Legend, Part I* (January–February), 1996. *Part II* (March–April).

Sports Illustrated. "A Straight Flush For Joe Burk," June 28, 1968, page 26–27.

Sports Illustrated. "Harry Parker and the World's Best Crew," June 28, 1965.

Time Magazine. "Sport: Rancocas Robot," July 11, 1938. Available at https://content.time.com/time/subscriber/article/0,33009 ,849089.00.html (accessed November 6, 2023).

WEBSITES

Brown, Dotty. "Lest We Forget Joe Burk." *Boathouse Row, The Book* website. Last modified October 15, 2019. https://boathouserow thebook.com/2019/10/15/lest-we-forget-coach-joe-burk/ (accessed September 1, 2023).

"Cornelius Dion O-Sullivan Memorial Site." U.S. Naval Academy Website. https://usnamemorialhall.org/index.php/CORNELIUS _D._O%27SULLIVAN,_LTJG,_USN (accessed September 1, 2023).

"Joe Burk Letters to George Pocock." Rowing History. http://www .rowinghistory.net/essays/joe-burk-letters (accessed September 1, 2023).

VIDEO TAPES

Biglow, John, curator. "1947: Giants of the Galley Washington Invitational 16 mm 16 HQ." YouTube, 1947. Curated by John Biglow, Yale.

CD AUDIO

Lydiard, Arthur. *Address at International Sports Specialist Symposium.* Fall 1963. Bud Winter Enterprises, 221 Canyon Drive, Suite B-2, Costa Mesa, CA 92627. www.BudWinter.com.

Notes

1   Thomas D. Hamm, *The Quakers in America* (Columbia University Press, 2003), (hereafter "Hamm"), page 26.

2   Pennsylvania Historical & Museum Commission website at www.phmc.state .pa.us/portal/communities/documents/1681-1776/pennsylvania-charter.html (accessed September 9, 2023).

3   Hamm, pages 27–8.

4   *The New York Times*, June 24, 1929, page 22.

5   *The New York Times*, "Rusty Callow Obituary," February 24, 1961.

6   *The Philadelphia Inquirer* (hereafter "*Inquirer*"), "Notre Dame Fracas Bunged Up Quakers," November 10, 1931, page 18.

7   The idea of focusing on the process of work and not the appearance of self is also a popular modern sports coaching technique. It is expressed today not as a monastic suppression of one's ego, but instead as an intense focus by each player on the specifics of the work that player is assigned. Recently retired Alabama football coach Nick Saban is famous for urging his players to *trust the process*—which he explains as the player focusing solely on executing *his job* in the midst of a contest, and ignoring the score and other players' roles during any action on the field. For coaches like Saban, this is the only thing that an athlete need focus upon during any contest. All else is irrelevant. It is a measure of Burk's intuitive genius that he would, alone on Rancocas Creek, develop and perfect this method of focusing that would decades later be hailed, albeit in a different sport, as a distinctive approach to what is now called "Sports Psychology."

8   *Inquirer*, "Ohio State Tilt Not So Rough Says Robbie, Scull Admits It Was," December 2, 1932, page 26.

9   George Pocock's son Stan remembered in his autobiography, Stanley Richard Pocock, *Way Enough!: Recollections of a Life in Rowing* (BLABLA Publishing, 2000), hereafter "Stan Pocock," that his father had made the oar for only a few instances, for Burk and for "Stub" McMillan, the five-man of the UW Olympic gold medal crew. "The idea behind using a big blade was that it slowed the drive of an extra-strong man, especially if he tended to tear the water, so that he would swing with the rest of the crew." Pages 177–8.

10   *Inquirer*, May 21, 1933, page 37

11   *Inquirer*, May 28, 1933, page 33.

12   *The Daily Pennsylvanian* (hereafter "*DP*"), October 16 and 23, 1933, page 1.

13   DP, October 27, 1933, page 1.

14   DP, October 30, 1933, page 1.

15   *Inquirer*, October 31, 1933, page 17.

16   DP, November 6, 1933, page 1.

17   DP, November 13, 1933, page 1.

18   *Inquirer*, "Penn Shows Form Grooming for Ohio," November 9, 1933, page 18.

19   DP, December 4, 1933, page 1.

20   DP, January 14, 1934, page 1.

21   DP, May 2, 1934, Page 1.

22   *Inquirer,* "Yale Oarsmen Triumph in Blackwell Regatta," May 6, 1934, page 25.

23   *Inquirer*, "Quaker Crews Score 3 Wins On Schuylkill," May 27, 1934, page 25.

24   *Brooklyn N.Y. Times Union*, June 13, 1934, page 13.

25   Peter Mallory, *The Sport of Rowing*, River and Rowing Museum, Henley-on-Thames, Great Britain, 2012 (hereafter "Mallory"), page 546.

26   Gordon Newell, *READY ALL!: George Yeomans Pocock and Crew Racing* (University of Washington Press, 1986), (hereafter "Newell"), page 18.

27   Newell, page 19.

28   Newell, page 20.

29   Newell, page 21.

30   Newell, page 98.

31   Modern rowers will find this figure lower than the best racing singles today. Hudson USP singles cost approximately $14,500 today.

32   James Burk, then at Moorestown High School but learning to row from his older brother. James Burk would row for Pennsylvania from 1936 to 1940. There exist photographs from this period in the Burk family scrapbooks which show Joe and Jim with a car topped with homemade boat racks. The family memory is that the brothers travelled to Florida to row, but no memory of details remains.

33   Pocock had likely been surprised to be paid in full for the first boat. He may well have told Burk that he need not pay in advance, thus Burk is here responding that he would send payment as directed by Pocock.

34   Foot stretchers are the term for the foot pedals attached to a cross bar in the boat in which the oarsman's feet are placed, and against which the oarsman pushes to move himself up and back during the rowing stroke.

35   "Out" meaning positioned toward the stern of the boat.

36   A 36-inch inseam is a long leg length for a 6-foot 2-inch oarsman.

37   *Inquirer*, July 4, 1936, page 14.

38   The Filled in Program statistics for this race, handwritten on the original Program from Princeton, is in the archives of the Malta Boat Club, thanks to the conservation efforts of Rick Stehlik, Archivist of the Club—who himself is a former bronze medalist in the lightweight double at World Rowing Championships of 1977.

39   Robert F. Kelly, "Splendid Race Establishes Washington Crew as U.S. Olympic Standard Bearer," *The New York Times*, July 6, 1936.

40   *DP*, January 13, 1937, page 3.

41   Dr. Reed Kindermann, Penn Crew '69 learned from Burk the precise locations of his training zone—and generously shared the details of these locations—still worthy of study by those interested in Burk's rise in sculling. The pier years ago had been known as "The Dung Pier," where local farmers would bring dung to be placed in barges and sold as fertilizer.

42   Interview with Peter Mallory.

43   There are a few notable exceptions. U.S.S.R. weightlifting champion Vasily Alekseyev won Olympic gold medals training alone in a room built onto his house in Russia. Coaches were no more than advisers to the powerful champion.

44   Under the overall supervision of the U.S. Rowing High-Performance Director, candidates for U.S. teams clustered in one of several area camps located around the U.S. There, the rowers training is guided by local coaches under the overall supervision of the High-Performance Director.

45   Steve Redgrave (with Nick Townsend), *A Golden Age: Steve Redgrave The Autobiography* (London: BBC Books, 2000), 175–221; Hugh Matheson and Christopher Dodd, *More Power: The Story of Jurgen Grobler* (London: HQ, an imprint of Harper Collins, 2018), passim. See also *Rowing (Rudern): The GDR Text of Oarsmanship*, by Dr. Ernst Herberger et al. (Toronto: Sports Books Publisher, 4th ed., 1990).

46   Mallory, page 556.

47   Correspondence with Roger Burk.

48   Roger Burk correspondence.

49   Interview with Kathy Burk McCaffery.

50   *Inquirer*, "Burk Wins Singles In Peoples Regatta," July 6, 1937, page 23.

51   *Inquirer*, "Burk Scull Victor at Canadian Henley," August 1, 1937, page 59.

52   I am grateful to Peter Mallory for the insight that at the time of race with Coulson, the traditional method of surging at the start to "break" an opponent was then in vogue.

53   *Inquirer*, "Joe Burk Invited to Canadian Meet," August 12, 1937, page 22.

54   *Inquirer*, "Penn A.C. oarsmen Called Out Today," February 29, 1938, page 15.

55   *Inquirer*, "Burk Retains Sculling Laurels," May 15, 1938, page 78.

56   *Inquirer*, "Joe Burk Victor By Eight Lengths," May 30, 1938, page 18.

57   Henry's younger brother Ernie Arlett also rowed in professional regattas, "winning races in eights, fours, pairs and singles." Ernie, during 1938 and 1939, was the boathouse supervisor for Leander Club, and a freelance coach for scullers and crews. In 1962, as we shall see in Chapter Eleven, he will appear on a bicycle at the starting line at Henley riding with Joe and Roger Burk following a Diamond Sculls race. He would later serve as boatman for the Rutgers crew, and sculling coach at Harvard's Weld Boathouse, and later establish the rowing program at Northeastern University in Boston. See Northeastern University post regarding Ernie Arlett at https://repository.library.northeastern.edu/downloads/neu:361001.

58   YouTube presentation can be found at https:///www.youtube.com/watch?v=wCFkNklrtc (accessed 7 November 2023).

59   Roger Burk noted in reading a draft of this book that George Pocock had told him the same story about his father, but that the meat was roast beef, rather than steak which Tytus remembered. Roger said roast beef was more traditional in the Burk household.

60   *Inquirer*, "Joe Burk Regain Schuylkill Navy Title, Unopposed in Sculls; PennAC Crews Win," June 18, 1939, page 14.

61   See historic images.com—1942 national champ.

62   See Friends of Rowing History (hereafter "FORH") at www.rowinghistory.net (accessed 5 March 2025), Joseph Burk Letters to George Pocock is under the Essays section on the first page.

63   *Inquirer*, "Joe Burk Wins Fourth U.S. Singles Rowing Title in Row," by Frank Bates, July 22, 1940, page 1.

64   Ibid.

65   Ibid.

66   Interview Kathy Burk McCaffery.

67   Robert J. Bulkley, *At Close Quarters: PT Boats in the United States Navy* (Arcadia Press, 2017; originally published in 1962), page 112.

68   Andrew Roberts, *The Storm of War: A New History of the Second World War* (Harper Collins, New York, New York, 2011), p. 214. Phelps' goal was the Navy, and the Army Air Corps which first refused Stewart—both of which had higher standards than the basic Army minimum criteria.

69   See Mallory, pages 1738–1746.

70   This proclivity to long-term thought is an underrated virtue. The late Charlie Munger, Vice Chairman of Berkshire Hathaway, attributed much of his own success as an investor not to greater insights, but to "having a longer attention span" than most. Munger: **"I think when you multi-task so much, you don't have time to think about anything deeply. You're giving the world an advantage you shouldn't do. Practically everybody is drifting into that mistake.** Concentrating hard on something that is important is . . . I can't succeed at all without doing it. I did not succeed in life by intelligence. I succeeded because I have a long attention span." See https://fs .blog/multitasking-giving-world-advantage (accessed 11 March 2024).

71   Pocock suspended his shell manufacturing during the war, and constructed specialized war equipment for the United States Government and its war contractors. When the troops returned from the war, collegiate rowing slowly restarted and Pocock resumed his shell construction business.

72   Doyle, William. *PT 109: An American Epic of War, Survival, and the Destiny of John F. Kennedy* (New York: Harper Collins, 2015).

73   Craig L. Symonds, *Nimitz at War: Command Leadership from Pearl Harbor to Tokyo Bay* (New York: Oxford University Press, 2022), 66.

74   The Navy acronym for the command was or CINCPAC, the same title used today.

75   Bulkley, page 103.

76   Bulkley, pages 112–113.

77   Bulkley, page 122.

78   Bulkley, page 122–123.

79   Action Report of J.W. Burk to The Commander, M.T.B. Squadron, dated 11 January 1944.

80 The correct designation was PT-127.

81 Correct number of barges destroyed was three.

82 Burk report on Actions on March 14, 1944.

83 Lt. (jg) James Burk is commemorated at the Manila American Cemetery, and with a commemorative marker at Arlington National Cemetery, Section MK, Site 155.

84 Burk's PT boat was fitted with three 12-cylinder Packard engines which ran on 100 octane aviation-grade gasoline.

85 The U.S. B-24 Liberator Bomber.

86 PT boat skippers and their crews frequently added to the firepower they had aboard, using whatever guns might be available at any one point.

87 Kathy Burk McCaffery confirmed that her father never heard the details of his bother Jim's wounds, and she did not make available the grim details of Jim's fatal wounds to her father when Jo Frkovich's book was published.

88 During the time the boats were passing through the Panama Canal.

89 By that time, Jim Burk's boat had been destroyed by friendly fire, and half the crew lost.

90 Peter Mallory, *The Sport of Rowing* (hereafter "Mallory"), page 659.

91 Now part of the Northeastern University's global university system.

92 The formal date of loss was listed by the Navy as the evening of April 8, 1943. He is listed among those lost at sea at the memorial located at the Manila American Cemetery. [See photo taken by Kay's grandson Kevin McCaffery. See https//:www.naval-history.net/WW2UScasaaDB-USNbyNameO.htm (accessed 3 June 2023).

93 *Inquirer*, September 8, 1944, page 23.

94 This is the only mention by Burk of a wish to switch theaters of operation and move from the Pacific to the Atlantic. By the date of Burk's letter, D-Day was three months past, the Germans had been driven from the Normandy area, and a second massive Allied ground offensive in Europe was beginning in the form of Operation Market Garden, the assault by the Twenty First Army Group led by British General Bernard Montgomery, aided by the largest airborne landing in history by the American 101st Airborne, and 82nd Airborne, and the British First Airborne divisions in Holland. Naval operations were not the focus in the theater during this time. It is not clear whether Burk was fully aware of these circumstances when he expressed the wish to Phelps.

95 Pennsylvania and Cornell used to have a tradition of holding their annual game on Thanksgiving Day. Penn vs. Cornell used to serve up Thanksgiving specials: "Penn and Cornell face off for the 127th time on Saturday At Franklin Field. Forty-three of the first 45 meetings were held on Thanksgiving Day," *Penn Today* at https://penntoday.upenn.edu/news/penn-vs-cornell-used -serve-thanksgivign-specials. (accessed 15 September 2023).

96 Burk letter to Phelps, dated January 12, 1945.

97 Ibid.

98 Burk letter to Phelps, April 5, 1945.

99 Symonds, page 399.

100 Symonds, page 401.

101   Marriage announcement in *The Social Way* of *The Philadelphia Inquirer* dated November 6, 1945.

102   Steve Gladstone, long time championship rowing coach at Harvard, Brown, California, Yale.

103   Jeff Fuglestad, Penn Oarsman, 1963–66.

104   *The Pennsylvania Gazette*, Volume 43, Number 2 (October 1944).

105   See the picture of the American Can Company industrial facility at Third Avenue at https;//calisphere.org/item/af6ce2131b05ea73073a31bd229d8a52/ (accessed 3 June 2023).

106   Steve Gladstone, a Burk mentee and longtime coach at Cal, heard from some of the older Cal alumni that it was generally understood that Joe had inquired about a job at Cal while he was residing in San Francisco. We can only imagine what the future of American rowing might have been had he gotten a job at Cal gather than going east to Yale to coach the freshman, and then on to Penn.

107   Manhattan College Website, History of Manhattan College found at https://manhattan.edu/about/history.php (accessed on 7 November 2023).

108   See Marist College archives at https://exhibits.archives.marist.ecu/s/regatta/page/Walz (accessed 12 August 2023).

109   See https://operations.nfl.com/gameday/technology/impact-of-television (accessed 2 October 2023).

110   See Marist College archives at https://exhibits.archives.marist.ecu/s/regatta/page/Walz (accessed 12 August 2023), and *Wisconsin Where They Row: A History of Varsity Rowing at the University of Wisconsin*, by Bradley F. Taylor (hereafter "Taylor").

111   Readers will recall that Bob Pearce was the Canadian sculling champion who had won the Diamond Sculls at Henley after being employed by Lord Dewar as a sales representative for Dewar's Scotch Whisky firm. See Chapter Seven.

112   Yale swimming coach and during 1947 to 1949, athletic director.

113   Burk Letters to Pocock dated January 12, 1947.

114   (Meriden, CT) *The Journal*, May 19, 1947, page 4.

115   The Harvard-Yale contest for the first year after World War Two, the 1946 race was held on the Charles.

116   See Photo 15.

117   (Meriden, CT) *The Journal*, June 19, 1947, page 14.

118   *NYT*, "Yale Crew in Seattle Race," June 5, 1947, page 33.

119   Thanks to John Biglow (Yale Varsity in the 1970s and member of the 1980 and 1984 U.S. Olympic Teams), this film is available at https://www.youtube.com.

120   Frank Cunningham, with Leslie Stillwell Strom, *The Sculler At Ease* (Seattle: Grandview Street Press, 1992).

121   *The Miami Herald*, "Yale Crew Conquers Penn by Yard in Bitter Regatta Duel: Kelly Easy Winner Over Two Eli Rivals," by Luther Evans, January 4, 1948, page 57.

122   *The Miami News*, AP Wire story, "Two of Yale Crew Injured, One Critically," January 5, 1948, page 14.

123   *The Day* (New London, Connecticut), April 28, 1947, page 12.

124   *The LaCrosse Tribune*, (AP Wire), May 11, 1947, page 18.

125   *New York Daily News*, in the column *Passing* Sentences by Hy Turkin, May 15, 1947, page 544.

126   (Meriden CT) *The Journal*, May 21, 1949,

127   *NYT*, "Harvard Triumphs by 20 Foot Margin," by Allison Danzig, June 26, 1948, page 13.

128   The coxswain in the Yale pair with was James "Jim" Beggs, Yale Varsity coxswain, who would later become Joe Burk's freshman coach at Penn.

129   *NYT*, "Kelly Is in Single Sculls for Olympic Post," page 136.

130   *NYT*, Sports of the Times, "Views on U.S. Rowing," by Allison Danzig, July 27, 1948.

131   "Yale and the Olympic Games," List of Yale Olympians, at https://news.yale.edu/sites/default/files/d6_files/imce/OLYMPICS.WEB_.pdf (accessed 12 August 2023).

132   *NYT*, "California Eight and Washington Four Annex Olympic Rowing Titles for U.S.," August 10, 1948, page 25.

133   Mallory, page 635.

134   *NYT*, "Yale Crew Victor In Florida Event," January 1, 1949, page 17.

135   *NYT*, "Harvard Eights Gain Title Sweep," *by Allison Danzig, May 15, 1949, page 181.*

136   *NYT*, "Yale Crew Breaks Record to Beat Harvard First Time in 11 Meetings," by Allison Danzig, June 25, 1949, page 1.

137   Taylor, Page 85.

138   *The Buffalo News*, "Eli Coach Takes to the Air To Get New Angle on Oarsmen," May 11, 19950, page 11.

139   Mallory, page 692.

140   *NYT*, "Harvard Varsity Favored Over Yale Today in 85th Thames Regatta," June 23, 1950, page 41.

141   *Boston Globe*, "Harvard Crews Win; Varsity's Margin 12 Feet," June 24, 1950, page 1.

142   *The Daily Pennsylvanian, April, 1950.*

143   *NYT*, "Callow Leaves Penn, Walsh a Navy Crew Coach," June 20, 1950, page 33.

144   Lyman Spencer "Pop" Perry, father of Lyman Perry, stroke of the 1960 Navy Olympic eight, Head of the Navy Athletic Department, was one of Navy Football's all-Americans in 1918.

145   Mallory, page 496.

146   Doing the longer and harder work earlier in the overall year-long training process—described in modern rowing parlance as "periodization," is now standard doctrine. Coaches break the season into a sequence of blocks of training leading to a final peak of performance at the race distance, with longer work at the beginning and shorter at the end.

147   See photo.

148   *The Yale Daily News*, "Rathschimdt Takes Place of Walz As Yale's Head Coach of Crew," by Richard Schumacher, September 13, 1950.

149   See Marist College archives at https://exhibits.archives.marist.ecu/s/regatta/page/Walz (accessed 12 August 2023), and *Wisconsin Where They Row: A History of Varsity Rowing at the University of Wisconsin*, by Bradley F. Taylor.

150   Readers can be forgiven from speculating whether Whitney—himself a WW2

veteran from the Navy Seebees—might not have found a father figure in Burk, the older PT Boat captain who had been his crew coach after the war. We cannot inquire of him, as Whitney died on September 18, 1985 at age 60, following heart surgery. See Find a Grave at https://findagrave.com /memorial/188595479/harry-payne-whitney (accessed 12 August 2023).

151   *The Daily Pennsylvanian* (hereafter "DP"), September 22, 1950, page 5.

152   DP, "New Mentor Goes into Action Rebuilding Crew in First Year," October 11, 1950, page 3.

153   DP, "Top Canadian Sculler Enter Penn Next Year," March 20, 1951, page 3.

154   DP, "Crew Loses to Eli By 4-Foot Margin," April 30, 1951, page 3.

155   DP, "Letter, Coach Burk Appeals," May 9, 1951.

156   DP, "Callow Has His Say; Former Quaker Crew Mentor Greets Campus From Annapolis," May 11, 1951, page 6.

157   DP, "Legendary Exploits of Joe Burk Could Make Him A Fiction Hero," May 14, 1951, page 3.

158   Peter Mallory, the author of *The Sport of Rowing* was also the author of the Penn Lightweight website, and he based the website on the content of that book.

159   Penn Men's Lightweight Rowing website, see https://pennathletics.com /news/2016/6/27/5771a3d9e4b0028e7235ac9d_131492760801596583 (accessed 17 August 2023).

160   NYT, "Penn Crew Leaves for Henley," June 26, 1951, page 34.

161   Mallory, page 662.

162   Lightweight rowing had not yet been organized as a separate category in European rowing.

163   *Inquirer*, "Sportscope," July 13, 1951, page 29.

164   *The Tampa Tribune*, "Pennsylvania Crew Wins Race in Germany," July 16, 1951, page 15.

165   DP, "Lightweight Crew Plans To Switch to Hutchison Gym," November 1, 1951, page 3.

166   *Inquirer*, "Navy Wins 18th; Harvard 2nd," May 17, 1952, page 65.

167   *Inquirer*, (Up Wire Story) "Steaks Spoil For Penn Crew," June 28, 1952, page 57.

168   *Inquirer*, December 8, 1952, page 18.

169   Mallory, page 673.

170   This phrasing is contained in Fred Lane's interview with the author.

171   *Inquirer*, "Friend, Ricky Operation Bring Penn Top Oarsman," by Leo Riordan, April 26, 1954, page 25.

172   *Inquirer*, "Penn Nips Yale In Blackwell; Columbia Third" (N.Y. Herald Tribune Wire), May 2, 1954, page 77.

173   *Daily News* (New York), "Quakers Seek Regatta Victory," May 9, 1954, page 114.

174   *Harvard Crimson*, "Navy Crew Wins 24th Race; Varsity Third," by Steven C. Scott, May 10, 1954.

175   NYT, "Navy Keeps Title In Sprint Regatta," by Allison Danzig, May 16, 1954, page 1.

176   NYT, "Penn Crew Outrows Cornell First Time," by Allison Danzig, May 30, 1954, page 121.

177   *NYT*, "Navy Eight Wins 28th Time In Row," May 30, 1954, page 121.

178   *NYT*, "Cornell Is Second," by Allison Danzig, June 20, 1954, page 1.

179   Conversation with Harry Parker.

180   Steve Gladstone relayed this story to the author with approval—saying he thought that Burk's allowing the smaller men time together to prove themselves was a way of slowly introducing a new element into the squad.

181   Nick Paumgarten interview.

182   Observation of Ken Dreyfus, Penn '69 Captain.

183   Mallory, page 667.

184   Fred Lane interview.

185   *Inquirer*, "Time, Defeat of Navy Causes Burk No Surprise: Penn Victory Patterned," by John Dell, May 6, 1955, page 29.

186   *The New York Times*, "Quakers Outrow Cornell For Eastern Sprint Title," by Allison Danzig, May 15, 1955, page 228.

187   Mallory, page 669.

188   Until 1950, the IRA had been four miles for the varsity, three for the JV, and two for the freshman, all rowed at Poughkeepsie where Burk himself had first watched a rowing race. By 1952, the location had changed to Syracuse and the waters of Lake Onondaga, and the varsity race distance was three miles.

189   *The Philadelphia Inquirer*, "Cornell Crews Sweep Regatta," by Irving T. Marsh, June 19, 1955. page 82.

190   *The Philadelphia Inquirer*, "2 Penn Crews Will Vie In European Regattas," by Irving T. Marsha, June 19, 1955, page 81.

191   See "NATO's Cold War Frontier in Europe," at https://www.nato.int/cps/en/natohq/declassified_185912.htm (accessed 9 December 2023).

192   Those Olympic rowing team members from the 1980 U.S. Team easily recall that their Olympic chances evaporated when President Carter declared the United States boycott of the Moscow Olympic Games. Those Olympic rowing athletes expecting to compete against the best rowers from Communist countries in 1984 at the Los Angeles Olympics were denied the chance by the boycott of the USSR, East Germany, and other Communist countries. For a complete list of Olympic boycotts, see https://wikipedia.ord/wiki/List_of_Olympic_Games-_boycotts. (accessed 1 August 2023).

193   Fred Lane interview.

194   A "canvas" in English rowing parlance is a unit of measure. It describes the canvas covered portion of the front of a shell—in an eight about twelve feet from the bow to the beginning of the boat's section where the oarsmen sit.

195   Fred Lane interview.

196   Mallory, page 685.

197   Still in existence and active as Rudergesellschaft "Hansa," Hamburg. See https://wwwcrwflags.com/fotw/flags/de@rghh.html (accessed 13 August 2023).

198   Still in existence and active since 1836 as De Hamberger und Germania Ruder Club von 1836. See https://der-club.de/en/start_en (accessed 13 August 2023).

199   *The Philadelphia Inquirer*, "Penn Eights Wins by 1 ½ lengths in Hamburg International Event," July 10, 1955.

200   Fred Lane interview. By November 3, 1943, RAF Bomber Command leader Sir

Arthur Harris had advised Prime Minister Winston Churchill that Hamburg, Essen, and Mannheim were three of thirteen cities that had been [by that date] "virtually destroyed." *Bomber Command*, by Max Hastings, Zenith Press, 1979, page 185.

201 Photo 17 has noted on the back the boating: Cox, John De Guise, stroke, Harry Parker, 7, Bruce Croco, 6, John Bergen, 5, Frank Betts, 4, Fred Lane, 3,—Foley, 2, Tom O'Brien, 1 John Weiss.

202 Harry Parker would not stroke the Penn Varsity until his senior year, 1957. *Philadelphia Inquirer*, "Delaware Valley Olympic Sketches: Representing You At Home," August 21, 1960, page 75.

203 *Clarion-Ledger*, Jackson, Mississippi, April 1, 1956, page 6.

204 *Hazleton Standard-Sentinel*, (Pa.), "Crack Penn Crew Could Go All the Way to Melbourne," April 17, 1956, page 17.

205 *Inquirer*, April 20, 1956, page 39.

206 *Inquirer*, "Princeton Wins Childs Cup; 'Promoted' Penn Is Second," by Ed Sinclair, Special to the Inquirer and the New York Herald Tribune, April 22, 1956, page 71.

207 *Inquirer*, "Yale Crew Upsets Penn, Wins 25th Blackwell Cup," April 29, 1956, page 85.

208 Brown, page 85.

209 Harry Parker would in 1984 suffer a very public failure of the double and quadruple sculling boats he selected as the 1984 National Team Sculling Coach when both boats were beaten by some of the same scullers whom Parker had cut from the squad. See *The Amateurs*, by David Halberstam, William Morrow and Company (1985).

210 *Inquirer*, "Harvard Crew Beats Penn, 2 Navy Eights," May 6, 1956, page 79.

211 *Clarion-Ledger* (Jackson, MS), "Eastern Sprints Won By Cornell Crew," by Whitney Shoemaker, (AP Wire), May 13, 1956, page 24.

212 *The Daily Olympian*, "Callow Opens Forest Fesitval With Plea For Sports Honesty," May 23, 1957, page 1.

213 https://dailyprogress.com/sports/college/ncaa-wants-to-pay-student-athletes/article_45941b1b-4800-577a-9949-f4f869086654.htm#:~:text=NCAA%20President%20Charlie%20Baker%20trust%20fund.

214 Steve Gladstone interview.

215 Mallory, page 689.

216 Stan Pocock, page 158.

217 Lyman Perry Interview.

218 *NYT*, "Navy Crew Loses Heat in Olympics," September 1, 1960, page 19.

219 Long time Coach Peter Raymond noted that it was widely known that Lake Albano's course was odd in that the water depth was different in different lanes, which could have a profound effect on relative boat speeds. For the Mexico City Olympics in 1968, West German coach Karl Adam was reported to have visited the Olympic rowing site the year before the 1968 Games, and found the depths uniformly more shallow than expected. In response, and based on the then German-known principles of fluid dynamics in rowing, he had the German eight-oared shell shortened to optimize that eight's resistance through the water. The German eight won the gold medal in 1968 in the following year.

220   *NYT*, "German Eight Triumphs, With Navy Finishing Fifth," by Allison Danzig, September 4, 1960, page 1.

221   Oxford language dictionary.

222   Stan Pocock, page 177.

223   Stan Pocock, page 155.

224   Personal communication of author with Peter Raymond, stroke of Parkers's 1968 Olympic coxless four, and six man of Parker's 1972 silver medal Olympic eight, Harvard lightweight coach, Radcliffe Crew Coach, and coach of the 1980 U.S. quad.

225   Written by Daniel James Brown, Penguin Books, 2013.

226   *The New York Times*, "Obituary," September 20, 1970, page 87. Princeton Rowing website, at https://rowing.princeton.edu/people/dutch-schoch/. (accessed 14 Jul/ 2021) Dutch Schoch died on September 19, 1970 while on the Springdale golf course at Princeton. At the time, his son, Fred was rowing for the varsity crew at the University of Washington, for the first of three years. Fred is now the executive director of the Head of the Charles Regatta in Boston—the largest rowing race of its kind in the world.

227   Interview with Fred Schoch.

228   Mallory, page 685.

229   Steve Gladstone interview.

230   *Inquirer*, in Time Out by John Dell, "Big Tennis Interest in Big Penn Crew," May 24, 1962, page 51.

231   *The New York Times*, "Cornell's Heavyweight Varsity Favored in Title Rowing Today," special to Times by Allison Danzig, May 19, 1962, page 22.

232   *The New York Times*, "Yale and Penn Share Title After Dead Heat in Rowing," by Allison Danzig, page 271.

233   *The New York Times*, "Penn, Yale Weigh Going To Henley," by Allison Danzig, May 22, 1962, page 44.

234   The New York Times, "Penn Beats Cornell By Two Feet," special to Times by Allison Danzig, May 27, 1962, page S 1.

235   *Philadelphia Daily News*, "Putting First Things First, Penn's Crew Has Thoughts Only of IRA," June 15, 1962, page 69.

236   *The New York Times*, "Cornell Varsity Rows To Victory," by Allison Danzig, June 17, 1962, page 153.

237   *The New York Times*, "Penn Crew Gains Semi-Finals In Challenge Cup at Henley," July 6, 1962, page 18.

238   River and Rowing Museum website, Henley-On-Thames, England, at https://collection.rrm.co.uk/persons/326.

239   Northeastern Rowing website, at https://nurarowing.com/coaches-history (accessed 10 February 2024).

240   *The New York Times*, "Poland Withdraws From Henley After Ace Rower is Disqualified," July 7, 1962, page 12.

241   Tibor G. Mahan was a Hungarian who immigrated to the United States in 1956, and coached at Vesper after 1960. He thought American rowing by 1960 was hampered by too low a rate of stroking as compared to European crews. See Mallory, pages 1359 et seq.

242   *Inquirer*, Frank Dolson in Time Out, "Rowing Enthusiasts Lead Tough Life," July 9, 1962, page 23.

243   *The Harvard Crimson,* January 17, 1963.

244   *Inquirer,* March 22, 1963, page 40.

245   *Pennsylvania Sunday News* (Lancaster), April 21, 1963, page 34.

246   *Boston Globe,* "H Coach Winner in Crew Bow" by John Ahearn, April 28, 1963, page 81.

247   Interview with Nick Bancroft.

248   *The Daily News* (New York City), "Cornell Trials to Crew Title," May 19, 1963, page 148.

249   Ibid.

250   *Binghamton Press and Sun-Bulletin,* "Beaten German Crew Wants To Take Wind Out of Red's Sail," May 21, 1963, page 23.

251   *The Daily News* (New York City), "Yale Oarsmen Thames Pick," June 15, 1963, page 192.

252   *The Boston Globe,* June 17, 1963, page 19.

253   *The Knoxville News-Sentinel,* June 15, 1963, page 6.

254   Dotty Brown, *Boathouse Row: Waves of Change in the Birthplace of American Rowing* (Philadelphia: Temple University Press, 2017), 97.

255   Perry's father, Lyman "Pop" Perry (1897–1975) was an all-American football player at the Naval Academy, career naval officer, and athletic director for the Academy 1942–1943. A photograph from Perry senior's days in 1932 in the Office of Naval Operations can be seen on Wikipedia.

256   Lyman Perry interview.

257   Lyman Perry interview.

258   *Evening Sun* (Baltimore), "Most Anything" (sports chat section) by Russell Cassell, June 17, 1963, page 29.

259   *Sunday News* (Lancaster, Pa.), June 23, 1963, page 33.

260   *Inquirer,* "Vesper BC Wins 6 Races, Captures Gallagher Trophy," by Frank Bates, July 5, 1963, page 26.

261   Lyman Perry interview.

262   Perry would years later succumb to the temptation and coach the Penn freshman lightweights for one year.

263   Neither Budd nor Clark responded to requests by the author for interviews.

264   Emory Clark, *Olympic Odyssey* (Lapeer, MI: Taylor Butterfield, 2014) (hereafter "Clark").

265   William A. Stowe, *All Together: The Formidable Journey to the Gold with the 1964 Olympic Crew* (Lincoln, NE: iUniverse, 2005) (hereafter "Stowe").

266   Clark, page 13.

267   Clark, pages 19.

268   Roger Burk interview.

269   Howard Greenberg interview.

270   *The New York Times,* "Penn Crew Tries Radical Changes," by Allison Danzig, May 1, 1964.

271   *Ibid.*

272   Correspondence with Joel Cantor and Dick Viall.

273   See https://www.row2k.com/feautres/3977/the-intercollegiate-rowing -asscoiation-regatta (accessed 5 March 2024). I am indebted to Joel Cantor for this context in which Burk's equipment choices are best understood.

274   Correspondence with Joel Kantor and Dick Viall.

275 Correspondence with Lyman Perry.
276 *The New York Times*, April 16, 1964, "Crew At Harvard Healthy, Hopeful: Varsity Rated as Potential Olympic Trial Contender," page 47,
277 *The New York Times*, Allison Danzig, "Harvard's Crew Sprint Champion," April —, 1965, p. 1
278 *The Portsmouth Herald* (reprinting the AP story), May 18, 1964, page 9.
279 Toby Ayer, *The Sphinx of the Charles: A Year at Harvard with Harry Parker* (Guilford, CT: Lyons Press, 2016).
280 *Sports Illustrated*, "FOUR X EIGHT = CREW OF THE DECADE", July 6, 1964.
281 *Inquirer*, "Penn-Laden College Crew Capture's Steward's Cup," by Frank Bates, Junes 7, 1964, page 93.
282 Stowe, page 81. Edmonds and Johnson would row in the coxless pair in the Tokyo Olympics. Edmonds had previous won a gold medal at the 1959 Pan Am Games. Johnson would row in the Vesper eight in 1965 and thereafter would row with Larry Hough in the coxless pair, winning two World Championships (1967 and 1969) and the silver medal at the Mexico City Olympics, missing the gold by mere feet against the East German pair.
283 Stowe, page 83.
284 Stowe, pages 83–85.
285 Stowe, page 85.
286 *Inquirer*, "New Crewmen Spur Triumph of Vesper Eight," by Frank Bates, June 28, 1964, page 80.
287 Lyman Perry interview.
288 NYT, "California, Harvard Top Choices in Olympic Rowing Trials Today," by Allison Danzig, July 8, 1964, page 30.
289 Stowe, page 95.
290 Stowe, page 97.
291 Lyman Perry interview.
292 NYT, "4 Olympic Gold-Medal Winners Are Eliminated in Rowing Trials," August 29, 1964, page 15.
293 NYT, "Harvard 4-Oared Crew Gains Olympic Berth in Trials Here," by Michael Strauss, August 30, 1964, page 211.
294 Presumably "per square inch," but no written confirmation of this assumption was found.
295 Interview, Stan Cwiklinski.
296 Interview, Dietrich Rose.
297 Mallory, page 960.
298 Mallory, page 1052.
299 Mallory, page 960.
300 *The Philadelphia Evening Sun*, November 3, 1964, page 25.
301 Mallory, page 925.
302 Stan Pocock, page 155.
303 Lyman Perry interview. As a Naval Academy graduate and officer, Perry obviously also approved.
304 *The Guardian*, "Obituary" by Pete Nichols, December 30, 2004
305 Later renamed Commonwealth Games in 1978.
306 Roger Burk interview.

307   Lyman Perry interview.

308   Arthur Lydiard address before the International Sports Specialist Symposium, *Bud Winter and Speed City Present Arthur Lydiard,* Bud Winter Enterprises, 221 Canyon Drive, Suite B-2, Costa Masa, CA 92627, (1963), Contact www.BudWinter.com.

309   *NYT*, "Hewlett of Harvard Sets Record in Heptagonal Run at Van Cortlandt Park," November 7, 1964, page 23; *NYT*, "Mottley Clips Mark Despite His Coach," by Frank Litsky, March 2, 1964, page 37.

310   Readers wishing to learn more about Lydiard and his impact on endurance sports may wish to consult the selected Bibliography.

311   Nick Paumgarten interview.

312   Remaining from the 1964 crews were Stowe, Budd, one Amlong, Foley, and Cwinkinski.

313   Fargo Thompson was the seven man of the 1962 Penn Henley crew.

314   Nick Paumgarten interview.

315   *Inquirer*, "Yale Rally Defeats Penn on Schuylkill After Dexel Wins," May 2, 1965, page 86.

316   *Inquirer*, "Harvard Beats Navy and Penn For Adams Cup," May 9, 1965, page 70.

317   *Inquirer*, "Harvard Oarsmen Win Crown," May 16, 1965, page 65.

318   *Inquirer*, "Cornell Rowers Beat Penn for Madeira Bowl," May 23, 1965, page 84.

319   *The Philadelphia Daily News*, "Penn Crew Really Wired For IRA Test," June 19, 1965, page 28.

320   *New York Daily News*, "Middies Sweep IRA Regatta," (UPI), June 20, 1965, page 135.

321   One example is *Psychology Today*, "The Sports Illustrated Cover Jinx," posted October 12, 2016.

322   Wolfram MathWorld, see https://mathworld.wofram.com /Reversionto the Mean.html (accessed 20 February 2024).

323   Students of rowing could profitably view the black and white video of the ABC Wide World of Sports broadcast of both races. The video is on a Harvard Athletic Department website: https://gocrimson.com/watch?Archive= 493&sport=9category=8&type=Archive (behind a paywall—$5.99 is well worth it for the impressive rowing by Ratzeburg, Vesper, and Harvard).

324   Bill Stowe personal communication.

325   Fargo Thompson interview.

326   Correspondence with Sean Colgan.

327   *NYT*, "Penn Rejects German Influence in Favor of U.S. Oars and Shells," by Allison Danzig, April 14, 1966, page S54.

328   Correspondence with Howard Greenberg.

329   Nick Paumgarten interview.

330   On October 5, 1965, the International Olympic Committee granted East Germany full recognition and the West and East German teams began competing as separate teams. East German rowing advanced mightily thereafter.

331   Steve Gladstone interview.

332   UPI Wire story, in *Nevada States Journal*, "Princeton Bows to Penn's Crew," April 25, 1966, page 25.

333   *The Boston Globe*, "Harvard's Crew Takes Adams Cup Third Time," May 8, 1966, page 56.

334   Correspondence with Dick Viall.

335   *The Daily Item* (Sunbury, PA), "Spotlight," by Ralph Bernstein, June 14, 1966, page 20.

336   *Sports Illustrated* Vault, at https://vault.si.com/vault/1966/06/06joeburks -blinking-black-box (accessed 24 August 2023).

337   *Sports Illustrated*, above.

338   *Sports Illustrated*, above.

339   *NYT*, "Wisconsin First In Rowing Upset," June 19, 1966, page 171 and 181.

340   Interview with Roger Burk.

341   Nick Paumgarten interview.

342   *NYT*, "Nicholas Paumgarten to Wed Miss Carol Marshall," June 24, April 7, 1966, page 45.

343   Paumgarten interview.

344   Gardner Cadwalader interview.

345   *NYT*, "Harvard's Crews Downs Penn for 4th Straight Adams Cup," May 7, 1967, page 231.

346   *Sports Illustrated*, May 22, 1967; *Boston Globe*, "Harvard Crew Wins 4th Sprint Title," by John Ahern, May 14, 1967, page 1.

347   Howard Greenberg interview.

348   Nick Paumgarten interview.

349   Nick Paumgarten interview.

350   *NYT*, "Penn Is Favored in I.R.A. Regatta," June 16, 1967, page S59.

351   *Inquirer*, "Penn Sweeps To IRA Crown, First Since 1900," June 18, 1967, page 73.

352   *Inquirer*, "Last Long Hours Of A 67-Year Wait," by Frank Dolson, June 18, 1967, page 85.

353   *Philadelphia Daily News*, "Sportspouri," June 22, 1967, page 61, third column.

354   *Philadelphia Daily News*, "Penn Out to Make Big Splash in Final Test," by Ed Conrad, June 30, 1967, page 68.

355   *Sports Illustrated*, "To Becky with love from all the Harvards," by Mike Riley, July 10,1967, Page 40.

356   Mallory, page 1211.

357   Mallory, page 1211.

358   *NYT*, "Harvard Defeats Penn, Navy In Adams Cup Race on Severn," May 5, 1968, page 375.

359   *NYT*, "Harvard Is First In Eastern Sprints," May 12, 1968, page 1.

360   See Madeira Cup History at https://cornellbigred.com/documents /2013/6/26Madeira_Cup.pdf (accessed 27 August 2023).

361   *The Philadelphia Daily News*, "A Tough Crew," by Stan Hochman, June 10, 1968, page 53.

362   *Sports Illustrated*, "A Straight Flush For Joe Burk," June 28, 1968, page 26.

363   Gardner Cadwalader interview.

364   "A prolific author of boys' sports fiction at the turn of the 20th century, Ralph Henry Barbour offered a range of engaging and easy to read stories, commonly centered around football and the importance of hard work and teamwork." American Literature. See https://american literature.com /authors/ralph-henry-barbour (accessed 28 August 2023). All his books are available on Project Gutenberg.

365   *The New Yorker*, "The Sporting Scene 0:00.005," August 10, 1968 page 71 (hereafter "Angell").

366   Angell, page 76.

367   Former 1967 Harvard captain Jake Fiechter had graduated and was attempting join the Olympic Team as the stroke of the Vesper eight.

368   Angell, page 81.

369   Angell, page 83.

370   Correspondence with Jim Dietz.

371   Cadwallader interview.

372   *Inquirer*, "Harvard Nips Penn By 4 Inches," by Frank Dolson, July 15, 1968, page 19.

373   *Inquirer*, "Harvard Nips Penn By 4 Inches," by Frank Dolson, July 15, 1968, page 19.

374   Nick Paumgarten Interview.

375   Mallory, page 1223.

376   Mallory, page 1224.

377   Mallory, page 1223.

378   Roger Burk interview.

379   *University of Cincinnati News*, "Dr. Art Evans recall 1968 Mexico City Olympics," July 26, 2021, at https://www.uc.edu/news/articles/2021/07 /dr-art-evans-recalls-1968-mexicoo-city-olympics.html (accessed 4 September 2023).

380   Frankly Penn '68 Heavyweight Crew, found at www.https://franklypenn .com/2017/09/15/68-penn-heavyweight-crew/ (accessed 1 Sept 2023).

381   Correspondence with Roger Burk.

382   Interview with Roger Burk.

383   See the discussions of the last seat racing before the 1969 IRA at the end of this chapter.

384   *Philadelphia Daily News*, "Burk Shuffling Another Top Hand?," by Ed Conrad, April 19, 1969, page 33.

385   *Philadelphia Inquirer*, "No Job Security For Penn Oarsmen," by Frank Dolson, April 24, 1969, page 31.

386   Like the varsity, the Penn freshman boat was starboard stroked. Clapp would go on to row in a faster boat for Harry Parker—he would join five Harvard oarsmen and the Harvard coxswain Paul Hoffman in the 1972 U.S. eight that would win the silver medal at the Munich Olympics.

387   *Inquirer*, "Penn Defeats Harvard, Navy for Adams Cup," by Frank Bates, May 4, 1969, page 3.

388   *Inquirer*, "Penn Favored To Win Sprints," May 10, 1969, page 23.

389   *The Boston Globe*, "Harvard Crew Whips Penn By 1 ½: Crimson Wins Five of 6 Races," by John Ahern, May 11, 1969, page 79.

390   The Globe comment read: "This is wholesale manipulation and rarely works so quickly. According to crew people, a shift such as that requires a couple of weeks to work out the kinks. For this boat, it required only one row, the morning trial."

391   Correspondence with Fritz Hobbs and Cleve Livingston. Note: This history would repeat itself in 1972. In the first National Team boat selected by the camp system of pooling all oarsmen together and selecting oarsmen one by one—Fritz Hobbs was originally positioned by the team coach, Parker, at the five seat, but just before the crew left for the Munich Olympics, Hobbs was moved to seven. The team would win the silver medal that year (Fritz Hobbs correspondence).

392   *The Boston Globe*'s headline indicated Harvard's margin of victory was one and one-half lengths, but the paper's page 87 picture near the finish line, as well as the time difference of 3.2 seconds indicates the margin was closer to three-quarters of a length.

393   *Sports Illustrated*, "Underdog Bites Back," by Hugh D. Whall, May 19, 1969, (hereafter "Underdog"), page 24.

394   UW New website at https://news.wisc.edu/black-student-strike/timeline/ (accessed 21 August 2023).

395   University of Pennsylvania protests at https://archives.upenn.edu/exhibits /penn-history/sit-in 1969/ (accessed 3 August 2023).

396   Harvard Magazine website at https://www.harvardmagazine.com /2019/02/1969-student-protests-vietnam

397   *The Ithaca Journal*, "Maderia Boatings," 24 May 1969, page 12.

398   *The Ithaca Journal*, "Penn Crew's Pace Slower," June 9, 1969, page 14.

399   *Inquirer*, "To the Henley Or the Jayvees," June 10, 1969 (hereafter "Henley/ Jayvees"), page 33.

400   Careful readers will note that the points assigned had changed from the 1967 system remembered with complete clarity by Captain Nick Paumgarten.

401   The leader of the Penn Heavyweights of that era was described variously as "The Captain" or "The Commodore."

402   Henley/Jayvees, page 34.

403   Henley/Jayvees, page 34.

404   *The Baltimore Sun*, "TRIP INCENTIVE TO PENN'S CREW: Henley Visit Hinges On Victory In IRA Row," June 16, 1969, page 27.

405   *Philadelphia Daily News*, "Henley Race Special For Burk," by Ed Conrad, page 36.

406   Leander Club Boathouse is located just after the finish line at Henley.

407   Katja Hoyer, *Beyond the Wall: A History of East Germany* (New York: Basic Books, Hatchette Book Company, 2023), 234–40. Whether the East German oarsmen who opposed the Penn Varsity at Henley in 1969 had been a part of the state sponsored administration of performance enhancing drugs which had been started in the country by this time is not known.

408   Henley Royal Regatta Records, 1969, page 13.

409   *Inquirer*, "Penn's Varsity, Frosh Outrowed in Henley Finals," (AP Wire), July 6, 1969, page 45.

410   A. E. Houseman, *To An Athlete Dying Young*.

411   *Philadelphia Inquirer*, "Joe Burk's Boys Will Remember," by Frank Dolson, July 16, 1969, page 34.

412   Roger Burk interview.

413   *Philadelphia Daily News*, "Making Burk Proud is Goal Of Nash Era for Penn Crew," by Ed Conrad, July 22, 1969, page 57.

414   Printed in the September 1969 *Penn Rowing News*.

415   University of Pennsylvania Archives, Citation of L.L.M. of Joseph William Burk.

416   Interview with author.

417   Rudyard Kipling, "If," Oxford University, 1918.

Printed in Dunstable, United Kingdom

66521167R00221